slow & easy

slow & easy

fast-fix recipes for your electric slow cooker

natalie haughton

WILEY

Wiley Publishing, Inc.

Published by John Wiley & Sons, Inc., Hoboken, New Jersey
Published simultaneously in Canada

For general information on our other products and services or for technical support, please contact our Customer Care Department within the United States at (800) 762-2974, outside the United States at (317) 572-3993 or fax (317) 572-4002.

Wiley also publishes its books in a variety of electronic formats. Some content that appears in print may not be available in electronic books. For more information about Wiley products, visit our web site at www.wiley.com.

Library of Congress Cataloging-in-Publication Data:
    Haughton, Natalie Hartanov.
    Slow & easy : fast-fix recipes for your electric slow cooker / Natalie Haughton.
        p. cm.
    Includes index.
    ISBN 978-0-470-22940-8 (paper : alk. paper)
        1. Electric cookery, Slow. I. Title.
    TX827.H3887 2008
    641.5'884—dc22
                                                            2007046846

Printed in the United States of America
10 9 8 7 6 5 4 3 2 1

contents

Learn all you need to know about the pot: why the slow cooker makes life so easy, what it's good for and what it's not, choosing the right size and model for your needs, and inside tips from a slow-cook expert.

Turn here for all your snacking and easy entertaining ideas. Throw a party with recipes like Party Taco Dip, Smoky Artichoke Dip, Sassy Spiced Pecans, and Hot Spiced Fruit Punch. And don't forget to pass the Mini Meatballs with Apricot Glaze.

Warm and comforting, homemade soup has never been easier. Just toss in the ingredients and take a hike. Whenever you return, you can ladle up steaming bowlfuls of Mexican Turkey Tortilla Soup, Sweet Corn Chowder, or Italian Minestrone that your whole family will enjoy.

New England Baked Beans with Molasses and Bacon, Curried Cauliflower with Potatoes and Peas, Apricot-Glazed Carrots, and even the best-ever Savory Sausage Stuffing.

breakfast and brunch   335

What better time to enjoy hands-free cooking than in the morning? Sweet and savory egg-based stratas layered with a variety of flavors, Chunky Chicken Hash, French Toast Bake, Overnight Oatmeal with Cinnamon and Bananas, and even Blueberry Coffee Cake allow you to entertain early with little effort and no mess.

preserves, chutneys, and salsas   365

No sterilizing, no processing, just easy toss-it-all-in recipes for a rainbow of colorful preserves. Jewel-like jars of preserves, chutneys, and salsas like Apricot-Pineapple Jam, Cherry-Apple Chutney, Corn and Black Bean Salsa, and Maple-Pumpkin Butter, perfect as condiments or charming homemade gifts, can be ready and waiting for you in the fridge.

great slow cooker desserts   379

Friends will be amazed when they learn these sweet treats came out of a pot. It's hard to make a single choice when there are so many fabulous desserts like Chocolate Fudge Cake with Peanut Butter Ganache, Pineapple-Coconut-Macadamia Cheesecake, Peach-Apricot Crumble, and Chocolate Crème Brûlée.

To my children, Alexis and Grant Haughton. Heaps of love and good eating!

acknowledgments

Special thanks to my family—husband, Fred, and children, Alexis and Grant Haughton—for their constant support, love, encouragement, and laughter throughout this project, even when I was frazzled. They never tired of sampling just one more dish, whether it was early morning, noon, or even late night, and their honest opinions provided valuable input. Alexis, my appreciation for your computer assistance, sharing your style, smile, and inspiration as well as your enthusiasm, which always added sparkle to my day.

My passion for food dates back to my growing-up years in Northern California where my mom and dad, Phyllis and Andrew Hartanov, encouraged my youthful experimentation in the kitchen (provided I cleaned up my mess). My mother was a fabulous cook who entertained often and constantly exposed us to something new, delicious, and interesting at the dining table. A big thank-you to them for the many fond memories of wonderful cooking and eating of my childhood.

Thanks to my Wiley editor, Justin Schwartz, who recognized the potential for new ideas with the electric slow cooker. Many thanks to editor, Susan Wyler, who had confidence in my cooking talents, expertise, and know-how. Also, my gratitude to Amy Golino, culinary analyst for Rival, for readily sharing slow cooker information.

I hope the recipes in this volume bring delicious dining to your table. Cheers and most of all, have fun!

celebrating a great way to cook

As a slow cooker fan from way back, I came to appreciate this versatile appliance early on. When my children were young, it was a lifesaver that allowed me the satisfaction of setting a tasty, nutritious, home-cooked meal in front of the family despite long hours at the office. Slow cooking is a subject that resonates with many home cooks. And these days, whether I'm preparing dinner for my husband, entertaining friends, or working on one of my cookbooks, I enjoy developing recipes that take advantage of what the slow cooker offers most: convenience and low, even heat.

Slow & Easy contains a vibrant collection of recipes that incorporate popular new ingredients and seasonings and a variety of international culinary heritages, so you'll never be at a loss for new ideas. They raise the soups, stews, and braises the slow cooker has always been celebrated for to a higher level. This book also takes the slow cooker interesting places it doesn't often go—into the realm of salsas, preserves, and fabulous desserts, especially cakes. There is a generous chapter filled with wonderful ideas for vegetables, beans, and whole grains, plus an entire chapter of pasta dishes and pasta sauces.

Electric slow cookers are a breeze to use, and they are cost, time, and energy efficient. For the most part, they require little or no tending. The pot is also economical, as many recipes rely on less expensive cuts of meat. It's a great tool for cooking dried beans; they don't need any presoaking. The slow cooker also does a great job with rice. For most all-purpose dishes, you'll get far and away the best results with converted long-grain rice—i.e., Uncle Ben's. Using ordinary white rice risks its being gummy and sticky. You can, however, make excellent risotto in the pot with Arborio rice, and it requires *no stirring!* Just be sure to time it closely so that it doesn't overcook. I've also included instructions for cooking brown rice and wild rice.

In keeping with contemporary taste as well as health concerns, these recipes call for unadulterated fruits and vegetables and only the simplest of processed foods, such as canned tomatoes and broth. In many instances, I've given hints for even more time-saving ways of cooking in the pot by using the already cut-up or prewashed vegetables sold in the produce departments of most supermarkets. Of course, as with any cooking, the quality of the ingredients you use will influence the results. I buy the best-quality produce, poultry, and meats I can and opt for organic whenever possible.

When all is said and done, slow cookers are extremely versatile. While they're ideal for long-cooking stews, chilies, soups, and many meats, they also lend themselves to some dishes that require shorter cooking times. It's amazing what you can use them for, if you keep an open mind. Ever thought of making chutney or jam in a slow cooker? How about lasagna, chocolate cake, or cheesecake? *Slow & Easy* explores them all.

put your pot to good use

Of course the pot is great for everyday food. But it can go much further. Whatever your level of cooking, whether you entertain once a week or once in a while, the slow cooker makes it easier. The appliance frees up the oven or stove-top for other dishes, especially during holidays and multicourse dinner parties. As a novelty, you can even plan a party based on serving the entire meal from start to finish in a variety of slow cookers, so there is no last-minute work at all. Potluck fans find the

usda recommended safe minimum internal temperatures

Although these are minimum temperatures, usually items cooked in the slow cooker will reach higher temperatures.

Beef, veal, lamb steaks, and roasts	145 degrees F
Ground beef, veal, lamb, and pork	160 degrees F
Pork chops and roasts	160 degrees F
Ham, fully cooked	140 degrees F
Fish	145 degrees F
Poultry breasts and whole poultry	165 degrees F
Ground poultry	165 degrees F
Egg dishes and casseroles containing eggs	160 degrees F
Meat and poultry casseroles, soups, and stews	165 degrees F

appliance a huge asset for soups and big pots of chili, and there's no arguing that electric slow cookers have starred on many a buffet table—at home, at schools, and at charity events. They also offer a welcome heat-free cooking option in summer.

Slow & Easy offers a variety of recipes designed to appeal to both veterans and first-time users of the appliance. It turns this hands-free style of cooking into easy, user-friendly, stylish, and delicious eating with the use of a variety of contemporary ingredients like balsamic vinegar, smoked paprika, ground chipotle chile, fresh ginger, roasted red peppers, edamame, and more.

You'll find global flavors here: Chunky Fresh Beet Soup, Beef Stifado,

Braised Lamb with Moroccan Flavors, Tangy Red Cabbage with Apples, Asian-Style Country Ribs, and several curries; not to mention all the popular Italian, Mexican, and down-home American recipes you'll encounter along the way. Shortcut Lasagna, Tamale Pie, and New England Baked Beans with Molasses and Bacon are just a few.

You've got the slow cooker—why not put it to work all the time? Tempting condiments like Mango-Ginger Chutney, Cranberry-Raspberry Relish, Fiery Green Pepper Jelly, and Apricot-Pineapple Jam are simple to make and store beautifully in the refrigerator or freezer with no processing necessary.

Chocolate-Pecan Bread Pudding, Chocolate Chip Cheesecake, Cinnamon-Raisin Rice Pudding, Rich Hot Chocolate, Pineapple-Carrot Cake, and Crème Brûlée lead the list of sweets from the slow cooker.

adding ingredients to the slow cooker

Though you may not be aware of it, any well-written recipe adheres to certain rules. Ingredients are conventionally listed in the order in which they are discussed in the instructions. If a number of ingredients are added at once, they are usually grouped by type—i.e., vegetables, liquids, seasonings—and within type by amount, with the larger amount first. In the case of the electric slow cooker, this is not always true.

When all the ingredients are simply added together and stirred to mix before cooking, these guidelines are appropriate, and the ingredients should be listed in this same fashion. However, because food resting on the bottom of the pot will inevitably receive a little more heat than the rest before the pot warms up and because some ingredients may exude a significant amount of moisture that you want to use to baste other ingredients, when foods are layered in the pot the order may seem random. It is not. Trust me, I've been cooking in the pot for many years, and this has all been carefully calculated to yield the very best results in flavor and texture.

know the limitations

To be fair, cooking in a slow cooker is not magic. Like any other kitchen appliance, the slow cooker has its limitations. To fully enjoy the advantages of the pot, you need to understand what it's good for and what it's not, so that you don't end up with any unwelcome surprises.

Don't even entertain the idea of using the pot for large tender roasts, like fillets of beef; expensive cuts of steak; pies; cookies; or most seafood dishes. Tough, inexpensive cuts of meat that need tenderizing are ideal for the slow cooker. Fish and shellfish require too short a cooking time to benefit from the slow cooker, though I've included about a half a dozen recipes that call for preparing the base in the cooker first and adding the seafood very near the end. With some exceptions, cheese and dairy dishes are poor candidates, too, as they have a tendency to toughen and separate. Foods that are best baked—like pies and cookies—or that are best grilled, broiled, or sautéed—like tender steaks and chops—are best prepared conventionally. But that still leaves you a world of flavors to explore.

simple by design

Meat and poultry do not brown in a slow cooker as they do when sautéed in a skillet or roasted in an oven. Many slow cooker books call for browning these meats and often onions on the stove-top before adding them to the pot. They insist browning develops a richer dimension of flavor in the finished dish. True, browning develops caramelization of the natural sugars in food and deepens color, but I find that after really long, slow cooking, the difference is usually negligible. So I've opted to keep things simple.

I purposely developed these recipes to be as easy as possible: That's where the "fast-fix" comes in. From my years as a food editor, I know that most people use the pot for convenience. So most of the dishes

slow-cooking savvy

Here's a quick reference guide to some of the dishes that are the most and least forgiving in the pot.

most forgiving foods

These dishes generally won't be ruined or compromised by a little extra cooking or warming time in the slow cooker. Use common sense and refer to recipes for guidelines and cooking settings, high or low.

Beef and pork chilis

Beef, pork, and lamb stews

Drinks and punches

Most types of soups, unless a recipe specifies otherwise due to an ingredient it contains (e.g., barley)

Larger pieces of meat such as brisket, corned beef, lamb shanks, and ribs

Pasta sauces

Beans and lentils

here require simply putting all the ingredients in the pot, stirring, and walking away. There are a few exceptions, however.

Bacon and ground beef, ground poultry, and sausage are browned first, either on top of the stove or under the broiler. This is as much for texture as for flavor; and it removes excess fat. There are also a few exceptions, like French Onion Soup, where caramelization is essential. But by and large, the recipes in this book are pared to the bone, and only one pot will need washing. Except for prepping your ingredients, once everything goes into the pot, your work is done.

more demanding dishes

These need to be cooked for the times and temperatures specified in the recipes. Stay near the pot at the end of the cooking time noted to avoid disappointing results. Once I ran an errand close to the end of the cooking time for a cake, and when I returned a half hour later (past the cooking time in the recipe), the cake was totally dried out, over-cooked, and inedible. Don't chance it.

Appetizers including dips, chicken wings, spiced nuts, and more

Brunch dishes including stratas, other egg dishes, coffee cakes, etc.

Desserts—from cakes and cobblers to crème brulées, cheesecakes, bread puddings, chocolate lava cakes, brownies, and much more

Rice and rice dishes, including risotto

Chicken dishes

Pasta dishes

Grains like polenta, quinoa, barley

Preserves, salsas, chutneys, and jams

Casseroles and bakes with pasta, tortillas, and the like

Asian-style dishes with vegetables

Many vegetable dishes

Well, sometimes there is one extra quick step. You may note that there are a lot of garnishes listed in these recipes. I often like to brighten both appearance and taste by punching up a finished dish with a color-ful garnish or a little extra flavor just before serving: chopped fresh herbs, another teaspoon of a spice, lemon juice, balsamic vinegar, sea salt, or freshly ground pepper. Whenever this is necessary, the recipe will give instructions for doing so. While you can always skip a garnish without hurting the taste or satisfaction you get from any dish, I err on the side of color. The extra step will take barely a minute.

keeping an eye on the pot

Don't assume that because you are using a slow cooker, timing is never crucial. Remember, some recipes are more forgiving than others—and not all dishes can take an extra hour or two of cooking. In the case of a soup, stew, or chili, don't panic if you don't arrive home exactly when the food is scheduled to be done; most of these sorts of dishes can tolerate some extra time without the quality and flavor being affected. That's not the case, however, with cakes and other desserts, pastas, egg-based dishes, chutneys, rice, and vegetables. Many of these take just a few hours, even on the low heat setting. So for texture as much as taste, plan to serve these foods when you know you'll be home near the end of the designated cooking time. Weekends offer lots of leeway. Even three or four hours of no-hands cooking gives you lots of time for errands or recreation.

tricks of the trade

I've been making great food in myriad slow cookers for so long, it's fun to share some of the tips I've learned from experience.

taking a peek

For years manufacturers have been telling consumers not to lift the lid during cooking. But I like to check and see what's going on below that cover. While it's prudent not to uncover the pot while it's heating up, many of my recipes encourage you to check and stir things up at least once. How else can you know what's happening in the pot, especially the first time you're cooking a recipe? If stirring is called for, do so very quickly and promptly replace the cover.

thickening in a slow cooker

Since slow cooking produces a lot of moisture, you need to plan ahead to thicken properly. Remember, during the long, gentle cooking, most of the juices and water are leached out of foods. And since there is little or no evaporation, ending up with enough body in sauces and gravies can be difficult in a slow cooker. Some of the liquid rises up as steam, but it hits the lid and falls right back down. You may be surprised when you start with what looks like a fairly thick stew and peek in five hours later to see your chunks of meat and vegetables swimming in a sea of juices.

Because the heat is so low, you cannot bring starch to a boil, which means it is difficult to thicken stews, sauces, and gravies at the end of cooking. Instead, thickening agents are best stirred in at the beginning. I use ingredients like tomato paste, quick-cooking tapioca, or a slurry of flour or cornstarch to thicken the juices that will exude as the food cooks. You can also remove the lid and cook a dish for another hour to encourage evaporation and thicken sauces slightly. The recipes in this book incorporate all these tricks.

If you want to design your own slow cooker recipes, it's almost always a good idea to use less liquid than in a conventional recipe. To help you choose your thickening option, here are the qualities of each:

Tomato Paste: One easy way to produce a lovely sauce is to use canned tomato paste. It has the advantage of adding flavor and color as well as body. The tomato paste is simply added with the other ingredients.

Flour: Another way to thicken during cooking is to toss meat and poultry pieces with flour, either all-purpose or "instant-blending," such as Wondra. Wondra has been processed so that the starch will immediately cook and thicken, so it's a great choice for the slow cooker. Flour can also be whisked into cold water, stock, or wine to make a slurry before stirring it into other liquid in the pot at the start of cooking. Be sure the slurry is smooth and free of lumps.

Cornstarch: If you want to end up with a clear finished sauce— in a sweet-and-sour dish, for instance—mix cornstarch with cold liquid prior to adding to the pot and cooking. Some cooks mix cornstarch into cold water and add it to the pot near the end of the cooking time, because it does not stand up to long cooking under conventional heat. But when testing the recipes for this volume, I found cornstarch could be added at the outset and cooked for several hours on either the low or high heat setting with excellent thickening results. One word of caution: The cornstarch must be heated long enough so that it is clear and thickened when stirred before serving.

Tapioca: "Minute," or precooked tapioca, is another good thickener, especially for fruits in fruit sauces, desserts, and cobblers where you want a high gloss. Simply mix with the fruits when you add them to the pot. Cook the fruit on high until bubbly so that the tapioca works its thickening magic.

Cornmeal: Yellow cornmeal is another possibility to stir into the pot during the last hour of the cooking time. Some diners object to the fact that the cornmeal can leave a slightly gritty texture in the finished dish. It's a personal choice.

Purees: Thickening soups or stew gravies by simply pureeing the liquid with some or all of the vegetables works well, too. You can do this in batches in a blender or food processor. If you have a hand-held immersion blender, many of the dishes can be pureed right in the pot.

Rice, Bread, or Bread Crumbs: Depending on the dish, a little un-cooked rice added at the beginning of the cooking time or cut-up bread pieces or bread crumbs added near the end of the cooking time can assist in thickening a mixture.

Roux: Basically, a roux is a blend of equal parts flour and butter—or sometimes oil—cooked until the roux is bubbly. Then hot liquid is whisked in and brought to a boil, stirring so the mixture is smooth and thickened by the starch, which has been released by the cooking process. A few minutes more of simmering ensures the lightest, most palatable sauce. For gumbo, the roux is cooked until almost milk chocolate in color; otherwise it is white or blond.

If your dish is done, and there's too much liquid or your sauce is not thick enough, here's an emergency fix. Drain the liquid from the pot into a large skillet. Bring to a boil over high heat, and then simply boil to reduce or thicken quickly. Or whisk in a flour or cornstarch slurry made with cold water. Alternatively, make a roux in the skillet first and then whisk in the hot liquid from the pot. Two tablespoons of butter and 2 tablespoons of flour cooked into a roux will thicken 1½ to 2 cups of liquid to a medium consistency. You can adjust from there, making your sauce thicker if you prefer.

which pot to choose

Since I hope you'll be using your pot a lot, it's worth choosing one that best suits your needs, though, to be truthful, it's hard to go wrong with such a simple appliance. Slow cookers are manufactured by numerous companies these days, including Rival, Hamilton Beach, Proctor-Silex, West Bend, Farberware, All-Clad, Cuisinart, General Electric, Corning-Ware, and KitchenAid. While the appliances come in myriad configurations and models, there are two basic types of slow cookers:

The most common and best-selling type is the original slow cooker design, in which the heating coils, or elements, are wrapped around and encased within the sides of the metal unit that houses the stoneware insert. (Each company has its own proprietary configuration of these elements.) This general configuration causes continuous, even heat to surround the food, cooking slowly to avoid any scorching or burning. The recipes in this book were all tested in pots using the wrap-around, continuous heat–style cookers.

Intermittent cookers offer the second option. Here the heating element or coil is located in an electric base that sits beneath the food container. During operation, it cycles on and off. Pots with this design are not recommended, as they tend to have hot spots and cook food less evenly, and sometimes even burn it.

Style-wise, electric slow cookers range from homey patterned designs and plain white to sleek stainless steel ready to take their place

eye appeal

If there is one drawback to slow cooker cuisine, it's in the lack of eye appeal. I'm a big believer in the maxim that first we eat with our eyes, so to me, it's important to embellish food from the slow cooker to make it as appealing and attractive as possible. Consider these colorful garnishes to dress up soups, stews, chilis, braised meats and poultry, appetizers, side dishes, and even desserts. Mix and match them to suit your personal taste and style and to give an extra flavor boost.

> Fresh herbs, such as cilantro, parsley, and chives, chopped or whole sprigs

> A drizzle of pesto sauce—basil, sun-dried tomato, artichoke, or olive

> Sliced or whole mushrooms

> Shredded carrots or zucchini

> Orange, lemon, or lime zest or twists

> Dried cranberries, tart cherries, apricots, or other dried fruits

> Grated, shredded, shaved, or crumbled cheeses, such as Cheddar, Parmesan, feta, blue cheese, or goat cheese

> Chopped hard-cooked eggs or egg whites

> Chopped tomatoes or tomato wedges or slices

next to modern commercial ranges and silent dishwashers. The choice is purely aesthetic.

On the other hand, size does matter. You'll find round and oval pots ranging in capacity from 1 to 8 quarts. People who use electric slow cookers regularly frequently own several models. That's because they are good for different purposes, and the investment is a small one.

For everyday cooking, I find the 4-quart pot to be the most practical. But you'll want to purchase a size that suits your personal dining needs and lifestyle and with features you find appealing. If you plan to use

- Chopped or julienne bell peppers
- Chopped or julienne jícama
- Chopped or sliced cucumbers
- Toasted sesame seeds
- Plain yogurt, sour cream, or crème fraîche
- Crispy cooked pancetta or bacon bits
- Guacamole
- Chopped fresh apples, peaches, or other fruits
- Whole fresh berries (strawberry, blueberry, raspberry, blackberry)
- Toasted whole, sliced, or chopped nuts
- Grated or chopped chocolate
- Shredded coconut
- Pomegranate seeds
- Diced or sliced avocado
- Chopped, sliced, or whole olives
- Assorted chutneys, such as mango, cherry, or apple-cranberry
- Crushed tortilla chips, potato chips, or crackers
- All kinds of salsas—pineapple, peach, tomatillo, tomato, etc.

the pot for entertaining, you may want to invest in a 6- to 7-quart pot as well. Also nice to own is a small 1½-quart model. It's great for cooking appetizers, fondues, and other small amounts of food.

As for extra features, slow cookers have come a long way with the introduction of an array of new bells and whistles, such as digital timers, sensory meat probes, programmable time and heat functions, and additional heat settings beyond the routine low, high, and warm heat settings that even the most basic models possess. These improvements are designed to give more flexibility to busy, contemporary cooks. Some pots automatically shift to a warm mode after the programmed cooking time is finished, so you can leave the house without worrying. Whether these extra features are worth the extra cost is largely a matter of personal preference.

stoneware inserts

Inside the metal housing of the electric slow cooker is a stoneware insert—the pot—which holds the food for cooking and can be removed for cleaning. You can serve from this pot, if you like.

The removable inserts in most pots are microwaveable, and oven-proof, usually up to 400°F depending on the manufacturer. Some of the latest models of slow cookers even allow you to cook in the stoneware insert on top of the stove, so you can brown something like ground meat and not have to dirty a second pan; it just stays right in the pot. However, this is not true for all pots, so be sure to read your manufacturer's instruction booklet before setting a stoneware insert over direct heat.

Never freeze the insert, or it will crack; and do not store food in the insert. The stoneware inserts and slow cooker covers should be washed after each use with hot soapy water. They are dishwasher safe. But the metal housing or bases should *never* be immersed in water.

not all slow cookers are alike

Be aware that these days, not all electric slow cookers are created equal. After extensive comparative testing in both new pots and older ones, I found a surprising number of idiosyncrasies from one pot to another, even with the high-end models.

It quickly became clear to me that the high-heat setting on one pot is not necessarily the same as "high" on another pot. Even some low-heat settings clearly cooked at a higher temperature than I was accustomed to. In fact, as a rule I found that many of the new generation of slow cookers operate at a higher temperature than a number of my older pots. No matter which setting I used, the dish was done sooner than expected. One test of a recipe I'd cooked for years on low for five-hours took half that time in a new pot. Since there are no coordinated industry standards and the cooking times can be variable, I've given a range of times in many recipes as well as a guideline of what you are going for in the finished dish.

get to know your pot

Like driving a new car, when you drive around the block before hitting the highway, it's a good idea to familiarize yourself with the idiosyncrasies of your own slow cooker and how it operates. Does it have any hot spots? Does it cook evenly? While variations usually don't matter, when you're cooking soups, stews, and chilis, they may make a difference with desserts, egg-based stratas, and other foods that cook for a relatively short period of time.

If your pot has a hot spot and you're cooking a cake, for instance, where it may be noticeable, use pot holders to rotate the stoneware insert in the metal housing for more even cooking and browning around the edges. Watch the pot closely in the beginning to get a handle on the timing and how it cooks.

Use recipe cooking times as guidelines. Many factors—such as size of the pot, volume of ingredients in the pot, density and temperature of the food, voltage, fluctuations in electrical wattage, and even altitude—can affect cooking times. Use common sense and check for doneness about a half an hour before the end of the shortest suggested cooking time specified in less forgiving recipes.

slow cooker safety

According to the United States Department of Agriculture, slow cookers are safe and cook food slowly at a low temperature from 170° to 280°F.

The direct heat from the pot, lengthy cooking time, and steam created within the covered pot combine to destroy bacteria and thus make it safe. See the chart on page 3 for minimum internal temperatures. An instant-read digital thermometer is the best way to check.

power outages

If the power goes off while you are out of the house, throw the food away, even it you think it's done. If you're at home and the food was completely cooked prior to the outage, it will remain safe in the cooker for up to 2 hours. After that it must be refrigerated.

holding food on the warm setting

Once the food has finished cooking, serve immediately (in most cases), or if the food is forgiving, switch the pot to the warm setting until serving time (2 hours maximum). Some pots automatically switch to the warm setting after cooking. Keep in mind, though, that over time, flavor and texture may be affected.

appetizers, dips, and drinks

When it comes to entertaining, the electric slow cooker can make it feel as if you've been given another pair of hands. While you focus on finger food and assembling cold appetizers and dips, the slow cooker offers a self-serve hors d'oeuvre station that includes warm dips and spreads, toasted spiced nuts, cocktail meatballs, and hot mulled beverages. Served right in the cooking pot, these savory appetizers can be set out and left on their own while you greet your guests.

I designed many of these recipes with a crowd of at least 10 or 12 in mind, because that's when many people need the most help. These are prepared in a 3- or 4-quart pot. However, some of the dips make such wonderful snacks that you might want to whip them up just for yourself and your family, I recommend a small 1½-quart electric slow cooker, which comes in two styles: a basic pot that only turns on to low; and a more conventional small cooker with a choice of heat settings.

appetizers, dips, and drinks

artichoke and roasted pepper spread with feta cheese

No need to add additional salt here, as the feta and olives contain plenty. Serve this savory spread with assorted crackers or thin baguette slices.

2 packages (8 ounces each) cream cheese, softened

⅓ cup heavy cream

1 garlic clove, minced

½ teaspoon dried basil

¼ teaspoon freshly ground black pepper

¾ cup chopped roasted red or red and yellow bell peppers, rinsed and drained if jarred

1 can (13.75 ounces) artichoke hearts, rinsed, well drained, and chopped

¾ cup coarsely chopped pimiento-stuffed olives

⅔ cup crumbled feta cheese

1. In a large bowl, combine the cream cheese, cream, garlic, basil, and black pepper. Mix until smooth and creamy. Stir in the bell peppers, artichoke hearts, and olives until well incorporated. Finally, blend in the feta cheese.

2. Transfer to a 1½-quart electric slow cooker. Cover and cook on the low heat setting for 1½ to 2 hours, stirring once or twice, until the spread is very hot throughout.

Cook's Notes

➤ For a milder spread, omit the feta cheese.

➤ This spread can also be made in a 1½-quart heat-proof casserole dish that fits in a 6-quart slow cooker. Place on top of a vegetable steamer or other rack in a 6-quart electric slow cooker. Cover and cook on the high heat setting for 2 hours. Then remove the cover and cook for 30 minutes longer.

smoky artichoke dip

Makes about 5 cups;
16 to 20 servings

Smoked Spanish paprika is one of the most versatile spices to arrive on the supermarket shelves in a long while. It is subtle and adds a pleasing hint of smokiness. Hint: This dip is loaded with gooey cheese. Avoid overcooking or it may become grainy. Serve with cut-up fresh vegetables and/or crackers for dipping.

1 pound shredded mozzarella cheese (about 4 cups)
½ cup freshly grated Parmesan cheese
1 cup sour cream
½ cup heavy cream
1 bag (14 ounces) frozen artichoke hearts, thawed,
    well drained, and chopped
1 red bell pepper, chopped
1 orange bell pepper, chopped
½ teaspoon smoked paprika
Freshly ground black pepper

1. In a 3- or 4-quart electric slow cooker, combine the mozzarella cheese, Parmesan cheese, sour cream, and heavy cream. Mix well. Stir in the artichoke hearts, red and orange bell peppers, and smoked paprika. Season with black pepper to taste.

2. Cover and cook on the low heat setting for 1½ to 1¾ hours, or until the cheese is melted and smooth, stirring once or twice during the cooking time.

3. Transfer to a serving bowl. Serve while still hot and runny.

The slow cooker makes a good server for hot beverages and dips and comes in handy for casual entertaining. Keep on the low or warm setting (once the food or drink is cooked) to maintain the proper serving temperature.

caponata

Makes about 3 quarts;
24 servings

Some books claim you cannot cook raw eggplant in a slow cooker, but this savory spread, tart and mildly sweet, belies that lore. The recipe makes enough for a big party. While this can be served warm, it is much better if left to cool to room temperature. Like many tomato-based dishes, it is even better the next day. Leftovers make wonderful topping for bruschetta or can be tossed with pasta for an instant sauce.

2 medium eggplant (1½ pounds total), finely diced

4 large celery ribs with leaves, finely diced

1 large onion, chopped

1 large green bell pepper

½ cup currants or ¼ cup currants and ¼ cup golden raisins

½ cup pitted green or pimiento-stuffed olives,
   coarsely chopped

¼ cup tiny nonpareil capers

3 tablespoons red wine vinegar

4½ tablespoons extra virgin olive oil

1 can (14.5 ounces) diced tomatoes

3 tablespoons tomato paste

1½ teaspoons salt

1 teaspoon dried oregano

¼ to ½ teaspoon crushed hot red pepper, to taste

1. Combine the eggplant, celery, onion, bell pepper, currants, olives, capers, vinegar, olive oil, tomatoes with their juices, tomato paste, salt, oregano, and hot pepper in a 6-quart electric slow cooker. Stir to mix well.

2. Cover and cook on the high heat setting for 3½ to 4 hours, or until the eggplant is tender, the onion is soft, and the flavors have melded.

Cook's Note

➤ The currants will add a touch of natural sweetness to the caponata. If it remains a little too tart for your taste, gradually add up to 1½ tablespoons brown sugar, a heaping teaspoon at a time.

edamame cheese dip with red and yellow peppers

**Makes about 5 cups;
16 to 20 servings**

t's always fun to find a new way to use an ingredient from another cuisine. Here easy-to-use Japanese edamame, shelled fresh soybeans, add a hit of color and great texture to a gooey cheese dip.

1½ cups frozen edamame (shelled soybeans), thawed
1 orange bell pepper, chopped
1 red bell pepper, chopped
1 pound shredded mozzarella cheese (about 4 cups)
½ cup freshly grated Parmesan cheese
1 cup sour cream
½ cup heavy cream
¼ to ½ teaspoon smoked paprika
Freshly ground black pepper

1. In a 3- or 4-quart electric slow cooker, combine the edamame, bell peppers, mozzarella cheese, Parmesan cheese, sour cream, heavy cream, and smoked paprika. Blend well. Season with pepper to taste.

2. Cover and cook on the low heat setting for 1½ to 1¾ hours, or until the cheese is melted and smooth, stirring once or twice during the cooking time. Do not overcook or the cheese will become grainy.

greek spinach dip

Makes 16 to 20 servings

This dip, with feta and spinach, has Greek overtones. Garnish with kalamata olives or chopped tomatoes. Serve with pita chips or crackers.

1 bag (16 ounces) frozen chopped spinach,
    thawed and well drained
2 packages (8 ounces each) cream cheese, softened
½ cup milk
½ teaspoon Greek seasoning mix or oregano
¾ cup crumbled feta cheese
1¼ cups shredded mozzarella or Monterey Jack cheese
½ cup pitted and coarsely chopped kalamata olives
½ red bell pepper, chopped, or ½ tomato, seeded and chopped

1. With your hands, squeeze as much moisture as possible from the spinach. In a bowl, mix together the cream cheese, spinach, milk, and Greek seasoning until well blended. Stir in the feta and 1 cup of the mozzarella cheese. Then mix in the olives and bell pepper. Turn into a 1½-quart electric slow cooker.

2. Cover and cook on the low heat setting for 2¼ to 2½ hours, or until the dip is hot. Sprinkle the remaining ¼ cup mozzarella over the top and serve.

hummus

You won't believe how easily you can make large quantities of delicious hummus with freshly cooked dried chickpeas, which are sometimes called garbanzo beans. Serve with vegetable dippers, such as carrot strips, red pepper strips, broccoli and cauliflower pieces, celery sticks, and baby tomatoes; pita crisps; or even tortilla chips.

1 package (16 ounces) dried chickpeas (garbanzo beans)
6 cups boiling water
½ cup fresh lemon juice
¼ cup extra virgin olive oil
⅓ cup plus 2 teaspoons chopped fresh parsley
¾ cup tahini
3 garlic cloves, crushed through a press
1 teaspoon smoked paprika
Seasoned salt and freshly ground black pepper

1. Rinse and drain the chickpeas. Place them in a 3½- or 4-quart electric slow cooker with the boiling water. (Do not add any salt as it will toughen the beans and they won't absorb water properly during cooking.)

2. Cover and cook on the high heat setting for 3¾ to 4 hours, or until the chickpeas are tender but still hold their shape. Drain off and discard the cooking liquid. Rinse the chickpeas with cold water and drain well. Let cool to room temperature.

3. In a food processor, combine the cooked chickpeas with the lemon juice, olive oil, ⅓ cup of the parsley, the tahini, garlic, smoked paprika, and 3 tablespoons of cold water. Puree until almost smooth, adding a little more water if necessary for good consistency. Add seasoned salt and pepper to taste. Cover and refrigerate the hummus until chilled. Serve with the remaining 2 teaspoons parsley sprinkled on top.

party taco dip

find this easy offering is always a hit at parties. It's like nachos without the chips. Instead, the chips are passed on the side for dipping. After cooking, transfer the dip to an attractive dish.

1 pound lean ground beef

½ medium onion, chopped

1 can (16 ounces) refried beans

1 jar (15.5 ounces) chunky salsa, mild or medium to taste

1 can (6 ounces) pitted ripe olives, drained and coarsely chopped

12 ounces shredded Mexican cheese blend or Cheddar cheese (about 3 cups)

1 tomato, chopped

½ cup guacamole

½ sour cream

1. In a large skillet, sauté the beef and onion over medium-high heat, stirring to break up the meat, until the beef is browned, 6 to 8 minutes. Drain off any excess fat.

2. Turn into a 3½- or 4-quart quart electric slow cooker. Stir in the refried beans, salsa, olives, and 2 cups of the cheese until well mixed.

3. Cover and cook on the high heat setting for 1½ to 2 hours or on the low heat setting for 3 to 4 hours.

4. Scatter the remaining 1 cup cheese and the chopped tomatoes over the hot dip. Dollop the guacamole and sour cream on top.

salsa-cheese dip

Makes 12 to 16 servings

Depending upon the variety of salsa you choose here, this dip can be made hot and spicy or mild. Also, if you like to experiment, try pineapple, chipotle, or even peach salsa for a change. Use a small 1½-quart electric slow cooker and serve the dip right from the pot, with a basket of tortilla chips on the side for dipping.

2 packages (8 ounces each) cream cheese, softened
1 container (12 ounces) refrigerated fresh tomato salsa
2½ cups shredded Mexican cheese blend
   (such as a combination of Monterey Jack, Cheddar,
   queso quesadilla, and asadero cheeses)
½ green, yellow, or red bell pepper, chopped
2 plum tomatoes, chopped

1. In a medium bowl, mix together the cream cheese and salsa until well blended. Stir in 2 cups of the cheese and the chopped bell pepper.

2. Turn this mixture into a 1½-quart electric slow cooker. Cover and cook on the low heat setting for about 2 hours, stirring once or twice, until the cheese is melted and the dip is hot.

3. Top with the remaining ½ cup cheese and chopped fresh tomatoes.

Cook's Note

➤ Store-bought shredded Mexican cheese blends vary depending on the brand. The exact mixture is not important.

nacho party dip

Easy and festive for a gathering of friends, this goes together in a jiffy. If you need more for a party, double the recipe and use a larger slow cooker on the low heat setting. If you like your dips extra hot, try substituting chipotle salsa for the salsa verde. Serve with yellow or blue corn tortilla chips for dipping.

**Makes about 4 cups;
10 to 12 servings**

½ pound lean ground beef or turkey

2 scallions, chopped

⅔ cup taco sauce

⅓ cup salsa verde

1 can (4 ounces) diced green chiles

½ cup coarsely chopped pitted ripe olives

2 cups corn kernels, drained canned or thawed frozen

¼ teaspoon freshly ground black pepper

1 cup shredded Mexican cheese blend or a combination of shredded Cheddar and mozzarella cheese

Cook's Note

➤ This marvelous dip can also be used as a nacho topping, a base for a tostada salad, or as a filling for tacos or burritos.

1. In a large skillet, cook the beef over medium-high heat, breaking up any large lumps, until browned, 6 to 8 minutes; drain off any excess fat. Stir in the scallions and cook for a few minutes longer. Stir in the taco sauce, salsa verde, green chiles, olives, corn, and pepper. Mix well. Transfer to a 1½-quart electric slow cooker.

2. Cover and cook on the low heat setting for 2 hours, or until the mixture is very hot and bubbling a bit around the edges.

3. Add ¾ cup of the cheese and stir to mix well. Sprinkle the remaining ¼ cup cheese over the top, cover, and cook for 5 minutes longer, until the cheese is melted.

warm pizza dip

Makes 16 to 20 servings

Easy, delicious, and flavorful—and best of all, enough for a crowd. This is one of those recipes that will be as popular with kids as with adults. Serve with crackers, pita crisps, potato chips, bread sticks, or toasted bread rounds.

2 packages (8 ounces each) cream cheese, softened
1½ cups pizza sauce, homemade (see page 110) or your
    favorite brand
Salt and freshly ground black pepper
1 can (2¼ ounces) sliced ripe olives, drained
¼ cup chopped fresh basil
2 cups shredded mozzarella cheese (about 8 ounces)
2 tablespoons freshly grated Parmesan cheese

1. In a bowl, combine the cream cheese and 1 cup of the pizza sauce. Beat with a wooden spoon until well blended. Season with salt and pepper to taste.

2. Spread the cream cheese mixture evenly over the bottom of a 3-quart electric slow cooker. Spoon the remaining ½ cup pizza sauce on top in an even layer. Sprinkle the olives, 2 tablespoons of the basil, 1 cup of the mozzarella cheese, and the Parmesan cheese over the sauce.

3. Cover and cook on the low heat setting for 1½ hours. Sprinkle the remaining 1 cup mozzarella cheese and 2 tablespoons basil on top.

4. Cover and continue cooking on low for 30 to 45 minutes longer, or until the dip is hot in the center.

reuben deli spread

This tasty party spread is designed to serve a crowd. It has all the flavors of a Reuben sandwich, except turkey pastrami is used instead of corned beef. And if you can't find turkey pastrami, smoked turkey makes a fine substitute. Serve with small slices of cocktail rye or pumpernickel bread or with rye crackers.

Makes 20 to 24 servings

3 packages (8 ounces each) cream cheese, softened
⅓ cup ketchup
2 tablespoons dill pickle relish
2 teaspoons yellow mustard
1 large jar (33.8 ounces) refrigerated sauerkraut, rinsed and
    well drained
½ pound turkey pastrami, chopped
1½ cups shredded Swiss cheese (about 6 ounces)

1. In a large bowl, mix together the cream cheese, ketchup, pickle relish, and yellow mustard. Stir in the sauerkraut, turkey pastrami, and 1 cup of the Swiss cheese until well blended.

2. Transfer the mixture to a 4-quart electric slow cooker. Spread it out evenly. Cover and cook on the low heat setting for about 2½ hours or on the high heat setting for about 1¼ hours, until hot throughout.

3. Stir with a large spoon, then top with the remaining ½ cup Swiss cheese. Cover and cook for 5 to 10 minutes longer, until the cheese on top is melted. Serve warm.

Cook's Note

➤ Do not add any salt to this recipe. The pastrami, ketchup, pickle relish, mustard, and sauerkraut contain plenty.

hot cheddar and white bean dip with ground meat and chiles

Makes 12 to 16 servings

f you use cannellini beans, they'll fall apart during the long, slow cooking, whereas black or pinto beans tend to hold their shape. Choose whichever suits you best. I take a shortcut here by using diced tomatoes with chiles already in the can to add a touch of spicy heat—no extra spices are required. Serve with a basket of tortilla chips.

1 pound lean ground beef or turkey

2 cans (15 ounces each) cannellini, black, or pinto beans, rinsed and well drained

1 can (10 ounces) diced tomatoes and green chiles

1 can (8 ounces) tomato sauce

1 can (6 ounces) pitted ripe olives, well drained and coarsely chopped

2 cups shredded sharp Cheddar cheese (about 8 ounces)

1 cup sharp Cheddar cheese, cut into ½-inch chunks

1. In a large skillet, sauté the ground meat over medium-high heat, stirring to break up any lumps, until browned, 5 to 7 minutes. Drain off any excess fat.

2. Transfer the browned meat to a 3- or 4-quart electric slow cooker. Add the beans, tomatoes and chiles, tomato sauce, olives, and shredded Cheddar cheese.

3. Cover and cook on the high heat setting for about 1½ hours or on the low heat setting for about 3 hours, until hot throughout.

4. Stir in the cheese chunks. Turn off the cooker, remove the insert, and let stand for 5 to 10 minutes. Stir again and serve.

south-of-the-border savory cheesecake

Makes 1 cheesecake;
12 to 16 servings

This easy recipe makes a whole cheesecake, which looks very pretty on a platter. I like to decorate it with multicolored mini peppers or with sprigs of cilantro. Since the cheesecake is cooked in advance and served chilled, it is a great choice for easy entertaining. Offer as an hors d'oeuvre at a cocktail party or slice into thin wedges and serve on small plates as a first course at a dinner party.

3 packages (8 ounces each) cream cheese, softened

3 large eggs

1⅓ cups chunky salsa

1 tablespoon all-purpose flour

1 tablespoon ground cumin

1 tablespoon chopped fresh or canned jalapeño pepper, or
    more to taste

¼ teaspoon salt

¼ teaspoon freshly ground black pepper

½ red bell pepper, chopped

½ green bell pepper, chopped

5 scallions, chopped

Sour cream, for garnish

1. In a large bowl, combine the cream cheese, eggs, ⅓ cup of the salsa, the flour, cumin, jalapeño, salt, and black pepper. Beat together with an electric mixer until well blended and smooth. Stir in the red and green bell peppers and the scallions, until well mixed.

2. Transfer to an 8-inch springform pan. Place on a vegetable steamer or other rack in a 5-quart round electric slow cooker. Do not add any water. Cover and cook on the high heat setting for 2¾ to 3 hours, or until the cake is almost set.

3. Turn off the cooker and remove the stoneware insert. Let stand until the springform pan is cool enough to handle. Remove the cheesecake from the insert and let stand until cooled to lukewarm, then refrigerate until thoroughly chilled, at least 4 or 5 hours.

4. Before serving, remove the sides of the springform pan. Spread the remaining 1 cup salsa over the top of the cheesecake. Garnish with sour cream.

Cook's Note

► You can just dollop the sour cream over the top of the cake. To make a more attractive design, thin the sour cream with enough milk so that it is the consistency of crème fraîche. Drizzle diagonal lines of the cream over the cake. Take a knife and draw it through the lines, first in one direction, then in the other, moving across the cake to create a sort of lattice pattern.

roasted red pepper cheesecake

Makes 1 cheesecake;
12 to 16 servings

Here's a show-stopping appetizer that's both colorful and tasty. It's garnished with sour cream and slices of pimiento-stuffed olives. Serve with crackers or toasted baguette slices.

¾ cup roasted red peppers, well rinsed and drained if jarred

2 packages (8 ounces each) cream cheese, softened

1 cup whole-milk ricotta cheese

2 large eggs

2 tablespoons all-purpose flour

2 tablespoons red wine vinegar

1½ tablespoons dried basil

1 garlic clove, crushed through a press

½ cup sliced pimiento-stuffed olives

Salt and freshly ground black pepper

Sour cream, for garnish

1. In a food processor, puree the roasted peppers. Add the cream cheese and ricotta and process until smooth. Add the eggs, flour, vinegar, basil, and garlic. Process until very well blended. Stir in the olive slices. Season with salt and pepper to taste.

2. Transfer the cream cheese mixture to an 8-inch springform pan. Place the pan on a vegetable steamer or other rack set in the bottom of a 5- to 6-quart round electric slow cooker. Do not add any water.

3. Cover and cook on the high heat setting for 2¾ to 3 hours, or until the cheesecake is set.

4. Turn off the cooker and remove the stoneware insert. Let stand until the springform pan is cool enough to handle. Remove the cheesecake from the insert and let stand until cooled to lukewarm, then refrigerate until thoroughly chilled, at least 4 or 5 hours.

5. Before serving, remove the sides of the springform pan. Place the cheesecake on a serving platter and garnish with dollops of sour cream topped with additional sliced pimiento-stuffed olives. Serve cut into thin slices.

cheese fondue stuffed bread

**Makes 1 loaf;
8 to 10 servings**

Here's a cheese dip that's a little like fondue, with the outside of the bread acting as a container for the melted cheese—while it cooks! This is a novel way to cook a cheese spread in a round sourdough loaf. The inside of the hollowed-out loaf is cut into cubes and used for dippers along with crackers or crudités.

1 round loaf (14 to 16 ounces) unsliced sourdough bread

1 package (8 ounces) cream cheese, softened

3 to 4 tablespoons heavy cream

1 teaspoon Worcestershire sauce

2 scallions (white and green parts), chopped

1 can (13.75 ounces) artichoke hearts, rinsed, drained, and chopped

⅓ cup chopped pimiento-stuffed olives

1 cup shredded sharp Cheddar cheese

¼ teaspoon freshly ground black pepper

Crackers and crudités

Cook's Note

➤ For an alternative way of serving, let the fondue cool until lukewarm, cut the entire bread into wedges (with the top on), and serve as sandwiches.

1. Cut a thin slice off the top of the bread loaf; reserve this "lid." With a curved serrated grapefruit knife or your hands, remove the soft inside of the loaf, leaving a shell about ¾ inch thick. Cut the inside bread into ½- to ¾-inch cubes and set aside.

2. In a medium bowl, combine the cream cheese, cream, and Worcestershire sauce. Blend with a fork until smooth. Stir in the scallions, artichokes, olives, Cheddar cheese, and pepper. Mix until well blended. Spoon the cheese mixture into the hollowed-out bread loaf. Set the lid in place.

3. Wrap the loaf tightly in a double thickness of heavy-duty aluminum foil. Place the wrapped loaf in a 5- or 6-quart electric slow cooker. Do not add any liquid.

4. Cover and cook on the high heat setting for 2 hours. Carefully remove the loaf from the slow cooker. Let stand for 5 to 10 minutes, then carefully unwrap. Place on a serving platter and remove the bread lid. Serve immediately, while the dip is hot and molten, with the bread cubes, crackers, and crudités for dipping.

bbq chicken wings

Makes 12 to 15 servings

Whip up an easy pot of these for chicken wing fans. They make a nice hot hors d'oeuvre or a great TV snack. If you're having a big party, double the recipe and cook in a 6-quart slow cooker. They are so tasty that no dipping sauce is needed.

> 3 pounds chicken wings
> Salt and freshly ground black pepper
> 1 cup hickory-flavored barbecue sauce
> ¼ cup honey
> ¼ cup red wine vinegar
> 2½ tablespoons Dijon mustard

1. Cut off the chicken wing tips and discard. Separate each wing at the joint into two pieces. Place the wing pieces on a broiler pan lined with aluminum foil for easier cleanup. Season with salt and pepper.

2. Preheat the broiler. Broil the wing pieces about 5 inches from the heat for 10 to 12 minutes per side, until nicely browned. Transfer to a 4-quart electric slow cooker.

3. In a bowl, whisk together the barbecue sauce, honey, vinegar, and mustard until blended. Pour over the chicken pieces in the pot and toss gently until completely coated. Cover and cook on the low heat setting for 4 to 4½ hours, or until the wings are tender. Serve hot.

cocktail smoked sausages

Retro food is back, if it has ever been gone, and these tiny sweet-and-spicy sausages are much like cocktail meatballs or miniature hot dogs. These are no worry, because they come already cooked. The time in the pot simply heats them up with no fuss and glazes them with a marvelous sweet-pungent sauce. Serve them hot, right from the pot. Be sure to put out a container of toothpicks, small plates or cocktail napkins, and your favorite mustard for dipping.

Makes 20 to 25 servings

3 pounds precooked mini smoked beef sausages

1 cup peach or apricot preserves

¼ cup bottled chili sauce

2 teaspoons prepared cream-style horseradish

1 teaspoon powdered mustard

1. Place the sausages in a 4-quart electric slower cooker. In a small bowl, combine the preserves, chili sauce, horseradish, and powdered mustard. Mix until all the ingredients are well blended. Pour over the sausages and toss until they are coated evenly with sauce.

2. Cover and cook on the high heat setting for 2½ to 3 hours or on the low heat setting for 5 to 5½ hours, until hot and bubbly. Remove the lid and cook for 20 to 30 minutes longer to reduce the sauce slightly.

smoky roasted cashews

can't stop eating these spiced nuts, with their fabulous smoky flavor and appealing crunch. Serve for nibbling with drinks at a cocktail party or before a dinner. Or enjoy as a snack anytime.

1 pound roasted unsalted whole cashews (4 cups)
1 tablespoon extra virgin olive oil
1½ teaspoons smoked paprika
½ teaspoon kosher or coarse salt
⅛ teaspoon cayenne pepper, or more to taste

1. Place the cashews in a 3-quart electric slow cooker. Add the olive oil and mix well. Add the smoked paprika, salt, and cayenne. Toss until the nuts are evenly coated with the spices.

2. Cover and cook on the high heat setting for 1 hour. Uncover and continue cooking on the high heat setting for 1 hour longer, stirring once or twice.

3. Transfer the spiced nuts to a dish and let cool. When cool, pack in an airtight plastic container and use within a week or two.

sassy spiced pecans

A little sweet and a little spicy, these are terrific with drinks at a party. They are also delicious as a garnish for salads.

Makes about 4 cups

6 tablespoons butter

1 tablespoon ground ancho chile

¼ teaspoon ground chipotle chile, or more to taste

1½ to 2 teaspoons granulated or brown sugar

½ teaspoon salt

1 pound pecan halves (4 cups)

1. Melt the butter in a glass or ceramic bowl in a microwave oven on high power for 45 seconds to 1 minute. Stir in the ancho and chipotle chile, sugar, and salt until well mixed.

2. Put the pecans in a 3-quart electric slow cooker. Pour the chile butter over the pecans and toss to coat evenly.

3. Cover and cook on the high heat setting for 1 hour. Uncover and continue cooking on the high heat setting for 1 to 1½ hours longer, stirring occasionally.

4. Spread out the pecans on a baking sheet to cool; line it with aluminum foil if you like to avoid cleanup. When cool, pack the spiced nuts in an airtight container and store in the refrigerator for up to 1½ months or in the freezer for up to 3 months.

mini meatballs with apricot glaze

**Makes 60 to 65 meatballs;
15 to 20 servings**

Cocktail meatballs have never gone out of fashion. They make great party fare and can be served right from the pot. If you prefer, the meatballs can be made ahead and frozen, then pulled out, thawed, and reheated with the sauce. While this is one recipe that requires some precooking outside of the pot, it is the long, slow simmering that give these fabulous meatballs their character.

1 large egg

1 cup fine dry bread crumbs

1 small onion, chopped

2 tablespoons chopped fresh parsley

½ teaspoon salt

½ teaspoon freshly ground black pepper

⅔ cup heavy cream or whole milk

2 pounds lean ground beef

⅔ cup apricot preserves

⅓ cup chipotle-mustard sauce, such as Frontera, or other grilling sauce

2½ tablespoons ketchup

Cook's Note

➤ Make this an instant recipe by purchasing 60 to 65 already cooked cocktail meat-balls and beginning at Step 3.

1. Preheat the oven to 450°F. In a large bowl, beat the egg lightly.
    Add the bread crumbs, onion, parsley, salt, pepper, and cream
    and mix until thoroughly blended. Add the beef and blend
    well. Using a 1¼-inch scoop, form the mixture into meatballs.
    Or roll into balls about the size of a walnut between the palms
    of your hands.

2. Place the meatballs on 2 jelly-roll or half-sheet pans lined with
    nonstick aluminum foil. Bake for 15 to 20 minutes, until the
    meatballs are browned and cooked through. If the baking
    sheet gets too greasy during baking, carefully drain off the
    excess fat.

3. Meanwhile, make a sauce by mixing together the apricot pre-
    serves, chipotle-mustard sauce, and ketchup until well blended.

4. Arrange half of the browned meatballs in a 4-quart electric
    slow cooker. Pour half of the apricot sauce over them. Add
    the remaining meatballs and pour the remaining sauce over
    the top.

5. Cover and cook on the low heat setting for about 4 hours or on
    the high heat setting for about 2 hours, until the meatballs are
    hot and glazed. Serve hot.

rich hot chocolate

Makes about 6½ cups;
10 to 12 servings

Be sure to use a dark, bittersweet chocolate here for a rich, smooth drink. There are lots of chocolate choices in supermarkets these days. Choose the best one you can for this incredible beverage. I use Trader Joe's bittersweet, but other 70 percent cacao products will work well, too. Since this is truly decadent, indulgent, and thicker than ordinary hot chocolate, serve smaller portions in cups, topped with whipped cream. Make a big batch for a winter grown-ups' party.

1 cup heavy cream
8 ounces bittersweet chocolate (70 percent cacao), cut into 1-inch
   pieces
4 cups whole milk
¼ cup sugar
Whipped cream, for topping

1. In a 2-quart glass measuring cup or a bowl, combine the heavy cream and chocolate. Heat in a microwave oven on high power for 1½ to 2½ minutes, until the chocolate is melted when stirred. Whisk to mix well. Whisk in 1 cup of the milk until blended.

2. Transfer the chocolate mixture to a 4-quart electric slow cooker. Whisk in the sugar and the remaining 3 cups milk.

3. Cover and cook on the high heat setting for 2 to 2½ hours or on the low heat setting for 4 to 5 hours, until the chocolate is very hot. Ladle into cups or small mugs and top with whipped cream.

hot mocha with cream

Makes about 9 cups;
9 or 10 servings

Make a pot of this to serve with dessert when company's coming. Serve topped with plenty of whipped cream, sweetened or not as desired.

8 cups hot brewed vanilla- or hazelnut-flavored coffee

½ cup unsweetened cocoa powder

½ cup sugar

½ cup brandy

½ cup Kahlúa or Bailey's Irish Crème

½ cup heavy cream, whipped

1. Pour the hot coffee into a 4-quart electric slow cooker. Whisk in the cocoa and sugar until well blended.

2. Cover and cook on the low heat setting for 2 to 3 hours or on the high heat setting for 1 to 1½ hours.

3. Just before serving, stir in the brandy and Kahlúa. Ladle into mugs or heatproof stemmed glasses. Garnish with a dollop of whipped cream and serve.

Cook's Note

➤ You can turn the whipped cream into chocolate whipped cream by beating in 1 teaspoon unsweetened cocoa powder and 1 tablespoon sugar.

hot spiced fruit punch

Makes about 8½ cups;
10 to 12 servings

Warm up on a winter night with this delicious and easy drink. It adds a wonderful aroma to the kitchen while it's heating.

1 large container (64 ounces) light apple-cranberry juice beverage
    or apple cider
1 can (12 ounces) frozen pineapple-orange juice concentrate
    (with lemon juice), thawed
2 cinnamon sticks
4 whole cloves
¼ teaspoon grated nutmeg
Thin orange slices, for garnish

1. In a 4- or 5-quart electric slow cooker, combine the apple-cranberry juice, pineapple-orange juice concentrate, cinnamon sticks, cloves, and nutmeg.

2. Cover and cook on the low heat setting for 5 to 6 hours, or until very hot.

3. Remove the cinnamon sticks and cloves. Ladle into heatproof glasses or mugs and garnish each with a slice of orange.

hot mulled wine

In fall and winter, nothing says hospitality like a cup of aromatic and fragrant warm spiced wine. The slow cooker does a great job of steeping the wine, spirits, and flavorings together without allowing them to boil.

Makes 9½ to 10 cups;
10 to 12 servings

2 bottles (750 ml each) dry red wine, such as merlot or pinot noir
2 cups orange juice
½ cup Triple Sec or Cointreau
¼ cup brandy
¼ cup sugar
3 cinnamon sticks
Lemon or orange slices, for garnish

1. Pour the wine, orange juice, Triple Sec, and brandy into a 4-quart electric slow cooker. Add the sugar and stir well to dissolve. Add the cinnamon sticks.

2. Cover and cook on the high heat setting for 3 to 3½ hours or on the low heat setting for 6 to 7 hours, until very hot. Remove the cinnamon sticks.

3. Ladle into heatproof glasses or mugs. Garnish with lemon or orange slices, if desired.

warm winter fruit punch

No one will feel cold after they've taken a sip of this wonderful warm drink that has tangy, tart undertones. There's plenty for an après-ski or pumpkin-carving party. If you want to spike the drink for adults, stir in about 1 cup rum or orange-flavored vodka just before serving.

1 container (64 ounces) grapefruit-tangerine juice or
    other citrus fruit drink
1 can (12 ounces) frozen white grape and raspberry juice
    concentrate, thawed
1 cup pineapple juice
4 to 5 tablespoons sugar
1 large orange, sliced, plus more for garnish (optional)
2 cinnamon sticks

1. In a 5-quart electric slow cooker, combine the grapefruit-tangerine juice, grape and raspberry juice concentrate, pineapple juice, sugar, orange slices, cinnamon sticks, and 2 cups of water. Mix well.

2. Cover and cook on the low-heat setting for 5 to 6 hours or on the high-heat setting for 2½ to 3 hours, until the beverage is very hot. Stir again. Remove the cinnamon sticks.

3. Ladle into mugs and serve hot, garnished with additional orange slices, if desired.

open-house party punch

This is a good choice for a warming drink during a holiday open house or other large gathering. Since the punch is warm, it's best served during the cold-weather months. For an adult crowd, you can spike the punch with a little vanilla-flavored rum, if you feel so inclined.

Makes about 3½ quarts;
20 servings

1 container (64 ounces) apple juice
1 can (12 ounces) frozen raspberry lemonade concentrate, thawed
1 can (12 ounces) frozen orange juice concentrate, thawed
⅔ cup packed light brown sugar
3 cinnamon sticks

1. In a 5- or 6-quart electric slow cooker, combine the apple juice, raspberry lemonade concentrate, orange juice concentrate, brown sugar, cinnamon sticks, and 4 cups of water. Mix well.

2. Cover and cook on the low heat setting for about 8 hours, until very hot. Just before serving, remove and discard the cinnamon sticks. Ladle into mugs or heatproof punch cups.

3. Refrigerate any leftover punch. Serve chilled, or reheat over low heat or in a microwave oven.

To make life as easy as possible, use shortcut food items to make cooking in the slow cooker even easier:

- canned beans
- rotisserie or grilled chicken
- canned diced tomatoes and tomato paste
- oven-ready lasagna noodles
- corn and flour tortillas
- prepared barbecue sauces in various flavors
- canned black olives and jarred pimiento-stuffed olives and roasted red peppers
- canned or frozen corn
- canned broth (opt for low sodium, fat free)
- sliced fresh or dried mushrooms
- frozen pearl onions
- frozen chopped spinach
- frozen peas or edamame (shelled soybeans)
- dried fruits
- packages or bags of prepared fresh vegetables, such as cut-up peeled squash, cut peeled carrots, and chopped onions, which are available in the refrigerated produce section of most supermarkets these days.

soups and chowders

Because most soups benefit from long, slow simmering, the electric slow cooker is not just an alternative to the stove-top; it's an excellent option that avoids the risk of too much evaporation. The pot excels in making soups based on vegetables, meat, and poultry, all of which benefit from the time and low temperature.

Seafood also does well when cooked at a low temperature, but not over time. For that reason, all the fish and shellfish chowders here call for letting the soup base steep unattended over a period of hours. Then the seafood is added and cooked for 30 or 40 minutes, until it is just done. During this last phase, you really should stick around and watch; overcooked seafood is tough and tasteless.

soups and chowders

chunky fresh beet soup

Makes 5 to 6 servings

Although the beets lose their deep purple color during the long, slow cooking and end up a paler red, this simple soup tastes fresh and delicious with a large dollop of sour cream and a sprinkling of chives or parsley for color. Accompany with a slice of olive bread for an easy supper on a busy day. The soup reheats beautifully.

3 pounds fresh beets, peeled and cut into ¾-inch cubes

6 cups chopped green cabbage (about 1 pound)

3 cups chopped carrots (about 6 carrots)

1 large onion, chopped

3 cans (14.5 ounces each) chicken or vegetable broth

½ teaspoon salt

¼ teaspoon freshly ground black pepper

3 to 4 tablespoons balsamic vinegar

Sour cream or plain yogurt and chopped fresh chives or
    flat-leaf parsley, for garnish

1. In a 6-quart electric slow cooker, combine the beets, cabbage, carrots, onion, broth, salt, and pepper.

2. Cover and cook on the low heat setting for 6½ to 7½ hours, until the beets are tender.

3. Stir in the vinegar. Season with additional salt and pepper to taste. Serve in soup bowls, garnished with a dollop of sour cream and a sprinkling of chives.

black bean soup

Makes 6 to 8 servings

No soaking, no blanching. This Mexican version of black bean soup turns out a rich, dark color because the beans are not soaked, simply rinsed and drained prior to cooking. For best results, after cooking puree half of the beans and liquid and return to the pot before serving. The pureed beans thicken the rest of the soup nicely. Serve with a dollop of sour cream and a garnish of chopped tomato and crumbled cooked bacon in each bowl.

1 package (16 ounces) dried black beans

1 large onion, chopped

2 tablespoons finely chopped Anaheim chile pepper

1 can (14.5 ounces) beef or chicken broth

1 can (14.5 ounces) diced tomatoes

1 bottle (12 ounces) beer

1 tablespoon ground cumin

1 tablespoon chili powder

2 garlic cloves, minced

Salt

1. Put the dried beans into a colander; rinse and drain well. Pick over to remove any grit.

2. In a 5-quart electric slow cooker, combine the beans, onion, chile, broth, tomatoes with their juices, beer, cumin, chili powder, garlic, and 3 cups of water.

3. Cover and cook on the low heat setting for 7 hours, or until the beans are tender.

4. Carefully remove half of the liquid and beans and puree in batches in a food processor or blender. Return the pureed mixture to the slow cooker pot. Season the soup with salt to taste.

Even though a recipe may call for a small amount of liquid (and it may seem like too little), don't be tempted to add more. Liquids do not evaporate or boil away during slow cooking. Generally assume you'll have more liquid at the end of cooking time, not less, due to the steam and condensation falling from the cooker cover back into the pot and the moisture exuded from the foods.

sweet-and-sour cabbage soup

Makes 6 to 8 servings

This hearty soup is like meatless stuffed cabbage you eat with a spoon. Like many cabbage- and tomato-based dishes, it tastes even better when reheated. Serve with buttered pumpernickel bread, if you like.

1 head green cabbage (2 to 2½ pounds), cored and coarsely chopped (about 10 cups)

1 large onion, chopped

3 cans (14.5 ounces each) chicken broth

1 can (28 ounces) peeled diced tomatoes

⅓ cup tomato paste

1 teaspoon salt

½ teaspoon freshly ground black pepper

⅓ cup balsamic vinegar

¼ cup packed brown sugar

Sour cream and chopped fresh chives, for garnish

1. In a 6-quart electric slow cooker, combine the cabbage, onion, broth, tomatoes with their juices, tomato paste, salt, pepper, vinegar, and brown sugar. Stir to mix well.

2. Cover and cook on the low heat setting for 7 to 8 hours, until the cabbage is very tender. Season with additional salt and pepper to taste.

3. Serve in soup bowls, garnished with a dollop of sour cream and a sprinkling of chopped chives.

lentil soup with canadian bacon

What this soup lacks in eye appeal, it makes up for in flavor. Garnish with a drizzle of balsamic vinegar or olive oil for added pizzazz. The soup reheats well. If it thickens too much upon standing, simply stir in a little more broth or water.

Makes 6 to 8 servings

1 package (16 ounces) dried lentils, rinsed, drained,
   and picked over
1 large onion, chopped
2 cups chopped celery
1½ cups chopped carrots
1 cup chopped Canadian bacon or baked ham
8 cups (64 ounces) chicken broth
2 teaspoons dried basil
½ teaspoon celery seeds
½ teaspoon seasoned pepper
Balsamic vinegar and/or extra virgin olive oil, for garnish

1. In a 5-quart electric slow cooker, combine the lentils, onion, celery, carrots, Canadian bacon, broth, basil, celery seeds, and seasoned pepper. Mix well.

2. Cover and cook on the low heat setting for 6½ to 7½ hours, until the lentils are tender.

3. To serve, ladle into soup bowls. Top with a small drizzle of balsamic vinegar and/or olive oil.

sweet corn chowder

Makes 5 to 6 servings

Everyone loves corn chowder, and this one, made in the slow cooker with frozen corn, is both easier than ever and good year-round. Serve for a starter or as a main course paired with a salad and thick slices of whole-grain bread.

1½ pounds Yukon gold or small white potatoes, peeled and cut into ½-inch dice

1 package (16 ounces) frozen white or roasted corn kernels, thawed

⅓ cup all-purpose flour

1 medium onion, chopped

2 celery ribs, chopped

1 garlic clove, minced

¾ teaspoon salt

4 cups homemade or 2 cans (14.5 ounces each) reduced-sodium, fat-free chicken broth

1 cup heavy cream

1 tablespoon Worcestershire sauce

¼ teaspoon freshly ground black pepper

¼ teaspoon ground chipotle chile

Chopped fresh parsley or chives, for garnish

1. Place the potatoes and corn in a 4-quart electric slow cooker. Sprinkle the flour over the vegetables and toss to mix well.

2. Add the onion, celery, garlic, and ¼ teaspoon of the salt. Stir in the broth. Cover and cook on the low heat setting for 7 hours, or until the potatoes are tender.

3. Stir in the cream, Worcestershire sauce, remaining ½ teaspoon salt, the pepper, and chipotle chile.

4. Cover and cook on the low heat setting for 1 to 1¼ hours longer. Ladle into soup bowls. Garnish with parsley.

Use completely—never partially— thawed foods in the slow cooker. If necessary, carefully thaw foods in a microwave oven on low power before adding to the pot. If using a commercially frozen slow cooker meal, prepare according to the manufacturer's instructions.

french onion soup

The one thing you cannot do in the slow cooker is brown foods. So to serve a really traditional gratinéed onion soup Parisian style, the onions must be caramelized on top of the stove first. At the other end, to make finishing easier, instead of broiling the cheese-covered bread on top of individual soup bowls in the oven, I grill the cheese bread separately and set it atop the bowls of soup.

2 tablespoons butter

4 very large Spanish onions, thinly sliced

1 teaspoon sugar

8 cups (64 ounces) chicken or beef broth

¼ cup dry or medium-dry sherry

2 tablespoons Worcestershire sauce

½ teaspoon freshly ground black pepper

¼ teaspoon salt

1 cup shredded Gruyère or mozzarella cheese

6 to 8 slices of peasant or sourdough bread,
    lightly toasted

1. In a large skillet, heat 1 tablespoon of the butter over medium-high heat until melted. Stir in half of the onions and ½ teaspoon of the sugar. Cover and cook for 5 minutes. Uncover, raise the heat to medium-high, and continue to cook, stirring often, until the onions are dark golden brown and caramelized, about 10 minutes longer. Transfer the browned onions to a 5- or 6-quart electric slow cooker. Repeat with the remaining butter, onions, and sugar (or use 2 skillets).

2. Add the broth, sherry, Worcestershire sauce, pepper, and salt. Cover and cook on the low heat setting for 4½ to 5 hours.

3. Preheat the broiler. Sprinkle the cheese over the bread slices to cover evenly. Broil about 6 inches from the heat until the cheese is melted and lightly browned, 2 to 3 minutes.

4. Ladle the soup into heatproof bowls. Float a cheese-covered bread slice on top of each and serve immediately.

For more flavor in soups and stews, use fat-free broth in place of water.

cheddared potato soup

Homey and warming, this chunky potato soup offers plenty of comfort as well as great taste. When they are available, Dutch yellow potatoes are great here; at other times, Yukon gold or other "buttery" potatoes make a fine choice. Also, be sure to use a good-quality aged Cheddar cheese.

1 medium onion, chopped

⅓ cup instant-blending flour, such as Wondra

4 cups chicken broth

2 pounds baby Dutch yellow potatoes or Yukon gold potatoes, peeled and cut into ¾- to 1-inch cubes

2 cups half-and-half

Seasoned salt and garlic pepper

1 to 1½ cups shredded sharp Cheddar cheese

½ cup crisply cooked crumbled bacon

½ cup finely chopped scallions

1. In a 5-quart electric slow cooker, combine the onion and flour, mixing well. Whisk in the broth until well blended. Add the potato cubes.

2. Cover and cook on the low heat setting for 5½ to 6 hours, until the potatoes are tender but not falling apart. Stir in the half-and-half.

3. Cover and cook on the low heat setting for 30 to 45 minutes longer, until very hot throughout. Season to taste with seasoned salt and garlic pepper.

4. To serve, ladle into soup bowls and top with the shredded cheese, crumbled bacon, and chopped scallions.

potato, carrot, and leek soup

Makes 5 to 6 servings

Toss this soup into the pot in a jiffy, and when dinner rolls around serve with thick bread slices and a green salad. This is a classic garden vegetable soup that I've given a little twist by using aromatic smoked paprika. Note that it's stirred in at the last moment to retain its bright flavor.

1 pound small white or red potatoes, preferably organic,
    scrubbed and cut into 1-inch pieces

4 large carrots, peeled and diced

2 medium leeks (white and tender green parts),
    rinsed well and chopped

2 cans (14.5 ounces each) chicken or beef broth

1 can (28 ounces) diced tomatoes

½ teaspoon salt

½ teaspoon freshly ground black pepper

2 to 3 teaspoons smoked paprika

Chopped fresh flat-leaf parsley, for garnish

1. In a 5-quart electric slow cooker, combine the potatoes, carrots, leeks, broth, tomatoes with their juices, salt, and pepper. Stir to mix well.

2. Cover and cook on the low heat setting for about 8 hours, or until the potatoes are tender.

3. Stir in the smoked paprika and season with additional salt and pepper to taste. Serve garnished with chopped parsley.

Cook's Note

➤ You can find smoked paprika in supermarkets in the spice section; it is a mild version. At specialty food shops, a greater variety is sold. Smoked Spanish paprika, sometimes called *pimentón de la Vera*, comes sweet, bittersweet, or hot. I recommend the sweet or bittersweet because the flavor is easier to control. You can always add a dash of cayenne pepper if you want to make a dish spicier.

spiced pumpkin soup

Makes 8 servings

Some tasters preferred this Southwestern-flavored soup without any cream stirred in, but suit yourself. Sprinkle the top with some shredded Cheddar cheese for a change of pace.

1 can (29 ounces) 100 percent solid pack pumpkin

4 cups canned or homemade chicken broth

1 medium onion, finely chopped

3 tablespoons light brown sugar

1 tablespoon ground cumin

1 teaspoon chili powder

½ teaspoon ground coriander

¼ teaspoon ground chipotle chile

½ teaspoon salt

Freshly ground black pepper

½ cup heavy cream (optional)

1. In a 4-quart electric slow cooker, combine the pumpkin, broth, onion, brown sugar, cumin, chili powder, coriander, ground chipotle, and salt. Mix well.

2. Cover and cook on the low heat setting for about 7 hours or on the high heat setting for about 3½ hours. Season with pepper to taste. Stir in the cream, if desired. Ladle into soup bowls and serve immediately.

spicy sweet pea soup

So that this beautiful, fresh-tasting soup can be made year-round, I make it with frozen peas, which freeze better than most vegetables. Green curry paste adds subtle heat. Refrigerate any leftovers and serve either chilled or gently reheated.

Makes 6 to 8 servings

2 teaspoons green curry paste

2 packages (16 ounces each) frozen petite peas, thawed

1 medium onion, chopped

1 or 2 garlic cloves, crushed through a press

Salt and seasoned pepper

Chopped fresh watercress or mint, for garnish

1. In a 4- or 5-quart electric slow cooker, stir the curry paste into 6 cups of water. Add the peas, onion, and garlic.

2. Cover and cook on the low heat setting for about 3 hours, until hot. Do not cook longer, or the peas will discolor.

3. Use a hand-held immersion blender to puree the soup in the pot. Or puree in batches in a blender or food processor. Season with salt and seasoned pepper to taste. Serve the soup hot or chilled, garnished with watercress.

split pea soup with ham

Makes 6 to 8 servings

This easily assembled soup is a great cold-weather choice, literally a meal in a bowl. If you have a meaty leftover ham bone, add it to the pot in place of the chopped ham in the recipe. Serve with whole-grain or rye bread.

1 package (16 ounces) dried green split peas, rinsed, drained, and picked over
4 carrots, peeled and chopped
3 celery ribs, chopped
1 red bell pepper, chopped
1 large onion, chopped
6 ounces smoked ham, chopped (about 1 cup)
¼ teaspoon salt
½ teaspoon freshly ground black pepper
¼ cup chopped fresh flat-leaf parsley
6 cups boiling water
1 teaspoon dried marjoram or thyme

1. In a 5-quart electric slow cooker, combine the dried peas, carrots, celery, red bell pepper, onion, half of the chopped ham, the salt, black pepper, and parsley. Pour in the boiling water.

2. Cover and cook on the high heat setting for 1 hour. Reduce the heat setting to low and continue cooking on low for 5 to 7 hours longer, or until the peas are soft and tender and disintegrate when stirred to make a thick soup.

3. Add the remaining chopped ham and the marjoram to the pot. Season with additional salt and pepper to taste.

creamy southwestern soup

T his vegetarian soup has an amazing creamy texture and heady flavor. Serve with soft, warm tortillas and a red cabbage slaw.

Makes 5 to 6 servings

1 can (14.5 ounces) diced tomatoes
1 can (15 ounces) pinto beans, rinsed and drained
1 package (16 ounces) frozen white corn kernels,
    thawed and drained
1 can (4 ounces) diced green chiles
1 garlic clove, crushed through a press
¼ teaspoon ground chipotle chile
4 cups vegetable broth
½ cup heavy cream
Salt and freshly ground black pepper
Chopped fresh cilantro, for garnish

1. In a 4- or 5-quart electric slow cooker, combine the tomatoes with their juices, beans, corn, green chiles, garlic, and ground chipotle. Stir in the broth.

2. Cover and cook on the low heat setting for 6 hours or on the high heat setting for 3 hours.

3. Remove 2 to 3 cups of the soup—liquid and vegetables—and puree in a blender or food processor. Stir the puree back into the remaining soup in the pot.

4. Stir in the heavy cream and season with salt and pepper to taste. Ladle into soup bowls and serve hot, garnished with chopped cilantro.

italian minestrone

Makes 6 to 8 servings

Here's a bit of a different take on the classic— with romaine lettuce for extra body. Be sure to top each serving with imported Parmesan cheese, Parmigiano-Reggiano, and a drizzle of extra virgin olive oil, just as they would in Italy.

1 medium onion, chopped

4 medium carrots, peeled and chopped (about 2 cups)

2 medium zucchini, chopped (about 2 cups)

3 celery ribs, chopped (about 1 cup)

1 medium-large red potato, peeled and cut into ½-inch dice

2 tablespoons chopped fresh flat-leaf parsley

5 tablespoons chopped fresh basil

2 garlic cloves, crushed through a press

3 cans (14.5 ounces each) diced tomatoes

2 cans (14.5 ounces each) chicken or vegetable broth

½ teaspoon salt

¼ teaspoon freshly ground black pepper

4 cups chopped romaine lettuce

1 can (15 ounces) small white beans, drained, then rinsed and drained well

Grated Parmigiano-Reggiano cheese and extra virgin olive oil, for garnish

1. In a 6-quart electric slow cooker, combine the onion, carrots, zucchini, celery, potato, parsley, 2 tablespoons of the basil, the garlic, tomatoes with their juices, broth, salt, and pepper. Stir to mix well.

2. Cover and cook on the low heat setting for 8 to 8½ hours. Stir in the remaining 3 tablespoons basil, the romaine lettuce, and the white beans. Cook for 10 minutes longer.

3. Serve the soup in big bowls, topped with cheese and a drizzle of olive oil.

If you need to change the timing of a recipe, generally figure that an hour on the high heat setting is equivalent to about two hours on the low heat setting. Do not tamper with cooking temperatures if a recipe specifies it must be cooked on only one setting.

ribollita

Makes 8 to 12 servings

talians say that *ribollita,* which means "reboiled," is not done until a spoon stands up in the pot. In that sense, this tremendously savory soup, thickened with bread, is really more of a vegetarian porridge. It's an ideal recipe for the slow cooker because it has to cook for such a long time. On top of the stove, ribollita cooks twice over two days. In the pot, it still takes a long time—about 15 hours—but you only need to check it a few times, and the results are superb.

This hearty soup will hold on the warm setting for several hours; or let cool and refrigerate, then reheat slowly on top of the stove. Serve in soup plates, with a cruet of extra virgin olive oil and a bowl of grated Parmesan cheese passed on the side.

1 cup chopped red onion

1 cup chopped carrots

1 cup chopped celery

3 cups chopped red cabbage

3 cups chopped cauliflower

3 cups chopped kale

3 cups chopped Swiss chard (leaves and some white stems)

1 large baking potato (12 ounces), peeled and chopped

1 can (15.5 ounces) cannellini beans, rinsed and drained

4 cups beef or chicken broth

1 cup dry red wine

1½ teaspoons salt

½ teaspoon dried oregano

¼ teaspoon crushed hot red pepper

¼ pound stale Italian or French bread, crusts removed

3 tablespoons extra virgin olive oil

1. In a 6- or 7-quart electric slow cooker, combine the chopped red onion, carrots, celery, red cabbage, cauliflower, kale, chard, potato, and beans. Add the broth, wine, salt, oregano, and hot pepper. Mix everything together as best you can. Pour 1 cup of water on top.

2. Cover and cook on the high heat setting for 8 hours. Stir in another 2 cups of water. Cook on high for 4 hours longer. If the liquid is well below the surface of the vegetables, add another 1 cup of water, but don't let the mixture become soupy.

3. Cut the bread into 1-inch cubes. If they are soft, spread out the cubes on a small baking sheet and bake in a 200°F oven for 5 to 10 minutes, until dry but not hard. Crumble the bread cubes over the ribollita in the pot. Add the olive oil and stir to mix.

4. Cover, reduce the heat setting to low, and cook for 2 hours. With a potato masher or large spoon, mash the vegetables 6 to 8 times to puree some of the beans and potatoes. Season with additional salt and hot pepper to taste. Raise the heat to high again and cook for 30 minutes longer.

butternut squash soup

Makes 5 to 6 servings

Rich tasting and gorgeous looking, this soup is a breeze to make. For convenience and to make it fuss-free, buy the butternut squash already peeled and cut into cubes.

2 packages (16 ounces each) peeled butternut squash cubes or
    6 cups peeled, seeded, and diced (1-inch pieces)
    butternut squash
2 cans (14.5 ounces each) chicken broth
1 medium onion, chopped
¼ teaspoon salt
¼ teaspoon freshly ground black pepper
2 to 3 tablespoons maple syrup
¼ teaspoon ground cinnamon
Sour cream, crème fraîche, or plain yogurt, for garnish

1. In a 5-quart electric slow cooker, combine the squash, broth, onion, salt, and pepper.

2. Cover and cook on the high heat setting for 3 to 4 hours or on the low heat setting for 6 to 8 hours, until the squash is very tender.

3. Use a hand-held immersion blender to puree the soup until smooth. Or puree in batches in a food processor or blender and return to the slow cooker. Stir in the maple syrup and cinnamon. Season with additional salt and pepper to taste.

4. To serve, ladle the hot soup into bowls. Top with a dollop of sour cream.

sweet potato soup

Makes 6 to 8 servings

This simple recipe will be even easier if you can find yams already peeled and cut up in your supermarket produce department, where they are usually sold in 1-pound packages.

2½ pounds yams, peeled and cut into 1-inch chunks
8 slices of bacon, cooked until crisp and crumbled
1 medium onion, chopped
5 cups chicken broth
1 tablespoon unsulphured molasses
½ teaspoon seasoned salt
¼ teaspoon freshly ground black pepper
⅔ cup heavy cream
2 tablespoons brandy

1. Place the yams in a 5-quart electric slow cooker. Add half of the bacon, the onion, broth, molasses, seasoned salt, and pepper.

2. Cover and cook on the low heat setting for 6½ to 7 hours, until the yams are tender.

3. Use a hand-held immersion blender to puree the soup in the slow cooker pot. Or in several batches, carefully transfer to a food processor or blender and puree until smooth; then return the soup to the slow cooker pot.

4. Stir in the cream and brandy, cover, and cook for 15 to 20 minutes longer, until hot throughout. Add additional seasoned salt and black pepper to taste. Ladle into soup bowls and garnish with a sprinkling of the remaining crumbled bacon.

vegetable-barley soup

Makes 6 to 8 servings

Barley soup, laden with lots of healthy vegetables, is hearty, homey fare. To maintain a good texture, use regular pearl barley, not instant, and be sure not to overcook it. The barley should retain a pleasing resistance to the bite.

2 cups chopped or shredded carrots

2 medium zucchini, chopped

1 large onion, chopped

3 celery ribs, chopped

⅓ cup uncooked pearl barley, rinsed several times and
   drained well

1 can (28 ounces) diced tomatoes

½ teaspoon seasoned salt

¼ teaspoon freshly ground black pepper

4 cups chicken or vegetable broth or water

¼ cup chopped fresh dill

1. In a 5- or 6-quart quart electric slow cooker, combine the carrots, zucchini, onion, celery, barley, tomatoes with their juices, seasoned salt, and pepper. Stir in the broth.

2. Cover and cook on the low heat setting for 7 hours, or until the barley is tender but not mushy.

3. Stir in the dill. Season with additional seasoned salt and pepper to taste. If you prefer a thinner soup, add up to 1 cup of additional broth or water. Serve hot.

garden vegetable soup with spinach and cheese

add the spinach during the last 15 to 20 minutes of cooking time to keep it from discoloring. The cheese sprinkled in at the end adds both flavor and body.

Makes 6 to 8 servings

1 large can (49 ounces) chicken broth

2 medium leeks (white and tender green parts), rinsed well, drained, and chopped

1½ cups finely chopped carrots

3 large plum tomatoes, chopped

2 tablespoons dried basil

½ teaspoon salt

½ teaspoon freshly ground black pepper

2 garlic cloves, crushed through a press, or ½ teaspoon garlic powder

1 bag (9 ounces) prewashed fresh spinach, chopped

¾ cup freshly grated Parmesan and Pecorino Romano cheese blend

1. In a 5-quart electric slower cooker, combine the broth, leeks, carrots, tomatoes, 1 tablespoon of the basil, the salt, pepper, garlic, and 2 cups of water. Mix well.

2. Cover and cook on the low heat setting for 6 to 7 hours, until the vegetables are tender.

3. Stir in the spinach and remaining 1 tablespoon basil. Cover and cook for 15 minutes longer. Season with additional salt and pepper to taste.

4. Ladle into bowls and serve immediately, topped with a generous sprinkling of grated cheese.

simple zucchini soup

Makes 6 to 8 servings

Rather than using flour or potato for body, this creamy vegetable soup is thickened with rice, though no one will know it is there. Garnish with a dollop of sour cream or plain yogurt and a fresh basil leaf or two. If you have any leftover, refrigerate in a covered container and serve the soup cold a day or two later.

2 pounds zucchini, coarsely chopped

1 medium onion, chopped

2 cans (14.5 ounces each) chicken broth

3 tablespoons converted long-grain white rice

¼ teaspoon ground chipotle chile

2 teaspoons dried basil

1 teaspoon salt

¼ teaspoon freshly ground black pepper

Sour cream and fresh basil leaves, for garnish

1. In a 4-quart electric slow cooker, combine the zucchini, onion, chicken broth, rice, ground chipotle, basil, salt, pepper, and 2 cups of water.

2. Cover and cook on the low heat setting for 5 to 6 hours, until the zucchini and onion are tender. Use a hand-held immersion blender to puree the soup until smooth. Or carefully transfer the hot soup in batches to a blender or food processor and puree; then return to the slow cooker.

3. To serve, ladle the hot soup into bowls. Top with a dollop of sour cream and a fresh basil leaf.

A hand-held immersion blender is a great tool for pureeing soups right in the slow cooker. It is much easier and less messy than transferring everything to a blender or food processor.

turkey sausage and vegetable soup

Makes 4 to 6 servings

These days, there are almost as many varieties of turkey sausage as there are of pork. They are a great leaner alternative. However, this soup can be made with any cooked smoked sausage. Serve garnished with a dollop of sour cream, if you like.

½ pound turkey kielbasa sausage, halved lengthwise, then cut into ¼-inch slices

3 celery ribs, chopped

1 onion, chopped

1 yellow bell pepper, chopped

1 to 1½ medium zucchini, chopped (about 1½ cups)

3½ tablespoons chopped fresh parsley

2 garlic cloves, crushed through a press

1 can (28 ounces) diced tomatoes

2 cans (14.5 ounces each) chicken or vegetable broth

1 can (28 ounces) pinto beans, rinsed and well drained

¼ teaspoon salt

¼ teaspoon freshly ground black pepper

Dash of cayenne pepper

1. Cook the sausage in a large nonstick skillet over medium heat, stirring occasionally, until lightly browned, 5 to 7 minutes. Drain off any excess fat.

2. Meanwhile, in a 5- or 6-quart electric slow cooker, combine the celery, onion, bell pepper, zucchini, 2 tablespoons of the parsley, the garlic, tomatoes with their juices, broth, beans, salt, black pepper, and cayenne. Add the sausage pieces and stir to distribute them evenly.

3. Cover and cook on the low heat setting for 8 to 9 hours. Serve garnished with a sprinkling of the remaining parsley.

mexican turkey tortilla soup

Makes 6 servings

Although raw turkey or chicken strips can be stirred into the broth mixture at the outset of cooking, the results are better when cooked meat is added for the last hour of cooking.

1 red bell pepper, chopped

1 green bell pepper, chopped

1 medium onion, chopped

1 cup diced fresh tomatoes

1½ cups corn kernels, thawed if frozen

1 can (4 ounces) mild diced green chiles

1 tablespoon plus 1 teaspoon ground cumin

½ teaspoon salt

¼ teaspoon freshly ground black pepper

1 large can (49 ounces) reduced-sodium,
    fat-free chicken broth

2 to 3 cups shredded cooked turkey or chicken breast

Juice of 1 lime

1 to 1½ cups tortilla chips or strips

1 cup shredded Monterey Jack or Cheddar cheese

Chopped fresh cilantro, diced avocado, and
    chopped tomatoes, for garnish

1. In a 4- or 5-quart electric slow cooker, combine the bell peppers, onion, tomatoes, corn, chiles, cumin, salt, and pepper; mix well. Carefully pour in the broth and stir.

2. Cover and cook on the low heat setting for 5 hours. Stir in the turkey. Cover and cook on the low heat setting for 1 hour longer. Stir in the lime juice.

3. Place a handful of tortilla chips and about 2½ tablespoons of the cheese in each of 6 soup bowls. Ladle in the hot soup. Garnish with a sprinkling of cilantro, avocado, and tomatoes and serve.

Cook's Note

➤ Instead of adding cooked turkey or chicken during the last hour of cooking time, stir 1½ pounds uncooked, skinless turkey breast cutlet strips or chicken breast strips into the broth mixture at the beginning of the cooking time. Cover and cook on the low heat setting for 6 hours, then stir in the lime juice and proceed as directed in Step 3.

manhattan clam chowder

Makes 8 to 10 servings

To avoid rubbery clams, add them during the last half hour or so of cooking. All you need to do is heat them up. Be sure to check occasionally and turn off the pot as soon as they are hot. Top the chowder with crisp crumbled bacon and serve with crusty bread or chowder crackers.

1 medium onion, chopped

3 celery ribs, chopped

1 large red or golden potato, peeled and diced

2 garlic cloves, crushed through a press

1 can (28 ounces) diced tomatoes

1 jar (8 ounces) clam juice

1 can (6 ounces) tomato paste

½ cup dry white wine

½ teaspoon dried thyme leaves

1 bay leaf

2 cans (6.5 ounces each) chopped clams in clam juice

Salt and freshly ground black pepper

6 slices of bacon, cooked until crisp and crumbled

1. In a 5-quart electric slow cooker, combine the onion, celery, potato, garlic, tomatoes with their juices, clam juice, tomato paste, wine, thyme, bay leaf, and 1½ cups of water. Mix well.

2. Cover and cook on the low heat setting for about 6 hours, until the potato is soft. Remove and discard the bay leaf. Add the clams with their juice and cook on low for 30 to 45 minutes longer, just until the clams are hot. Season with salt and pepper to taste.

3. Ladle the chowder into bowls. Sprinkle the crumbled bacon liberally over the top and serve immediately.

Never attempt to cook food on the warm setting: it will not reach a temperature high enough to kill bacteria and is dangerous.

shrimp chowder

Seafood is not the pot's strongest suit, but by making the chowder base first and then adding already cooked shrimp, you can produce a thick, savory soup your whole family will love. Serve, if you like, with chowder crackers or saltines, and pass a bottle of hot sauce on the side.

1 large onion, chopped

3 celery ribs, sliced

2 pounds golden potatoes, peeled and cut into 1-inch cubes

¾ cup finely chopped or shredded carrots

6 tablespoons instant-blending flour, such as Wondra

1 cup dry white wine

2 garlic cloves, crushed through a press

1 teaspoon salt

½ teaspoon freshly ground black pepper

2 cups half-and-half or light cream

¾ pound cooked, shelled, and deveined shrimp

4 slices of lean bacon, cooked until crisp and crumbled

Chopped fresh tarragon or parsley, for garnish

1. In a 5-quart electric slow cooker, combine the onion, celery, potatoes, and carrots. Sprinkle on the flour and toss to coat the vegetables evenly. Stir in the wine, garlic, and 2 cups of water. Season with the salt and pepper.

2. Cover and cook on the low heat setting, stirring once if you are around, for 6 hours, or until the potatoes are tender.

3. Increase the heat setting to high. Stir in the half-and-half and shrimp and cook uncovered, stirring occasionally, for 30 to 40 minutes, or until hot throughout.

4. Stir in the cooked bacon. Serve hot, garnished with chopped tarragon.

easy slow cooker vegetable stock

Makes about 2 quarts

Homemade vegetable stock is a great base to have on hand whenever you are preparing soups or stews. And the slow cooker is ideal for making stock with no fuss. You can go to sleep and not worry about the stove being on. After the stock cools slightly, divide it among pint containers and refrigerate for up to three days or freeze for up to three months.

1 large onion, cut into 12 wedges
¾ cup coarsely chopped carrots
2 celery ribs, coarsely chopped
1 leek (white and tender green parts), rinsed well and sliced
¼ cup fresh parsley sprigs
1 teaspoon salt

1. Combine all the ingredients in a 5-quart electric slow cooker. Add 8 cups (2 quarts) of water.

2. Cover and cook on the low heat setting for about 8 hours. Strain through a fine-mesh strainer, pressing on the vegetables to extract as much liquid as possible. Discard the vegetables.

3. Use the stock immediately, refrigerate, and use within 3 days, or freeze for up to 3 months.

pasta and pasta sauces

In the past, many people have said you cannot make pasta in the pot, but guess what? They were wrong! After extensive testing, I found that you can use small dried ravioli, fresh tortelloni, and no-cook lasagna noodles to create marvelous pasta dishes that will draw your guests in as soon as you remove the lid from the pot. I've also included a broad selection of pasta sauces in tempting flavors like wild mushroom, basil-artichoke, gorgonzola, and sweet pepper.

My fresh tomato sauce, which incorporates both fresh and dried basil, offers an easy way to turn a bounty of late-season tomatoes into homemade sauce, to use at once or to freeze in pint containers and pull out whenever you want a cheerful reminder of summer in the middle of winter. How is it different from your favorite brand, which requires only a twist of the wrist? You know exactly what's gone into your family's food—no preservatives, no thickeners, no heavily processed ingredients.

pasta and pasta sauces

mini ravioli with tomato sauce and basil

Makes 4 servings

Here's an easy dinner I turn to on busy weekends because it doesn't take much prep time. Even though the ravioli are dried, they go right into the pot without any precooking.

1 jar (26 ounces) tomato-basil marinara or pasta sauce

1 can (28 ounces) diced tomatoes

½ cup dry red wine

2 tablespoons dried basil

3 cups dried mini ravioli with cheese (about 12 ounces)

1 medium onion, chopped

¼ cup chopped fresh basil

¼ cup shredded mozzarella or grated Romano cheese

1. In a large bowl, mix together the marinara sauce, tomatoes with their juices, wine, and dried basil. Ladle 1 cup of the sauce into the bottom of a 4-quart electric slow cooker.

2. Add the ravioli, distributing them evenly. Sprinkle the onion over the pasta. Top with the remaining sauce. Do not stir.

3. Cover and cook on the high heat setting for 2½ to 3 hours, until the pasta is tender. Do not overcook, or the ravioli will lose their shape and become mushy.

4. Just before serving, stir in the fresh basil. Serve topped with mozzarella cheese.

gorgonzola and walnut ravioli bolognese

Makes 4 servings

Doctored-up jarred sauce, some cheese, and frozen edamame or peas transform ready-made fresh ravioli into an easy, delicious dinner. Just be sure not to overcook. And pass extra Parmesan cheese on the side.

1 jar (24 to 26 ounces) Bolognese pasta sauce

¾ cup dry white wine

2 Roma or other large plum tomatoes, seeded and chopped

1 package (about 9 ounces) fresh small or medium
    gorgonzola and walnut ravioli or another favorite flavor
    (do not use giant size)

½ cup shredded mozzarella cheese

3 tablespoons freshly grated Parmesan cheese

1 cup frozen shelled edamame (soybeans) or peas, thawed,
    rinsed, and well drained

1. In a large bowl, combine the pasta sauce, wine, and tomatoes. Mix well. Ladle about 1 cup of the sauce into a 4-quart electric slow cooker, spreading it to cover the bottom evenly. Top with the ravioli and then another 1 cup of sauce. Sprinkle the mozzarella and Parmesan cheeses over the ravioli. Add the edamame in an even layer and top with the remaining sauce.

2. Cover and cook on the high heat setting for 2¼ to 2½ hours, until the pasta is tender and the sauce is hot. Do not overcook, or the pasta will become mushy.

For best results, fill slow cookers half to two-thirds full (some desserts will fill the pot less at the beginning of cooking). When in doubt, refer to the manufacturer's instruction manual that came with your pot.

shortcut lasagna

Makes 6 to 8 servings

This is the easiest way to make lasagna—with uncooked oven-ready lasagna noodles. My family loves the way it turns out. Serve with a big tossed green salad and dinner is on. This is a good choice for potlucks, too.

1 pound lean ground beef

1 medium onion, chopped

3 garlic cloves, minced

1 can (28 ounces) tomato puree

1 can (14.5 ounces) diced tomatoes

2 tablespoons dried basil

1 teaspoon dried oregano

Salt and freshly ground black pepper

1 container (15 ounces) whole-milk ricotta cheese

¾ cup freshly grated Parmesan cheese

2 tablespoons chopped fresh Italian parsley

9 uncooked oven-ready lasagna noodles
(from an 8-ounce package)

4 cups shredded mozzarella cheese (1 pound)

1. In a large skillet, cook the beef and onion over medium-high heat, stirring often, until the meat is broken up and lightly browned and the onion is softened, 6 to 8 minutes. Drain off any excess fat. Stir in the garlic, tomato puree, diced tomatoes with their juices, basil, and oregano. Season the meat sauce with salt and pepper to taste.

2. In a bowl, mix together the ricotta cheese, ½ cup of the Parmesan cheese, the parsley, and a generous grinding of pepper.

3. Spread about 1½ cups of the meat sauce over the bottom of a 5-quart electric slow cooker. Cover with 2 to 2½ uncooked lasagna noodles, breaking them to fit in a single layer. Top with one-third of the ricotta mixture, spreading it over the pasta as evenly as possible. Sprinkle 1 cup mozzarella over the ricotta. Repeat these layers two more times. Then top with half of the remaining meat sauce, a final layer of noodles, the remaining 1 cup mozzarella, and the rest of the sauce, spreading it evenly.

4. Cover and cook on the low heat setting for 4 to 5 hours, until the noodles are tender. Sprinkle the remaining ¼ cup Parmesan cheese over the top. Let the lasagna cool and set for 15 minutes before serving right out of the pot. Be sure to dig down for each serving, so everyone gets all the layers.

three-cheese and black bean lasagna with mexican flavors

Makes 8 to 10 servings

The longer this stands after cooking, the easier it is to cut and serve, and the more prominent the individual layers appear. For widest all-round appeal, especially for kids, use mild, not hot, salsa. Pass bowls of sour cream and guacamole on the side.

1 can (28 ounces) diced tomatoes

1 jar (24 ounces) mild chunky salsa

1 can (8 ounces) tomato sauce

2 cans (15 ounces each) black beans, rinsed and well drained

1 container (15 ounces) whole-milk ricotta cheese

1 package (16 ounces) frozen chopped spinach, thawed
    and squeezed dry

4 cups blended shredded Monterey Jack and Cheddar cheese
    (1 pound)

Salt and seasoned pepper

1 package (8 ounces) oven-ready lasagna noodles

1. In a large bowl, combine the tomatoes with their juices, the salsa, tomato sauce, and black beans. Mix well. In a medium bowl, combine the ricotta cheese, spinach, ½ cup of the blended cheeses, and salt and seasoned pepper to taste. Mix well.

2. Spread 1½ cups of the tomato-bean mixture over the bottom of a 6-quart electric slow cooker. Add a single layer of the un-cooked lasagna noodles, breaking them to fit as necessary. Spread one-third of the ricotta mixture evenly over the pasta. Sprinkle 1 cup of the shredded cheese blend on top of the ricotta. Spoon one-quarter of the remaining tomato-bean mixture on top. Repeat the layers two more times. Then add a final layer of noodles and the remaining tomato-bean mixture, spreading it evenly over all.

3. Cover and cook on the low heat setting for 4½ to 5 hours, until the noodles are tender. Sprinkle the remaining ½ cup shredded cheese blend on top, cover, and cook for about 5 min-utes longer, until melted. Let the lasagna cool for at least 10 minutes before serving.

vegetable lasagna casserole

Make 8 to 10 servings

f you dislike making lasagna the traditional way, streamline chores by using uncooked oven-ready noodles, which work well in this slow cooker version. Layering is quick and easy. Don't be tempted to add salt to the sauce mixture, because the dish really doesn't need any. There is plenty in the pasta sauce and cheese. Leftovers reheat well in a microwave oven.

2 jars (24 to 26 ounces each) garden vegetable pasta sauce

1½ cups chopped zucchini

1 container (15 ounces) small-curd cottage cheese, low-fat if you like

3 tablespoons prepared pesto sauce

¼ teaspoon freshly ground black pepper

8 to 9 oven-ready lasagna noodles (from an 8-ounce package)

4 cups packed fresh baby spinach leaves, washed and well drained

1 package (16 ounces) shredded mozzarella cheese (about 4 cups)

¼ cup whole fresh basil leaves

1. In a large bowl, combine the jarred pasta sauce, zucchini, and ½ cup of water. Stir to mix well. In a medium bowl, blend together the cottage cheese, pesto sauce, and pepper.

2. Spread 1½ cups of the zucchini-sauce mixture in the bottom of a 5-quart electric slow cooker. Add a single layer of the uncooked lasagna noodles, breaking them to fit as necessary. Spread one-third of the pesto cottage cheese over the noodles. Cover evenly with 2 cups of the spinach and 1 cup shredded mozzarella. Top with one-quarter of the remaining sauce. Add another layer of lasagna noodles, half the remaining cottage cheese, all the remaining spinach, another 1 cup of the mozzarella cheese, and one-third of the remaining sauce. For the third layer, use another layer of noodles, the remaining cottage cheese, all of the basil, another 1 cup mozzarella, and half the remaining sauce. Top with the remaining noodles and sauce.

3. Cover and cook on the low heat setting for about 4½ hours, or until the noodles are tender. Sprinkle the remaining 1 cup mozzarella cheese evenly over the top. Cook, uncovered, for 5 to 10 minutes longer, until the cheese is melted. Let stand for 10 to 15 minutes to allow the lasagna to set up before serving.

tortelloni bake

Tortelloni are large tortellini. Because of their size, they hold up better in the pot. Serve with a green salad and garlic bread.

1 jar (24 to 26 ounces) roasted red pepper marinara sauce,
    or your favorite flavor
1 can (14.5 ounces) diced tomatoes
½ cup dry white wine
1 tablespoon dried basil
1 teaspoon sugar
1 teaspoon Worcestershire sauce
½ teaspoon fennel seeds
1 package (16 ounces) frozen chopped spinach, thawed
    and squeezed dry
1 red bell pepper, seeded and chopped
1 package (9 or 10 ounces) refrigerated fresh pesto or sausage
    tortelloni, or your favorite flavor
⅓ cup freshly grated Parmesan or shredded mozzarella cheese

1. In a large bowl, combine the marinara sauce, tomatoes with their juices, wine, basil, sugar, Worcestershire sauce, and fennel seeds. Stir to mix well. Ladle 1 cup of the sauce into a 4-quart electric slow cooker, spreading it evenly over the bottom.

2. Cover the sauce with the spinach. Then scatter on half of the red bell pepper. Arrange the tortelloni evenly in the pot. Top with the remaining red pepper. Pour the remaining sauce evenly over all.

3. Cover and cook on the low heat setting for 4 to 4½ hours, until the tortelloni are cooked through but the pasta is not mushy. Sprinkle with the Parmesan cheese and heat for 5 to 10 minutes longer, until melted.

With the right instructions, both rice and pasta can be cooked in the slow cooker with success. In most cases, converted rice offers the best results. Dried beans can be made in the slow cooker with no soaking or precooking. To be sure they soften properly and are most digestible, it is best to cook beans first covered simply with water until they are tender. Then they are rinsed and drained, after which flavorings, sugar, salt, and acidic foods, such as tomatoes, can be added to the pot.

slow mac and cheese

Makes 8 to 10 servings

This makes a lot on purpose. Everyone comes back for more. It's a good dish to tote to a potluck, especially if there are going to be kids around. Don't expect this to be bright orange, like much of the packaged kind. It's the real deal: creamy, gooey, and delicious!

1 pound small elbow macaroni

1 package (8 ounces) cream cheese

3 cups whole milk

2 tablespoons Dijon mustard

1 teaspoon Worcestershire sauce

½ teaspoon salt

½ teaspoon freshly ground black pepper

2¾ cups shredded Cheddar cheese, sharp or mild as you prefer

1. Cook the macaroni in a large pot of boiling salted water, stirring occasionally, until it is *al dente,* tender but still firm, about 7 minutes. Drain into a colander, rinse briefly, and drain well. Transfer the macaroni to a 5-quart electric slow cooker.

2. In a large glass bowl, heat the cream cheese in a microwave oven on high power for 30 to 45 seconds, until softened and smooth when blended with a wire whisk. Heat the milk in a glass container in the microwave on high power for 5 to 6 minutes, until very hot but not boiling. Whisk the hot milk into the cream cheese until blended and smooth. Whisk in the mustard, Worcestershire sauce, salt, and pepper. Add 2 cups of the cheese and stir until well mixed.

3. Pour the cheese sauce over the macaroni in the pot and mix well. Cover and cook on the low heat setting for 1½ to 1¾ hours, until most of the milk has been absorbed and the mac and cheese is very hot throughout but still moist.

4. Season with additional salt and pepper to taste. Top with the remaining ¾ cup Cheddar cheese. Cover and cook for about 10 minutes longer, until the cheese melts.

Cook's Note

➤ For variety, another easy melting cheese, such as Manchego, fontina, or Gruyère can be substituted for the Cheddar. Or try a mix.

fresh tomato sauce

Makes about 6½ cups

Most of the time, canned tomatoes offer a convenient way to whip up homemade tomato sauce easily. But for that very special short season, in late summer and early fall, when either your garden or the farmer's market is exploding with all kinds of wonderful, sweet, juicy tomatoes, here is a recipe that takes full advantage of them. And it freezes beautifully, so you can return to summer for a moment—at least for a meal—all year long.

Cook's Note

➤ For variation when serving, add cut-up artichoke hearts, chopped roasted red peppers, or sliced fresh mushrooms. A pound of ground beef or Italian sausage, cooked until browned, can also be added at the beginning.

5 pounds fresh tomatoes, peeled, cored, and cut into large dice
1 can (6 ounces) tomato paste
⅓ cup dry red wine
¼ cup chopped fresh Italian parsley
1 tablespoon dried basil
¼ cup chopped fresh basil
1 teaspoon sugar
Salt and freshly ground black pepper

1. In a 4-quart electric slow cooker, combine the tomatoes, tomato paste, wine, parsley, and dried basil.

2. Cover and cook on the low heat setting for 4 to 5 hours. Remove the cover, raise the heat to high, and cook for 30 minutes longer.

3. Stir in the fresh basil and sugar and season with salt and pepper to taste.

artichoke pasta sauce

Artichokes are meaty vegetables with sweet over-tones that make them particularly satisfying. As much as I love them, preparation of fresh arti-chokes can be tedious, so I developed this sauce to use convenient canned artichoke hearts. They produce a really good, easy, versatile sauce for pasta, vegetables, grilled poultry, or fish. It can also be used as a topping for pizza.

Makes about 8 cups

2 cans (13.75 ounces each) artichoke hearts
1 large onion, chopped
1 garlic clove, crushed through a press
3 cans (14.5 ounces each) diced tomatoes
1 can (6 ounces) tomato paste
½ cup chopped fresh basil
½ teaspoon freshly ground black pepper
Pinch of sugar
Kosher salt

Cook's Note

➤ This recipe makes 2 quarts of sauce, which will be more than you need unless you're having a party; leftovers freeze beautifully.

1. Drain the artichokes, rinse them well, and drain again. Coarsely chop the artichokes.

2. In a 4-quart electric slow cooker, combine the chopped arti-chokes, onion, garlic, tomatoes with their juices, tomato paste, ¼ cup of the basil, the pepper, and the sugar. Stir to mix well.

3. Cover and cook on the low heat setting 5 to 6 hours. Just before using, stir in the remaining ¼ cup basil and season with salt to taste. Refrigerate any extra sauce in a covered container and use within 3 days; or freeze and use within 3 months.

easy pizza sauce

Makes about 3¾ cups sauce, enough for 2 or 3 pizzas, depending on size

Pizza sauce has a slightly different quality than pasta sauce: It's deeper, more intense, and thicker. This easy version, paired with purchased bread dough, Boboli bases, or even pita rounds, allows you the fun of making pizza at home. Choose whichever additional toppings your family enjoys. For even more convenience, whip up a double batch of sauce and keep some in the freezer to use on short notice.

1 can (28 ounces) crushed tomatoes with added puree
2 cans (6 ounces each) tomato paste
1 tablespoon extra virgin olive oil
⅓ cup chopped fresh basil
Salt

Cook's Note

➤ For the best flavor, use imported Italian tomatoes or a high-quality domestic brand.

1. In a 3-quart electric slow cooker, combine the crushed tomatoes with their juices, tomato paste, and olive oil. Stir to mix well.

2. Cover and cook on the high heat setting for 2½ to 2¾ hours or on the low heat setting for 5 to 6 hours.

3. Stir in the fresh basil and season with salt to taste. Let the sauce cool; then refrigerate in a covered container for up to 3 days or freeze for up to 3 months.

pasta sauce puttanesca style

Makes 6½ cups

Use this fast-to-make, classic sauce to top your favorite cooked pasta, or polenta or steamed vegetables.

2 cans (28 ounces each) crushed tomatoes with added puree

1 large onion, chopped

1 garlic clove, crushed through a press

1 cup coarsely chopped pitted kalamata olives

⅓ cup drained capers

1½ teaspoons dried basil

¼ crushed hot red pepper, or more to taste

¼ teaspoon sugar

¼ teaspoon seasoned salt

¼ teaspoon freshly ground black pepper

¼ cup chopped fresh basil

1. In a 4-quart electric slow cooker, combine the crushed tomatoes, onion, garlic, olives, capers, dried basil, hot pepper, sugar, seasoned salt, and black pepper. Mix well.

2. Cover and cook on the low heat setting for 6 to 7 hours. Remove from the heat and stir in the fresh basil. Season with additional salt and black pepper to taste. Keep refrigerated in a covered container for up to 3 days or freeze for up to 3 months.

meat sauce with tri-color peppers

Makes about 7 cups, enough for 8 to 10 servings

This colorful sauce is excellent over any pasta, but because it is so chunky, it takes well to thicker shapes, like penne and rotelle, or even shells. It's also good over steamed zucchini or other vegetables. Serve with shaved Parmesan cheese. My daughter likes this sauce so much that she likes to eat it by itself, without any pasta!

1 pound lean ground beef

½ pound sweet or hot Italian sausage, casings removed

1 large onion, chopped

1 can (28 ounces) diced tomatoes

1 can (6 ounces) tomato paste

¾ cup dry red wine

1½ tablespoons dried basil

1 to 2 garlic cloves, crushed through a press

2 teaspoons Worcestershire sauce

1 teaspoon fennel seeds

Pinch of sugar

½ teaspoon salt

¼ teaspoon freshly ground black pepper

3 large bell peppers—1 red, 1 green, and 1 yellow—cut into thin julienne strips

Cook's Note

➤ For a bright flavor, sprinkle a big handful of chopped fresh basil over the dish just before serving.

1. In a large skillet, sauté the beef and sausage over medium-high heat, breaking up any large lumps of meat, until browned and cooked through, 6 to 8 minutes. Drain off any excess fat. Stir in the onion and cook until softened, 3 to 5 minutes longer.

2. Transfer the meat and onion mixture to a 4- to 5-quart electric slow cooker. Add the diced tomatoes with their juices, tomato paste, wine, basil, garlic, Worcestershire sauce, fennel seeds, sugar, salt, and pepper. Stir in the bell peppers.

3. Cover and cook on the low heat setting for 4½ to 5 hours, or until the sauce is bubbling. Season with additional salt and pepper to taste.

It is easiest to fill and layer the slow cooker with liquid and other ingredients when the stoneware insert is already set in the base.

chunky italian beef sauce with zucchini

Makes 10 servings

Besides looking appealing, this substantial sauce has wonderful flavor enhanced with fennel seeds and basil. Serve over hot cooked pasta or polenta. Be sure to add a sprinkling of freshly grated Parmesan cheese.

3 pounds boneless beef round steak

2 medium onions, cut into thin slices

1 large red bell pepper, cut into julienne strips

1 jar (26 ounces) tomato and basil pasta sauce

1 can (6 ounces) tomato paste

½ cup dry red wine

2 teaspoons dried basil

1 teaspoon fennel seeds

1 tablespoon Worcestershire sauce

2 medium zucchini, coarsely chopped

¼ teaspoon salt

¼ teaspoon freshly ground black pepper

1. Trim all excess fat from the beef. Cut the meat into ¾- to 1-inch cubes.

2. In a 5-quart electric slow cooker, combine the beef, onions, and bell pepper. In a bowl, combine the pasta sauce, tomato paste, wine, basil, fennel seeds, and Worcestershire sauce. Whisk to blend. Pour over the beef mixture in the slow cooker and stir to mix.

3. Cover and cook on the low heat setting for 7½ to 8 hours, or until the meat is tender.

4. Stir in the chopped zucchini and season with the salt and pepper. Cover and cook for 30 to 45 minutes longer, until the zucchini is crisp-tender.

Cook's Note

➤ The advantage of buying a whole round steak and cutting it up rather than buying precubed meat is that it is easy to trim off all the fat around the outside.

wild mushroom sauce with pancetta and rosemary

Makes about 8 cups

Pancetta is unsmoked Italian bacon, which imparts a full, rich flavor to sauces and stews. It's sold packaged in the deli section of many supermarkets, either sliced or finely diced. In the slow cooker, it is best added at the end, so the sauce does not become too fatty. Bacon makes a fine substitute. Serve over polenta or pasta.

1 ounce dried mixed wild mushrooms, porcini, or other imported dried mushrooms

1 can (28 ounces) crushed tomatoes with added puree

1 can (28 ounces) diced tomatoes

½ pound fresh cremini mushrooms, trimmed and halved or sliced into thirds

½ cup dry red wine

1 teaspoon dried rosemary, crumbled

½ teaspoon salt

¼ teaspoon freshly ground black pepper

3 ounces diced pancetta or 4 to 6 slices of bacon

1. Rinse the dried mushrooms, put them in a small bowl, and cover with hot water. Let stand until softened, 10 to 15 minutes. Lift out the mushrooms and squeeze to remove excess moisture. Trim off any hard bits.

2. In a 3½- or 4-quart electric slow cooker, combine the rehydrated mushrooms, crushed tomatoes, diced tomatoes with their juices, fresh mushrooms, wine, rosemary, salt, and pepper. Cover and cook on the low heat setting for about 5 hours.

3. Cook the pancetta in a large skillet over medium heat, stirring or turning, until lightly browned and crisp, 5 to 7 minutes. Drain on paper towels. If using bacon, crumble into small bits.

4. When the sauce is done, stir in the cooked pancetta. Season with additional salt and pepper to taste.

ranchero sauce

This Mexican-flavored sauce is easily made and great to have on hand stashed in the freezer. Mixed with rice, slices of grilled steak, and cheese, it makes a mean burrito. Stir into cooked ground meat to make a taco filling. Or spoon the zesty sauce over pasta, rice, grilled sausages, chicken, enchiladas, or quesadillas.

1 medium onion, chopped
3 cups chopped bell peppers, preferably a mix of
   green, red, and yellow
½ cup chopped celery
2 garlic cloves, crushed through a press
1 can (4 ounces) diced green chiles
1 can (28 ounces) diced tomatoes
1 jar (16 ounces) chunky salsa
1 can (6 ounces) tomato paste
2 teaspoons ground cumin
¼ teaspoon pico de gallo Mexican seasoning
¼ teaspoon sugar
3 tablespoons chopped fresh cilantro (optional)
Salt

1. In a 4-quart electric slow cooker, combine the onion, bell peppers, celery, garlic, chiles, tomatoes with their juices, salsa, tomato paste, cumin, and pico de gallo seasoning.

2. Cover and cook on the low heat setting for 6 to 7 hours.

3. Stir in the sugar and cilantro, if desired. Season the sauce with salt to taste.

chicken, turkey, and seafood

Poultry does especially well in the electric slow cooker, since these days so many of us prefer to remove the skin to reduce fat. Long, slow cooking keeps chicken and turkey moist and tender. In fact, it's an excellent way to prepare turkey breast. Once it's cooked, the turkey can be carved and served drizzled with a sauce or salsa, or chilled and used for sandwiches.

Because you probably have so many recipes for slow cooker chicken and turkey already, I've made a real effort here to offer some interesting, more international dishes that provide variety and new flavors. Turkey Molé, with chocolate, chiles, raisins, and prunes, is a Mexican classic. Mediterranean Chicken with Artichokes, Mushrooms, and Sun-Dried Tomatoes; Chicken Cacciatore; and Balsamic Chicken Breasts with Roasted Red Peppers are just a few of the exciting ideas you'll find in this chapter.

Seafood is one type of food that is tricky in the slow cooker. The delicate proteins need such quick, gentle cooking that you can't just throw fish or most shellfish into the pot and walk away, even when it's set to low. I've solved this by offering a few saucy seafood dishes, including a gumbo, in which the base is cooked for hours and then the seafood is added near the end of the cooking time.

chicken, turkey, and seafood

simple savory chicken breasts

When you don't want to heat up the oven, here's an easy way to cook chicken breasts to have on hand for other uses. For convenience and to save time, make a batch or two in the slow cooker on weekends while you're running errands. It's less expensive than buying rotisserie chicken.

Makes 8 servings

2½ pounds skinless, boneless chicken breast halves
1½ teaspoons chicken seasoning (such as McCormick) or lemon pepper
¼ cup balsamic vinegar

1. Rinse the chicken breasts and pat dry with paper towels. Trim off any visible fat.

2. Place half of the chicken breasts on the bottom of a 3- or 3½-quart electric slow cooker. Sprinkle with half of the chicken seasoning and drizzle with 1 tablespoon of the vinegar. Add the remaining chicken breasts, sprinkle with the remaining seasoning, and drizzle with another 1 tablespoon vinegar.

3. Cover and cook on the high heat setting for 2½ hours, or until the chicken is cooked through. Do not overcook, or the chicken will be dry. Remove the chicken to a platter, discarding the liquid in slow cooker. Drizzle the remaining 2 tablespoons vinegar over the chicken.

Cook's Note

➤ If you have left-overs or prefer to use the chicken for another purpose, let the meat cool, then wrap well and refrigerate for up to 3 days or freeze for up to 3 months.

balsamic chicken breasts with roasted red peppers

Makes 4 to 6 servings

Balsamic vinegar and jarred roasted peppers are put to good use in a simple but tasty dish that's attractive to boot. Serve with roasted or mashed potatoes and fresh, crisp-tender green beans. Don't skip the balsamic vinegar reduction in the beginning; intensifying the flavor is the trick that makes this such a flavorful dish.

¾ cup balsamic vinegar

1 jar (15 ounces) roasted red peppers

3 medium onions, cut into wedges

6 skinless, boneless chicken breast halves,
    trimmed of all fat

Use lean cuts of meat and skinless, boneless chicken breasts wherever possible. Remove skin and trim as much fat as possible from poultry and meats prior to cooking to avoid ending up with lots of fat swimming in the pot.

1. Add the vinegar to a nonreactive medium skillet and boil over medium-high heat until reduced by half, 3 to 5 minutes.

2. Drain the roasted peppers and rinse and then drain well. If the peppers are whole, cut them into large pieces or strips.

3. In a 4-quart electric slow cooker, layer half of the onions and half of the roasted peppers. Top with all the chicken breasts. Cover the chicken with the remaining onions and peppers. Drizzle half of the reduced balsamic vinegar over the top.

4. Cover and cook on the high heat setting for 1 hour. Reduce the heat setting to low and cook for about 2 hours longer, or until the chicken is cooked through. Transfer the chicken, onions, and peppers to a serving platter. Heat the remaining balsamic reduction in a glass or ceramic bowl in a microwave oven for 30 seconds and drizzle it over the chicken.

mustard-glazed chicken breasts

Makes 12 to 14 servings

Any leftovers can be reheated in the oven the next day or saved for chicken salad, sandwiches, casseroles, or tacos. Ground chipotle chile, which is smoked dried jalapeños, can be found on supermarket spice shelves.

4 pounds skinless, boneless chicken breasts
½ teaspoon ground chipotle chile
3 tablespoons Dijon mustard or honey mustard
2 tablespoons honey mustard salad dressing

Consumers with food-safety questions can call the toll-free USDA Meat and Poultry Hotline at (888) 674-6854. Recorded food-safety messages are available 24 hours a day. Or go online to www.fsis.usda.gov or www.askkaren.gov.

1. If the breasts are whole—two joined together—separate them. Trim off all excess fat. Rinse the chicken and dry with paper towels. Lightly dust the top of each chicken breast with a little pinch of chipotle chile and rub it in. Brush the mustard over the chicken to coat lightly.

2. Stack the chicken breasts, mustard side up, in a 4-quart electric slow cooker. Drizzle the salad dressing over the chicken.

3. Cover and cook on the high heat setting for about 2½ hours or on the low heat setting for 5 to 5½ hours, until the chicken is tender and cooked through. Do not overcook, or the meat will be dry and tough.

4. Serve the chicken warm. Refrigerate any leftovers, well wrapped, for up to 3 days or freeze for up to 3 months.

pulled barbecued chicken

Makes 6 servings

f you like pulled pork, but you're avoiding meat, here's a good way to fix chicken. It's easy and everybody loves it. Serve over toasted buns, with coleslaw and baked beans.

2 pounds skinless, boneless chicken breasts

1 large onion, chopped

1 can (6 ounces) tomato paste

¼ cup red or white wine vinegar

⅓ cup packed brown sugar

1 tablespoon Worcestershire sauce

¼ teaspoon ground chipotle chile

½ cup ketchup

1 teaspoon smoked paprika

Seasoned salt and freshly ground black pepper

Toasted sourdough rolls or hamburger buns

If you freeze leftovers, thaw in the refrigerator or microwave oven, not at room temperature.

1. Trim any visible fat from the chicken breasts and cut the meat into thin strips. Place the chicken strips in a 5-quart electric slow cooker. Toss with the onion.

2. In a small bowl, stir together the tomato paste, vinegar, brown sugar, Worcestershire sauce, chipotle chile, and ½ cup of water until well blended. Add to the pot and stir to mix with the chicken and onion.

3. Cover and cook on the low heat setting for 4 to 5 hours, or until the chicken is falling apart. Pull the chicken apart into large shreds with two forks.

4. Stir in the ketchup and smoked paprika. Add seasoned salt and black pepper to taste. Serve over toasted split buns.

Variation

Add 1 can (15 ounces) red kidney or pinto beans, rinsed and well drained, along with the onion at the beginning of the cooking time.

mediterranean chicken with artichokes, mushrooms, and sun-dried tomatoes

Makes 5 to 6 servings

White wine and sun-dried tomatoes are two sophisticated ingredients that turn skinless, boneless chicken breasts into an elegant dish that's good enough for company. Because mushrooms have a tendency to darken as they stand after cooking, this dish is best served the day it is made. Accompany with rice or noodles and a salad of baby field greens.

2 pounds skinless, boneless chicken breast halves

¾ cup dry white wine

3 tablespoons cornstarch

1 teaspoon dried basil

½ teaspoon freshly ground black pepper

1 can (14.5 ounces) diced tomatoes

1 package (12 ounces) frozen artichoke hearts, thawed and drained, or 1 can (13.75 ounces) artichoke hearts, rinsed, drained, and halved

8 ounces fresh cremini mushrooms, thickly sliced

1 medium onion, chopped

¼ cup julienne slices oil-packed sun-dried tomatoes

3 tablespoons drained capers

Salt

1. Pat the chicken breasts dry with paper towels. Trim off any visible fat.

2. In a medium bowl, stir together the wine, cornstarch, basil, pepper, and tomatoes with their juices until well mixed. Transfer to a 5-quart electric slow cooker.

3. Stir in the artichokes, mushroom slices, onion, sun-dried tomatoes, and capers until well mixed. Place the chicken breasts on top and gently push them down to submerge them partway in the sauce mixture. Spoon some of the sauce up and over the chicken.

4. Cover and cook on the high heat setting for 2¾ to 3 hours or on the low heat setting for about 5 to 5½ hours, stirring once halfway through the cooking time, if possible, until the chicken is cooked through and the sauce is thickened. Stir after the cooking is completed. Season with salt to taste.

lemony chicken with olives and capers

Makes 6 servings

Mild chicken takes well to tart flavorings, and this dish incorporates a number of them—lemon, vinegar, capers, and briny olives—for a complex, enticing taste, mellowed by slow cooking in the pot. Serve with your favorite green vegetable and mashed potatoes or hot cooked rice.

⅓ cup fresh lemon juice

¼ cup dry white wine

2 tablespoons red wine vinegar

2 tablespoons extra virgin olive oil

¾ cup pimiento-stuffed Spanish olives

¼ cup capers with a little of the juice

2 tablespoons dried oregano

2 garlic cloves, minced

3 bay leaves

½ teaspoon salt

¼ teaspoon freshly ground black pepper

3 tablespoons cornstarch

2½ pounds skinless, boneless chicken breast halves, trimmed of all fat and patted dry

Chopped fresh flat-leaf parsley and thin slices of lemon, for garnish

1. In a medium bowl, mix together the lemon juice, wine, vinegar, olive oil, olives, capers, oregano, garlic, bay leaves, salt, and pepper. Stir in the cornstarch until thoroughly blended.

2. Ladle about one-quarter of the olive-caper mixture over the bottom of a 4-quart electric slow cooker. Arrange half of the chicken breasts in the pot; then pour half of the remaining mixture over the chicken. Top with the rest of the chicken breasts and pour the remaining olive-caper mixture over the chicken.

3. Cover and cook on the high heat setting for 2½ to 3 hours, until the chicken is tender and cooked through. Stir the sauce in the pot around the chicken to blend thoroughly. Using tongs, remove the chicken to a platter.

4. Discard the bay leaves from the sauce in the pot. Spoon the sauce with the olives and capers over the chicken. Garnish with chopped parsley and lemon slices.

Cook's Note

➤ I like this sauce very lemony. If it tastes too tart for your palate, stir in a few pinches of sugar.

chicken with apricots, raisins, and butternut squash

Makes 6 servings

This sunny looking citrus-flavored chicken dish, with chunks of butternut squash, is fresh and wonderful. Raisins and dried apricots add sweetness. Serve over steamed rice, with a sprinkling of chopped parsley for garnish.

2 pounds skinless, boneless chicken breasts

1 medium onion

2 tablespoons olive oil

1¾ cups orange juice

2 tablespoons brown sugar

3 tablespoons instant-blending flour, such as Wondra

2½ pounds butternut squash, peeled, seeded, and
    cut into ¾- to 1-inch cubes

½ cup chopped dried apricots

3 tablespoons raisins

½ teaspoon salt

¼ teaspoon freshly ground black pepper

1. Trim any visible fat from the chicken and cut the breasts into thin strips. Quarter the onion lengthwise and cut crosswise into thin slices.

2. In a large skillet, heat 1 tablespoon of the olive oil until hot. Add half the chicken strips and sauté over high heat until golden brown, 3 to 5 minutes. Using a slotted spoon, transfer to a 5-quart electric slow cooker. Repeat with the remaining oil and chicken. Then brown the onion in the same skillet over medium-high heat until golden, about 5 minutes. Add to the slow cooker pot.

3. Pour 1 cup of the orange juice into the skillet and bring to a boil, scraping up any brown bits with a wooden spoon or spatula. Stir in the brown sugar until dissolved; pour into the slow cooker pot.

4. In a small bowl, whisk together the flour with the remaining ¾ cup orange juice until smooth and blended; stir into the pot. Add the squash chunks, apricots, and raisins. Season with the salt and pepper. Toss to mix well.

5. Cover and cook on the high heat setting for 2½ to 3 hours or on the low heat setting for 5 to 6 hours, until the squash is tender. Season with additional salt and pepper to taste.

spicy chicken chili with red and white beans

Makes 6 servings

Since both chicken and beans are mild in flavor, a white chili like this usually benefits from a good dose of heat. The punch is delivered here by a combination of canned green chiles, which are mildly hot, and ground chipotle chile, which is very hot. Adjust the heat to your taste by varying the proportions.

1½ pounds skinless, boneless chicken breasts

2 cans (15 ounces each) cannellini or other white beans, rinsed and drained well

1 can (15 ounces) light red kidney beans, rinsed and drained well

1 large green or red bell pepper, chopped

1 medium onion, chopped

1 can (4 ounces) diced green chiles

¾ cup chicken broth

4 teaspoons ground cumin

1 to 2 teaspoons ground chipotle chile, to taste

1 teaspoon dried oregano

Salt

Sour cream and chopped red onion, for serving

1. Trim all the fat from the chicken. Cut the meat into large bite-size chunks.

2. In a 4-quart electric slow cooker, combine the chicken chunks with the cannellini and kidney beans, bell pepper, onion, green chiles, broth, cumin, chipotle chile powder , and oregano. Mix well.

3. Cover and cook on the low heat setting for 7 to 8 hours, until the chicken is cooked through. Season with salt to taste. Serve topped with sour cream and chopped red onion.

Herbs and spices often become diluted and lose their flavor with long slow cooking, so don't be concerned if a recipe calls for a generous amount at the outset. Be sure to taste a finished dish before serving and adjust the seasonings as needed, adding more fresh herbs, spices, a drizzle of olive oil or balsamic vinegar, or a splash of citrus juice as necessary. And, of course, do season with salt and pepper as desired just before serving.

grilled chicken and black bean chili

Makes 6 servings

Serve with rice and top with shredded Monterey Jack cheese and chopped tomatoes and scallions. If you have any leftovers of this wonderful chili, which is unlikely, they can be put to good use as a base for tostada salads or in tortilla wraps, burritos, or tacos.

3 cans (15 ounces each) black beans, rinsed and drained
1 jar (15.5 ounces) chunky salsa, mild, medium, or hot
1 can (6 ounces) tomato paste
½ large red bell pepper, coarsely chopped
½ large green bell pepper, coarsely chopped
3 skinless, boneless chicken halves, grilled and
   cut into chunks (3 cups)

Cook's Note

➤ Many super-markets now carry grilled chicken breasts already cut up into chunks.

1. In a 4-quart electric slow cooker, combine the beans, salsa, tomato paste, and red and green bell peppers. Add 1 cup of water and mix well. Cover and cook on the low heat setting for 5 hours.

2. Stir in the grilled chicken and cook for 10 to 15 minutes longer, or until the chicken is heated through.

soft chicken tacos with pineapple salsa

Makes 5 to 6 servings

Pineapple is actually grown in Mexico, so don't think this isn't authentically flavored. To vary the recipe from time to time, you can substitute another flavored salsa for the pineapple. I like to serve this easy dish with an iceberg lettuce, radish, and white onion salad tossed with lime juice and oil.

2 cups corn kernels, canned or thawed frozen
1 jar (12 ounces) pineapple salsa
5 to 6 boneless, skinless, chicken breast halves (2 pounds)
1 to 2 teaspoons ground ancho chile
Salt and freshly ground black pepper
10 or 12 flour tortillas (6 to 7 inches in diameter)

1. In a small bowl, mix together the corn and half of the pineapple salsa. Spoon half of this mixture evenly over the bottom of a 4-quart electric slow cooker.

2. Season the chicken breasts with the ancho chile and place on top of the corn and salsa mixture in the slow cooker. Spread the remaining corn mixture over the chicken and spoon 2 tablespoons of the pineapple salsa on top.

3. Cover and cook on the high heat setting for 2½ hours or on the low heat setting for 5 hours, until the chicken is tender and cooked through. Remove the chicken breasts to a platter.

4. Stir the remaining salsa into the mixture in the slow cooker. Season with salt and pepper to taste. Spoon the corn-salsa mixture over the chicken. Serve with warm flour tortillas.

slow cooker roast chicken

Makes 8 to 10 servings

t takes the same amount of time to cook two chickens as one, and this way, you've got enough home-cooked chicken for dinner, with plenty leftover for sandwiches, salads, tostadas, and tacos. When cleaning the chickens, be sure to remove as much fat as possible. Cook them with or without the skin. When the chickens are done, there will be plenty of delicious juices in the pot. Skim off the fat and freeze the broth for sauces, soups, or stocks.

2 whole chickens (3½ to 4 pounds each)
1 teaspoon paprika
½ teaspoon ground ancho chile
½ teaspoon ground cumin
¾ teaspoon salt
½ teaspoon freshly ground black pepper
1½ to 2 tablespoons buffalo wing sauce,
 such as Frank's Red Hot

When lifting the cover off the slow cooker,
do so carefully and away from you, as the blast
of steam can be very hot.

1. Remove the giblets and neck bones from the chickens. Trim off as much fat as possible. Rinse the chickens inside and out and drain well; pat dry with paper towels. Place the chickens, breast sides up, side by side in a 6-quart oval electric slow cooker.

2. Mix together the paprika, ancho chile, cumin, salt, and pepper. Sprinkle half of the seasoning mixture over the top of each chicken, rubbing it in evenly. Drizzle the buffalo wing sauce over the chickens.

3. Cover and cook on the high heat setting for 3½ to 4 hours, until the chickens are tender and the juices run clear when the thickest part of the thigh is pricked. The internal temperature of the meat should be at least 165°F. Remove the chickens to a large platter and let stand until cool enough to handle.

4. Meanwhile, carefully pour the juices from the slow cooker into a plastic container, cool, cover, and refrigerate. When the liquid chills, you'll be able to remove the fat from the top easily. The chicken broth will keep in the refrigerator for up to 3 days or in the freezer for at least 3 months.

5. Carve the chicken or chickens you want to serve. Refrigerate any leftovers for up to 3 days.

Cook's Note

➤ If you want to cook only one whole chicken, use a 4-quart electric slow cooker. It will take 3 to 3½ hours on the high heat setting.

chicken cacciatore

Many people like the succulence of dark-meat chicken thighs, but if some of your family members prefer white meat, you can make this same recipe with skinless, boneless chicken breasts or offer a choice with half breasts and half thighs. Serve with pasta or polenta.

2 medium onions, halved and thinly sliced

1 can (28 ounces) diced tomatoes

1 can (6 ounces) tomato paste

¾ cup dry white wine

2 garlic cloves, crushed through a press

1 teaspoon dried rosemary, crushed

½ teaspoon kosher salt

¼ teaspoon freshly ground black pepper

Pinch of crushed hot red pepper

8 skinless, boneless chicken thighs (about 2½ pounds)

⅓ cup instant-blending flour, such as Wondra

1 cup pitted ripe olives, drained

1. In a 5-quart electric slow cooker, combine the onions, tomatoes with their juices, tomato paste, wine, garlic, rosemary, salt, black pepper, and hot pepper. Stir to blend the tomato paste with the rest of the ingredients.

2. Rinse the chicken thighs with cold water and pat dry. Trim off all excess fat. Dredge the thighs in the flour to coat all over; gently shake off any excess. Submerge in the tomato mixture in the pot, spooning some of the liquid up and over the chicken.

3. Cover and cook on the low heat setting for 4½ to 5½ hours, until the chicken is tender and cooked through. Stir in the olives. Season with additional salt and black pepper to taste.

Cook meat and other foods to the tenderness desired. Check for doneness using a sharp small knife or fork—is the food fork-tender, is it falling apart, or does it pierce it easily with no resistance?

braised chicken with tarragon and vinegar

Makes 6 to 8 servings

Piquant and tantalizing, this recipe is based on a French dish the great chef Fernand Point called *poulet diable*. I like to use boneless thighs, because it's much easier to dig out all the excess fat. Serve with mashed potatoes, or a puree of potatoes and parsnips, and steamed green beans.

2 pounds skinless, boneless chicken thighs (8)

2 pounds small skinless chicken drumsticks (8)

3 tablespoons thinly sliced garlic

¾ cup chicken broth

½ cup plus 1 to 2 tablespoons red wine vinegar

¼ cup dry white wine or dry vermouth

2 tablespoons tomato paste

1½ teaspoons dried tarragon

1 teaspoon salt

½ teaspoon freshly ground black pepper

2 tablespoons unsalted butter, softened

2 tablespoons all-purpose flour

1. Trim all excess fat from the chicken thighs. Put the chicken thighs and drumsticks and the garlic in a 4-quart electric slow cooker.

2. In a medium bowl, combine the broth, ½ cup of the vinegar, the wine, tomato paste, 1 teaspoon of the tarragon, the salt, and black pepper. Whisk until blended. Pour over the chicken and cook on the low heat setting for 3½ to 4½ hours, or until the chicken is tender and cooked through. The internal temperature of the meat should register at least 165°F on a digital thermometer.

3. Using tongs, remove the chicken pieces. Pour all the liquid in the pot into a medium saucepan. Return the chicken to the pot, cover, and leave on low. Boil the liquid in the saucepan, skimming the fat off the top, until reduced by about one-third, 12 to 15 minutes.

4. In a small bowl, blend the butter and flour to make a smooth paste. Gradually stir into the boiling liquid and boil, whisking, until the sauce is thickened and smooth. Stir in the remaining ½ teaspoon tarragon and 1 to 2 tablespoons vinegar to taste. Pour the sauce over the chicken and continue to cook on low, covered, for 15 to 20 minutes.

chicken and vegetables with peanut sauce

Makes about 6 servings

This interesting, colorful stew adapts beautifully to the slow cooker. I think it's originally Senegalese, and it's a real party pleaser. Serve over steamed rice.

2 pounds skinless, boneless chicken, preferably
   half thighs and half breasts

2/3 cup crunchy peanut butter

1 can (14.5 ounces) diced tomatoes

1/4 cup all-purpose flour

1/4 to 1/2 teaspoon cayenne pepper, to taste

1/2 teaspoon seasoned salt

2 garlic cloves, crushed through a press

1 medium onion, chopped

1 large red bell pepper, chopped

1 1/4 pounds yams or sweet potatoes, peeled and
   cut into 3/4-inch pieces

1 package (6 ounces) prewashed fresh baby spinach

1. Pat the chicken dry with paper towels. Trim off any visible bits of fat. Cut the meat into 1-inch chunks.

2. In a medium bowl, combine the peanut butter, tomatoes with their juices, flour, cayenne, seasoned salt, and garlic. Stir until well blended.

3. In a 5- or 6-quart electric slow cooker, combine the onion, bell pepper, yams, and chicken chunks. Pour in the peanut butter mixture and toss to mix thoroughly. Cover and cook on the low heat setting for 4½ to 5½ hours, until the yams are tender and the chicken is cooked through.

4. Stir in the spinach until wilted, 3 to 5 minutes. Add more seasoned salt if needed.

ragout of chicken with root vegetables

Makes 4 to 6 servings

We often think of root vegetables in fall and winter, but late summer offers up tiny turnips, baby carrots, and new potatoes that translate into a wonderful stew. In cold months, simply cut larger vegetables into halves or quarters. For color, sprinkle with a tablespoon of chopped parsley, chervil, or chives before serving.

2 pounds skinless, boneless chicken thighs

1 to 1¼ pounds new potatoes, scrubbed

½ pound small boiling onions, peeled, or
    medium onions cut into ¾-inch wedges

½ pound baby carrots or larger carrots, peeled and
    cut into 1½-inch lengths

½ teaspoon dried thyme leaves

¼ teaspoon ground allspice

1 teaspoon salt

¼ teaspoon freshly ground black pepper

2 tablespoons all-purpose flour

¾ pound baby turnips, peeled, or larger turnips,
    halved or quartered

6 whole garlic cloves, peeled

1 cup reduced-sodium chicken broth

½ cup dry white vermouth

1½ to 2 tablespoons heavy cream (optional but nice)

1. Cut the chicken thighs in half and trim off any visible fat. Halve any potatoes that are larger than 1½ inches in diameter.

2. Make a bed of the onions on the bottom of a 4-quart electric slow cooker. Add the carrots, then the chicken. Season with the thyme, allspice, salt, and pepper. Sprinkle the flour evenly over the chicken. Add the potatoes, turnips, and garlic. Pour in the broth and vermouth.

3. Cook on the low heat setting for 5½ to 6 hours, or until the chicken is cooked and the vegetables are tender when pierced with the tip of a small knife.

4. With a slotted spoon, transfer the chicken and vegetables to a serving dish. As you do so, measure out 1 cup of mostly onions, with 1½ potatoes, a couple of pieces of carrot, and 1 piece of turnip and place in a food processor. Pour in the cooking juices and puree until smooth. Add the cream, if desired. Season with salt and pepper to taste. Pour the sauce over the chicken and vegetables and serve.

braised turkey breast with green beans and potatoes

Makes 6 to 8 servings

This is a simple way to cook a turkey breast, in a colorful one-pot meal. The smoked paprika colors the turkey beautifully and adds a deeper dimension to the flavor. Serve slices topped with the juices from the pot along with the vegetables.

1½ pounds small red potatoes, preferably organic, scrubbed and halved or quartered

3 cups fresh green beans, trimmed and cut into 1½-inch pieces, or frozen haricots verts, thawed

1 medium onion, halved and sliced

1 red bell pepper, chopped

½ cup dry white wine

1 teaspoon smoked paprika

1 teaspoon seasoned salt

½ teaspoon freshly ground black pepper

1 turkey breast half (3 to 3½ pounds), skinned and boned (2 to 2½ pounds after trimming)

1. In a 6-quart electric slow cooker, combine the potatoes, green beans, onion, bell pepper, wine, and half of the smoked paprika, seasoned salt, and pepper. Mix well.

2. Sprinkle both sides of the turkey breast liberally with the remaining smoked paprika, seasoned salt, and pepper. Set the turkey on top of the vegetables in the pot.

3. Cover and cook on the low heat setting for 6½ to 7 hours, or until the turkey and potatoes are tender and the turkey is white throughout with no trace of pink. The internal temperature should register at least 165°F on a digital thermometer.

4. Transfer the turkey to a cutting board, cover loosely with aluminum foil, and let stand for 10 minutes. Carve the turkey breast on the diagonal into thin slices. Arrange on a deep platter. Spoon the vegetables around the turkey and ladle some of the juices from the pot on top.

turkey breast with cranberry chutney and squash

Makes 6 servings

For Sunday dinner or a small Thanksgiving, here's a great dish with a medley of your favorite flavors in one pot. If you have a second pot, try the Savory Sausage Stuffing (page 332) so you'll have all the trimmings.

2 packages (1 pound each) butternut squash cut into
   1-inch cubes, or 2½ pounds butternut squash, peeled,
   seeded, and cut into 1-inch cubes (about 6 cups)
1 jar (9 ounces) apple-cranberry chutney
½ cup assorted dried fruit bits or pieces
2 tablespoons frozen orange juice concentrate, thawed
2½ tablespoons instant tapioca
1 turkey breast half (2½ pounds), skinned and boned
   (about 1½ pounds after trimming)
½ teaspoon ground chipotle chile
Seasoned salt and freshly ground black pepper

1. Place the squash cubes in a 5-quart electric slow cooker. In a bowl, mix together the chutney, dried fruit pieces, orange juice concentrate, tapioca, and ½ cup of water. Pour over the squash in the pot. Toss together until well mixed. Place the whole turkey breast on top and dust with the chipotle chile.

2. Cover and cook on the low heat setting, stirring once during cooking to spoon the sauce up and over the turkey, for 5 to 6 hours, until the turkey is cooked through but still moist and the squash is tender but holds its shape. Remove the turkey to a carving board.

3. Gently stir the squash and sauce. Season with salt and pepper to taste. Carve the turkey into thin slices and serve with the squash and sauce.

poached turkey breast

Makes 4 to 5 servings

Turkey benefits from the gentle, slow heat of the electric cooker. You'll find it turns out beautifully, with little shrinkage. This low-fat recipe is excellent if you want to serve the turkey plain or sliced for sandwiches. Or you can use the meat for pasta sauces, salads, casseroles, or soups. Be sure to strain the broth and use it as stock; it can be refrigerated for up to three days or frozen for up to three months.

1 large turkey breast fillet (about 1 pound)

2 cups chicken broth or water

1 onion, quartered

1 celery rib, cut into 1½-inch lengths

6 sprigs of parsley with stems

¼ teaspoon dried thyme leaves

1 teaspoon salt

½ teaspoon whole black peppercorns

Cook's Note

➤ If you want to increase this recipe, you can follow it as is, but use 2 turkey breast fillets. Just make sure they are completely submerged; add more broth or water, if necessary.

1. Rinse the turkey and pat dry with paper towels.

2. In a 3- or 4-quart electric slow cooker, combine the broth, onion, celery, parsley, thyme, salt, and peppercorns. Pour in 2 cups of water. Cover and cook on the high heat setting for 30 minutes.

3. Add the turkey breast. Cover, reduce the heat to low, and cook for 2½ to 3 hours, or until the turkey is tender but still juicy; there should be no pink in the center.

4. If not serving at once, turn off the pot, uncover, and let the turkey cool in the broth for 30 minutes. It will remain moister this way. Then remove from the liquid, wrap well, and refrigerate for up to 3 days.

Be aware that poultry requires less cooking time than most beef, pork, or lamb—and does not, in most instances, require all day or anywhere near that to cook. Cook poultry in the evenings, on weekends, or when you're around the house for a few hours, so you can check it and avoid overcooking.

turkey molé

Makes 4 to 6 servings

In Mexico, there are as many recipes for mole as there are cooks. This is a simplified mole poblano, designed expressly for the slow cooker. You'll find the play of sweet, hot, and spicy extremely appealing, especially as a foil for the mild turkey meat.

This recipe makes enough sauce that if you want to double the amount of turkey you can without changing the recipe. If you do so, leave out the bone so there will be plenty of room for all the meat. Serve with rice and sautéed zucchini, or wrap in flour tortillas with thinly sliced white onion and sprigs of cilantro.

1 turkey breast on the bone (2 to 2½ pounds)

1 can (14.5 ounces) diced tomatoes

¾ cup lager beer or chicken broth

2 ounces semisweet baking chocolate, broken up

3 tablespoons yellow cornmeal

1 small onion, finely chopped

2 garlic cloves, finely chopped

¼ cup raisins

8 pitted prunes

2½ tablespoons toasted sesame seeds

1 tablespoon ground ancho chile

½ teaspoon ground chipotle chile

1½ teaspoons salt

1½ teaspoons ground cinnamon

2 dashes of ground cloves

1. Cut the turkey off the bone, but reserve the bone; it will add extra flavor and body to your sauce. Remove the skin and trim off any visible fat.

2. In a 4-quart electric slow cooker, combine the tomatoes with their juices, beer, chocolate, cornmeal, onion, garlic, raisins, prunes, 2 tablespoons of the sesame seeds, the ancho chile, chipotle chile, salt, 1 teaspoon of the cinnamon, and the cloves. Stir to mix. Tuck the bone down into the sauce and place the turkey breast on top. Spoon some of the sauce ingredients up and over the turkey.

3. Cover and cook on the low heat setting for 3¾ to 4 hours, until the turkey is tender and cooked through and the sauce is thick. The internal temperature should register at least 165°F on a digital thermometer.

4. Remove the turkey to a cutting board and carve into thin slices. Add the remaining ½ teaspoon cinnamon to the sauce and, using a hand-held immersion blender, puree until smooth. Or puree the sauce in a blender or food processor. Pour over the turkey and sprinkle the remaining 1½ teaspoons sesame seeds on top.

turkey chop suey with peanut sauce

Makes 6 servings

Serve over hot cooked rice or Chinese noodles for a satisfying supper. Or top with crispy chow mein noodles. My family likes to wrap the chop suey in iceberg lettuce cups.

1½ pounds ground turkey

¼ teaspoon salt

¼ teaspoon freshly ground black pepper

4 scallions, chopped

4 celery ribs, thinly sliced

4 cups chopped Napa cabbage

3 cups fresh bean sprouts, rinsed and drained (¾ pound)

1 can (8 ounces) whole water chestnuts, rinsed, drained, and chopped

½ cup peanut butter, smooth or chunky

⅓ cup hoisin sauce

2 tablespoons soy sauce

1 tablespoon fresh lime juice

½ cup chicken broth

Chopped peanuts and thinly sliced scallion greens, for garnish

1. In a wok or large skillet, cook the turkey over high heat, breaking up the ground meat into small pieces, until well browned, 5 to 6 minutes. Season with the salt and pepper.

2. Transfer the turkey to a 5-quart electric slow cooker. Add the scallions, celery, cabbage, bean sprouts, and water chestnuts. Mix well.

3. In a medium bowl, combine the peanut butter, hoisin sauce, soy sauce, and lime juice. Mix until well blended. Gradually stir in the broth. Pour half of the peanut sauce over the turkey and vegetables in the pot and toss to mix well. Drizzle the remaining sauce over the top.

4. Cover and cook on the low heat setting for 4½ to 5 hours, until hot. Transfer to a serving platter and sprinkle chopped peanuts and scallions on top.

turkey and potato casserole

Makes 6 servings

This is a good choice for a potluck or buffet, and it's easy on the cook. Serve over rice or wrap up in warm flour tortillas.

1 pound ground turkey

1 medium onion, chopped

1 can (28 ounces) diced tomatoes

1 can (6 ounces) tomato paste

4 medium golden potatoes (about 1½ pounds), peeled and finely diced

1 jar (7 ounces) roasted red peppers, drained and coarsely chopped

⅔ cup golden raisins

2 or 3 garlic cloves, minced

1 teaspoon dried oregano

2 teaspoons Worcestershire sauce

Dash of your favorite hot sauce, or more to taste

¾ teaspoon salt

¼ teaspoon freshly ground black pepper

Toasted slivered almonds and chopped fresh parsley, for garnish

Cook's Note

➤ All golden potatoes used to be Yukon gold. Now they come with many names, butter potatoes and golden potatoes being just a couple.

1. In a large skillet, cook the turkey and onion over medium-high heat, stirring often and breaking up the turkey until well browned, 7 to 8 minutes.

2. Transfer to a 4- or 5-quart electric slow cooker. Add the tomatoes with their juices, tomato paste, potatoes, roasted peppers, raisins, garlic, oregano, Worcestershire sauce, hot sauce, salt, and pepper. Mix well.

3. Cover and cook on the low heat setting for 6½ to 7½ hours, or until the potatoes are tender. Serve garnished with toasted slivered almonds and parsley.

almost-instant barbecued turkey and beans

H ere's a barbecued turkey and bean stew that's great for spooning over your favorite rolls or toasted potato buns, just like a sloppy Joe. Serve with coleslaw and potato salad or chips.

Makes 4 servings

1 pound turkey breast cutlets, cut into 1-inch pieces
1 can (15 ounces) pinto beans, rinsed and well drained
1 can (14.5 ounces) diced tomatoes
1 medium onion, chopped
1 cup hickory-flavored barbecue sauce
Salt and freshly ground black pepper

1. In a 4-quart electric slow cooker, combine the turkey pieces, beans, tomatoes with their juices, onion, and ½ cup of the barbecue sauce. Mix well.

2. Cover and cook on the low heat setting for about 5 hours, or until the turkey is cooked through and tender. Stir in the remaining ½ cup barbecue sauce and season with salt and pepper to taste.

turkey and mixed vegetables asian style

Makes 4 to 5 servings

Because of all the water in many of these vegetables, you'll find they fill up the pot. But you'll be surprised at how much they cook down. Serve over steamed rice to soak up all the good juices.

1 pound turkey breast tenderloins

¼ cup plus 2 tablespoons hoisin sauce

3 tablespoons soy sauce

2 tablespoons dry sherry

¼ cup chicken broth

1 tablespoon rice vinegar

¼ to ½ teaspoon Asian chili paste with garlic

¼ teaspoon ground ginger

2 tablespoons cornstarch

4 cups chopped bok choy

1 head of Napa cabbage (about 1 pound), chopped

5 celery ribs, diagonally sliced

1½ cups chopped fresh bean sprouts

5 scallions, chopped

1 red or orange bell pepper, chopped

4 ounces snow peas, trimmed and cut into thin julienne strips

Sea salt and freshly ground black pepper

1. Cut the turkey tenderloins into thin strips. In a medium bowl, combine ¼ cup of the hoisin sauce, 2 tablespoons of the soy sauce, the sherry, broth, vinegar, chili paste with garlic, and ginger. Stir to mix well. Blend in the cornstarch. Add the turkey pieces and toss to coat.

2. In a 6-quart electric slow cooker, combine the bok choy, cabbage, celery, bean sprouts, scallions, and bell pepper. Mix well. Add the turkey with all its sauce and toss with the vegetables to distribute evenly.

3. Cover and cook on the low heat setting for 4½ to 5 hours, or until the turkey is cooked through and tender. Stir in the remaining 2 tablespoons hoisin sauce and 1 tablespoon soy sauce, the snow peas, and salt and pepper to taste. Cover and cook for 5 to 10 minutes longer, until heated through.

seafood stew with halibut, scallops, and shrimp

Makes 6 to 8 servings

The sauce takes no time to toss into a slow cooker, and then you let it lazily simmer away. Be sure to add the seafood only during the last 45 minutes, so it won't become tough. Serve with toasted peasant bread rubbed with garlic and brushed with extra virgin olive oil.

1 can (28 ounces) diced tomatoes

¾ cup chopped roasted red peppers (about 7.5 ounces)

1 leek (white and pale green parts), rinsed well to remove dirt and finely chopped

2 garlic cloves, finely grated

1 tablespoon extra virgin olive oil

¼ teaspoon crushed hot red pepper

1 pound large or medium shrimp, shelled and deveined

½ pound bay scallops

½ pound halibut steak, cut into ¾-inch chunks

Grated zest of 1 lemon

⅓ cup chopped fresh parsley

Sea salt and freshly ground black pepper

1. In a 4-quart electric slow cooker, combine the tomatoes with their juices, roasted peppers, leek, garlic, olive oil, and hot pepper. Cover and cook on the low heat setting for 4½ to 5 hours to make the base.

2. Raise the heat to high. Stir in the shrimp, scallops, halibut chunks, lemon zest, and parsley. Cover and cook on the high heat setting for about 45 minutes, until the seafood is cooked through but still tender.

3. Season with salt, black pepper, and additional hot pepper to taste. Ladle into bowls and serve at once.

Keep perishable foods refrigerated until preparation time. If you plan to cut up fish, meats, and vegetables in advance, store them separately in the refrigerator so bacteria won't begin multiplying.

shrimp and sausage gumbo

Makes 6 to 8 servings

Gumbo is sort of a cross between soup and stew. Some versions are served thin as a first course. This thicker, heartier-style gumbo can be offered as a substantial soup, but I like to ladle it over rice for a tasty one-pot meal.

There are all kinds of gumbos with various combinations of sausages, seafoods, meats, and vegetables. To thicken gumbo, some use okra, cooked right in the dish, while others use filé powder, sprinkled over the top of the gumbo when served or stirred into the gumbo just before serving. Filé powder should not be heated. The basic recipe here features andouille chicken sausage, but hot Italian can be substituted.

3 tablespoons vegetable oil

3 tablespoons all-purpose flour

1 pound fully cooked andouille chicken sausage,
    halved lengthwise and sliced ¼ inch thick

2 medium onions, chopped

2 green bell peppers, chopped

4 celery ribs, chopped

1½ cups chicken broth

1 can (14.5 ounces) diced tomatoes, drained

2 cups frozen cut okra, thawed

⅛ teaspoon cayenne pepper

1 pound shelled and deveined cooked medium shrimp

Sea salt and freshly ground black pepper

1. In a large heavy skillet, make a roux by whisking together the oil and flour until well blended. Cook over medium-high heat, whisking constantly, until beige, 3 to 5 minutes. Reduce the heat to medium and cook, whisking constantly, until the roux turns the color of milk chocolate (6 to 8 minutes longer), being careful not to burn it. Immediately scrape into a 5-quart electric slow cooker.

2. In another large skillet, quickly brown the sausage pieces over medium-high heat, stirring often. Drain and pat with paper towels to remove as much excess fat as possible. Add to the pot.

3. Add the onions, bell peppers, celery, broth, tomatoes, okra, and cayenne; mix well. Cover and cook on the low heat setting for about 8 hours or the high heat setting for about 4 hours, until slightly thickened.

4. Add the shrimp and cook on the low heat setting until they are hot, about 30 to 40 minutes. Season with salt and black pepper to taste.

shrimp veracruz style

Makes 4 to 5 servings

Because of all the savory sauce, this dish is best served over hot cooked pasta or steamed rice. If there's extra sauce, it makes a wonderful topping for grilled or broiled fish, such as halibut, swordfish, or red snapper.

1 can (14.5 ounces) diced tomatoes
3 large plum tomatoes, diced and drained
1 small onion, chopped
1 can (6 ounces) pitted ripe olives, drained and coarsely chopped
3 tablespoons drained capers
1 teaspoon ground cumin
1 garlic clove, crushed through a press
¼ teaspoon freshly ground black pepper
Pinch of sugar
1 pound shelled and deveined cooked jumbo or large shrimp
¼ cup crumbled feta cheese or queso fresco

1. In a 4-quart electric slow cooker, combine the canned tomatoes with their juices, plum tomatoes, onion, olives, capers, cumin, garlic, and pepper. Mix well.

2. Cover and cook on the low heat setting for 4 to 5 hours.

3. Stir in a pinch of sugar. Add the shrimp, cover, and cook on the high heat setting for 35 to 45 minutes, or until hot throughout. Serve with the feta cheese sprinkled on top.

Cook's Note

➤ Feta cheese may not sound as if it's from Mexico, and of course, it's not, but it's the closest cheese to the Mexican queso fresco, which is not available all over.

beef, pork, and lamb

Meats do exceptionally well in the slow cooker because the controlled method lets the protein fibers tenderize slowly with little shrinkage. By cooking in the pot, the low temperature is automatically regulated, which keeps the proteins relaxed and loose and stretches a pound of meat about as far as it can go. Flavor has time to develop, and good texture is easy to achieve. The only caveat is that in some recipes, if the meat is surrounded by heat for much longer than the recipe calls for, it will eventually begin to fall apart. In the cases of pulled barbecued meat and chilis, or in the Leg of Lamb Braised in Red Wine, which steeps for eight hours, the meat ends up so tender you can eat it with a spoon, which is the intention.

In most cases, initial browning can be skipped. One exception to this is ground meats—beef, turkey, or sausages—which for best color and flavor do better when seared first. The extra step also allows you to drain off excess fat. By far the majority of the recipes you'll find here, however, are as quick-fix as elsewhere in the book.

beef, pork, and lamb

beef stifado

Makes 5 to 6 servings

Even if the name is unfamiliar, the cinnamon and feta cheese here might tip you off that this savory stew is of Greek origin. Serve with rice or roasted potatoes and braised greens or steamed broccoli.

1½ pounds boneless beef top round

2 tablespoons all-purpose flour

1 pound small white pearl onions, peeled

1 can (6 ounces) tomato paste

⅔ cup dry red wine

2 tablespoons balsamic vinegar

2 garlic cloves, crushed through a press

3 whole cloves

1 cinnamon stick

2 bay leaves

1 cup halved baby tomatoes or coarsely chopped plum tomatoes

½ cup crumbled feta cheese

1. Trim any excess fat from the beef. Slice the meat into 1-inch cubes or diagonally across the grain into thin strips. Place in a 4-quart electric slow cooker. Sprinkle the flour over the beef and toss to coat evenly. Mix in the onions.

2. In a small bowl, mix together the tomato paste, wine, vinegar, and garlic until well blended. Add to the meat and stir gently. Submerge the cloves, cinnamon stick, and bay leaves in the pot.

3. Cover and cook the stew on the low heat setting for 6 to 7 hours, or until the meat is tender but not falling apart.

4. Remove and discard the whole cloves, cinnamon stick, and bay leaves. Stir in the tomatoes. Serve topped with feta cheese.

savory meat loaf

Makes 8 to 10 servings

Lean ground meat is the best choice for the slow cooker. To keep it moist with the long, low heat, I use plenty of eggs, bread crumbs, and milk. This creates a loaf that slices beautifully. Leftovers are delicious reheated or cold in sandwiches.

3 large eggs

3 cups soft white bread crumbs (from 3 to 4 slices)

1 teaspoon salt

½ teaspoon freshly ground black pepper

1 large onion, chopped

1 green bell pepper, chopped

3 tablespoons minced fresh parsley

1¼ cups milk

3 pounds ground beef sirloin or ground round

Glaze (recipe follows)

1. In a large bowl, beat the eggs lightly. Add the bread crumbs, salt, black pepper, onion, bell pepper, parsley, and milk and mix well. Add the ground beef and lightly mix with your hands until thoroughly incorporated. Pack the meat loaf into a 4-quart oval electric slow cooker.

2. Cover and cook on the high heat setting for 2¾ to 3 hours or on the low heat setting for 6 to 6½ hours, until the meat loaf is cooked through.

3. Spread the glaze evenly over the top and continue cooking on the high heat setting, covered, for 20 minutes. Turn off the pot and let the meat loaf cool in the pot for 10 to 15 minutes to allow it to set up. Using two metal spatulas, carefully transfer the loaf to a platter. Cut the loaf into slices to serve. Refrigerate any leftovers; they'll make great sandwiches.

glaze

In a small bowl, combine ½ cup ketchup, 2 teaspoons brown sugar, 1 teaspoon yellow mustard, and 2 tablespoons red wine vinegar. Stir to mix well.

tamale pie

Makes 6 servings

Everyone loves this dish: savory chili beef mixed with corn and ripe olives, topped with a cornmeal crust and lots of Cheddar cheese. What's not to like? To save time here, use a sliced roll of prepared polenta instead of making the topping from scratch. Be sure to pass a bottle of hot sauce on the side.

1 pound lean ground beef

1 medium onion, chopped

1 green bell pepper, chopped

1½ tablespoons chili powder

1 tablespoon ground cumin

½ teaspoon salt

½ teaspoon freshly ground black pepper

1 can (28 ounces) crushed tomatoes

1 cup coarsely chopped ripe olives (6-ounce can)

1¾ cups corn kernels (fresh, frozen, or canned)

1 log (18 ounces) ready-to-heat, precooked polenta,
  preferably organic

1 cup shredded sharp Cheddar cheese

Sour cream and chopped fresh cilantro, for garnish

1. In a large skillet, sauté the ground beef with the onion over medium-high heat, breaking up any large lumps of meat, until lightly browned, 7 to 8 minutes, Drain off any excess fat.

2. Stir in the bell pepper, chili powder, cumin, salt, and black pepper. Cook for another 2 minutes to toast the spices. Stir in the tomatoes, olives, and corn. Mix well.

3. Cut the polenta roll crosswise into 10 to 12 rounds about ¾ inch thick. Use half of the slices to line the bottom of a 4-quart electric slow cooker, trimming the rounds as necessary to fit. Spoon the meat mixture over the polenta, spreading it evenly. Top with the remaining polenta slices.

4. Cover and cook on the low heat setting for 4 to 4½ hours. Remove the lid and sprinkle the cheese over the top of the tamale pie. Raise the heat setting to high and cook with the cover ajar for 10 minutes, or until the cheese is melted. Serve the tamale pie hot, garnished with sour cream and chopped cilantro.

beefy bean chili

Makes 6 servings

This chili is easy to toss together in a flash. Pinto beans are traditional in southwestern chili, so that's what's suggested here, but you can use any kind: black, white, or kidney. Just before serving, taste the dish and refresh, if needed, with a little extra chili powder and cumin. Pass white or brown rice, if you like, and a basket of tortilla chips on the side. Accompany with an avocado salad.

1¼ to 1½ pounds lean ground beef

1 large onion, chopped

3 cans (15 ounces each) red kidney beans, pinto beans, or black beans, rinsed and well drained

1 can (14.5 ounces) diced tomatoes

1 can (10 ounces) diced tomatoes and green chiles

1 can (6 ounces) tomato paste

2 tablespoons chili powder

1½ tablespoons ground cumin

½ teaspoon salt

½ teaspoon freshly ground black pepper

Chopped fresh tomatoes and shredded Cheddar cheese

Cook's Note

➤ If you're making this for picky children, you may want to use a can of plain diced tomatoes in place of the tomatoes with green chiles.

1. In a large skillet, cook the beef and onion over medium-high heat, stirring often, until the beef is browned and crumbly, 7 to 8 minutes. Drain off any excess fat. Transfer the beef and onion to a 4-quart electric slow cooker.

2. Add the beans, diced tomatoes with their juices, diced tomatoes with green chiles and their juices, tomato paste, chili powder, cumin, salt, and pepper. Mix well.

3. Cover and cook on the low heat setting for 5½ to 6 hours. Serve hot, topped with chopped tomatoes and shredded cheese.

slow picadillo

Makes 4 servings

Here's a dish that takes even better to the slow cooker than the top of the stove. All the wonderful flavors have plenty of time to meld, and the gentle heat keeps the meat moist and tender.

1 pound ground sirloin (90 percent lean)

1 teaspoon salt

¼ teaspoon freshly ground black pepper

1½ cups chopped onion

¾ cup finely diced green bell pepper

1½ teaspoons ground cumin

½ teaspoon dried oregano

1 cup sherry, preferably medium-dry amontillado

1 can (6 ounces) tomato paste

¼ cup plus 2 tablespoons raisins

1 tablespoon plus 1 teaspoon nonpareil capers,
    plus 1½ teaspoons brine from jar

½ cup small Spanish pimiento-stuffed olives

¼ cup slivered almonds

1. Season the meat with salt and pepper. Spread out in a 7 × 11 metal baking dish and broil as close to the heat as possible, turning once, for 8 to 10 minutes, until lightly browned.

2. In a 3- or 4-quart electric slow cooker, scatter 1 cup of the chopped onion over the bottom of the dish. Top with the bell pepper. Crumble the meat into the pot in an even layer, leaving some larger chunks. Season with 1 teaspoon of the cumin and the oregano.

3. Pour the sherry over the meat. Spread the tomato paste over the beef. Add the raisins, capers with their brine, and 1 cup of water. Stir to mix. Cover and cook on the low heat setting for 5 hours. Stir once or twice if it is convenient.

4. Add the olives, almonds, and remaining ½ teaspoon cumin. Continue to cook on low for 30 to 60 minutes. Switch to warm for up to 2 hours, until ready to serve.

beef lettuce wraps

Makes 4 to 5 servings

Wrap delicious, spicy ground beef in cool iceberg lettuce cups for an enticing appetizer or light entree. You can also pile the beef mixture on shredded lettuce or top with shredded iceberg lettuce, slivered pea pods, and thinly sliced red peppers and drizzle with sesame dressing for a warm main-course salad.

1½ pounds extra-lean ground beef

4 scallions, chopped

¼ cup dry sherry

1 can (8 ounces) sliced water chestnuts, drained and chopped

2 cups chopped fresh white mushrooms

1 garlic clove, crushed through a press

3 tablespoons hoisin sauce

1 tablespoon soy sauce

1 teaspoon Asian sesame oil

½ teaspoon Asian chili paste with garlic

Dash of sugar

1½ tablespoons cornstarch

Salt and freshly ground black pepper

Iceberg or Bibb lettuce leaves

Cook's Note

➤ Unless otherwise indicated, "sesame oil" always refers to the amber-colored Asian sesame oil, sometimes called toasted sesame oil. The cold-pressed kind you find in health-food stores has little flavor.

1. In a large skillet, cook the ground beef with the scallions over medium-high heat, stirring to break up any lumps of meat, until well browned, 6 to 8 minutes. Drain off any excess fat.

2. Turn the beef mixture into a 4-quart electric slow cooker. Pour 2 tablespoons of the sherry into the skillet and cook over high heat for 30 seconds, scraping up any browned bits with a wooden spatula. Pour over the beef.

3. Add the water chestnuts, mushrooms, and garlic. Whisk together the remaining 2 tablespoons sherry with the hoisin sauce, soy sauce, sesame oil, chili paste with garlic, sugar, cornstarch, and ½ cup of cold water until well blended and smooth. Add to the pot and stir to mix well.

4. Cover and cook on the high heat setting for about 2 hours or on the low heat setting for about 4 hours. Season with salt and pepper to taste. Serve with a stack of lettuce leaf "cups." Spoon some of mixture into each lettuce leaf, roll up, and eat.

Variation

Use 1½ pounds ground chicken breast instead of beef. Brown in 1 teaspoon sesame oil along with the scallions. Proceed as directed.

asian flavors beef and vegetables

Makes 4 to 5 servings

With Asian overtones and supermarket-accessible ingredients, this makes an easy one-pot meal. When checking for doneness, be sure the snow peas are still slightly crisp but the rice is tender. To perk up the flavor, stir in another tablespoon each of soy sauce and hoisin sauce just before serving.

1 pound lean ground beef

1 large onion, cut into 1-inch chunks

5 celery ribs, sliced

1 red bell pepper, chopped

1 yellow bell pepper, chopped

½ pound fresh snow peas, ends trimmed and
   cut lengthwise in half

½ cup converted long-grain white rice

1 cup beef or chicken broth

2 tablespoons hoisin sauce

1 tablespoon soy sauce

Sea salt and freshly ground black pepper

1. In a large skillet, sauté the beef and onion over medium-high heat, breaking up any large lumps of meat and stirring often, until the beef is well browned and the onion softened, 7 to 8 minutes. Drain off any excess fat.

2. In a 4-quart electric slow cooker, combine the celery, red and yellow bell peppers, snow peas, and rice. Add the beef and onion and stir to mix. Add the broth, hoisin sauce, and soy sauce. Mix well.

3. Cover and cook on the low heat setting for 3 to 3½ hours, or until the rice is cooked through but the snow peas are still somewhat crisp. Season with salt and pepper to taste.

barbecued beef with pinto beans

Makes 6 to 8 servings

This fast-fix dish comes together so effortlessly. Just dump everything into the pot and forget about it as you go about your day. For a hearty meal, serve with plenty of hot cornbread and coleslaw or a tossed green salad.

1½ to 1¾ pounds boneless beef round

6 cups cooked pinto or Great Northern beans, well drained (see page 281), or 2 cans (29 ounces each) pinto beans, rinsed and well drained

1 large onion, chopped

1½ cups hickory-flavored barbecue sauce

Salt and freshly ground black pepper

1. Trim any excess fat from the beef round. Cut the meat into 1-inch cubes. Place in a 5-quart electric slow cooker.

2. Add the beans, onion, and 1 cup of the barbecue sauce. Stir gently to mix with the beef without breaking the beans.

3. Cover and cook on the low heat setting for 7 to 8 hours, or until the beef is tender. Stir in the remaining ½ cup barbecue sauce. Season with salt and pepper to taste.

chili beef with mushrooms

S erve this lovely rich stew over hot egg noodles. Garnish with dollops of sour cream and a dusting of chopped parsley.

Makes 8 servings

2 pounds boneless beef top round steak

2 tablespoons instant-blending flour, such as Wondra

1 tablespoon chili powder

1 teaspoon paprika

1 large onion, halved and cut into thin slices

1¼ cups sliced fresh white mushrooms

¾ cup chili sauce

½ cup dry white wine

1 garlic clove, crushed through a press

1½ teaspoons Worcestershire sauce

Salt

1. Trim any excess fat from the steak. Slice the beef diagonally across the grain into thin strips. Place in a 5-quart electric slow cooker.

2. Sprinkle the flour, chili powder, and paprika over the meat. Toss to coat the strips with the flour and seasonings. Add the onion and mushrooms. In a small bowl, stir together the chili sauce, wine, garlic, and Worcestershire sauce. Pour into the pot and mix well.

3. Cover and cook on the low heat setting for about 8 hours or on the high heat setting for about 4 hours, until the meat is tender. Season with salt to taste.

beef and three-bean stew

f you like slow cooker recipes that you can just throw into the pot before work, this is a great choice. I like to serve the stew like a sloppy Joe, ladled over toasted hamburger buns or sourdough rolls. Coleslaw makes a fine accompaniment.

2½ pounds flat-cut brisket of beef

1 can (15 ounces) kidney beans

1 can (15 ounces) black beans

1 can (15 ounces) pinto beans

1 cup ketchup

3 tablespoons cider vinegar

1 tablespoon Worcestershire sauce

¼ cup packed brown sugar

¼ teaspoon smoked paprika

2 teaspoons instant coffee, dissolved in 2 tablespoons water

½ teaspoon salt

¼ teaspoon freshly ground black pepper

1. Trim as much fat as possible from the beef brisket.

2. Drain all three types of beans into a colander. Rinse thoroughly under cold running water; drain well. Transfer the beans to a 5-quart electric slow cooker.

3. In a bowl, combine the ketchup, vinegar, Worcestershire sauce, brown sugar, smoked paprika, and instant coffee dissolved in water. Pour half of this sauce over the beans and toss together. Place the brisket on top of the beans. Season the meat with the salt and pepper. Spoon about two-thirds of the remaining sauce over the meat. Pour the rest around the brisket.

4. Cover and cook on the low heat setting for 8 to 8½ hours, or until the brisket is falling-apart tender. Remove the brisket to a plate and let stand until cool enough to handle. Either shred the beef with two forks or coarsely chop the meat. Return it to the pot and stir to mix with the beans and sauce.

beef stew with red wine

Makes 8 servings

Simple beef stews like this one lend themselves to long, slow simmering. Red wine adds a nice dimension of flavor. The best choice would be a cabernet or merlot.

1¾ to 2 pounds beef top round steak or boneless beef for stew

6 carrots, peeled and cut into ¼-inch slices

4 medium waxy potatoes, such as Red Bliss or Yukon gold, peeled and cut into ½- to ¾-inch cubes

3 celery ribs, sliced

2 medium onions, cut into ¾-inch dice

¼ cup all-purpose flour

¾ teaspoon salt

¼ teaspoon seasoned pepper

1½ to 2 cups dry red wine

2 tablespoons Dijon mustard

Pinch of sugar

2 bay leaves

1. Trim all excess fat from the beef. Cut the meat into 1-inch cubes.

2. In a 6-quart electric slow cooker, mix together the carrots, potatoes, celery, and onions. Place the flour, salt, and pepper in a large, zippered plastic bag. Add the beef cubes, seal the bag, and toss until the beef is evenly coated with the seasoned flour. Add the meat and any loose flour to the slow cooker. Spoon some of the vegetables up and over the beef.

3. In a glass bowl or large glass measuring cup, whisk together the wine, mustard, and sugar until thoroughly mixed. Pour evenly over the beef and vegetables. Submerge the bay leaves on opposite sides of the pot.

4. Cover and cook on the low heat setting for 6½ to 7½ hours, until the potatoes and beef are tender but the beef still holds its shape. Remove and discard the bay leaves before serving.

autumn beef stew with yams

Makes 4 to 6 servings

Yams are usually paired with poultry, but laced with a sweet-tart sauce, they go beautifully with beef as well. To make this an almost-instant dish in terms of preparation, pick up a couple of packages of peeled, cut-up, ready-to-cook yams, if your supermarket stocks them. A small handful of chopped parsley, if you have it on hand, will brighten the color of the stew just before serving.

1 pound boneless beef top round steak

2¼ pounds yams, peeled and cut into 1-inch chunks, or
    2 packages (1 pound each) ready-to-cook yam pieces

1 large onion, chopped

1 cup barbecue sauce

2 tablespoons instant-blending flour, such as Wondra

½ cup apricot-pineapple preserves

Seasoned salt and freshly ground black pepper

Cook's Note

➤ There are many brands and blends of seasoned salt on the market. I like to use them for extra flavor and to reduce the need for a long list of herbs and spices. Some purists might protest. In any of the recipes that call for seasoned salt, you can substitute regular or sea salt.

1. Trim as much fat as possible from the beef and cut the meat into thin strips. Place in a 4-quart electric slow cooker and add the yams and onion.

2. In a small bowl, stir the barbecue sauce and flour into the apricot-pineapple preserves until well blended. Pour over the beef and vegetables. Toss gently to coat evenly.

3. Cover and cook on the low heat setting for 7½ to 8 hours or on the high heat setting for about 4 hours, until the beef and yams are tender. Add seasoned salt and black pepper to taste.

slow beef bourguignon

Makes 6 to 8 servings

Slow is a smart way to prepare this great classic stew. The green beans, or haricots verts if you can find them, are added near the end of the cooking to maintain their color. While bacon would normally cook with the meat, you end up with more flavor in a slow-cooked preparation when crisply cooked strips are crumbled onto the finished dish.

2 pounds boneless beef top round steak, cut about 1-inch thick

¼ cup all-purpose flour

½ teaspoon salt

½ teaspoon freshly ground black pepper

1½ pounds waxy potatoes, such as Red Bliss or Yukon gold, peeled
   and cut into 1-inch pieces

1 package (14 ounces) frozen petite whole onions, thawed

1 pound carrots, peeled and cut into ¾-inch pieces

1 cup sliced fresh cremini mushrooms

1 teaspoon dried thyme leaves

1 cup dry red wine

3 cups frozen haricots verts or green beans, thawed and
   halved crosswise

3 tablespoons chopped fresh flat-leaf parsley

5 to 6 slices of bacon, cooked until crisp and crumbled

1. Trim all excess fat from the beef. Cut the meat into 1-inch cubes.

2. In a 6-quart electric slow cooker, combine the beef cubes, flour, and salt and pepper. Toss to coat the pieces of meat evenly. Add the potatoes, onions, carrots, mushrooms, and thyme. Mix well. Pour in the wine.

3. Cover and cook on the low heat setting for 6 to 8 hours, stirring once halfway through the cooking time, if possible, until the beef and vegetables are tender.

4. Stir in the haricots verts, cover, and cook on low for 20 to 30 minutes longer. Serve hot, garnished with a sprinkling of parsley and crumbled bacon.

thai-style beef with peanut sauce

Makes 5 to 6 servings

Red bell pepper is a must for color in this tantalizing dish. I sometimes add a cup or so of trimmed fresh snow peas during the last 30 to 45 minutes of cooking time. Serve over steamed rice and top with chopped scallions and peanuts.

2 pounds lean boneless beef top round steak

1 medium onion, chopped

1 large red bell pepper, cut into strips

1 can (8 ounces) sliced water chestnuts, rinsed well and drained

1 jar (7 ounces) Thai peanut satay sauce or

¾ cup Asian peanut sauce

1½ tablespoons soy sauce

1 tablespoon balsamic vinegar

½ teaspoon ground ginger

3 tablespoons instant-blending flour, such as Wondra

2 tablespoons peanut butter, crunchy or smooth

1. Trim all excess fat from the beef. Cut the meat into thin strips.

2. In a 4-quart electric slow cooker, combine the beef, onion, bell pepper, and water chestnuts. In a bowl, blend together the peanut sauce, soy sauce, vinegar, ginger, and flour. Pour over the beef and vegetables in the slow cooker and mix well.

3. Cover and cook on the low heat setting for about 7 hours, until the beef is tender. Stir in the peanut butter.

tuscan beef stew

Makes 6 servings

Rich and hearty, this is great for warming the soul. Because canned cannellini beans are delicate, they are added near the end of the long, slow cooking, so that they don't break up. Serve the stew with pasta or polenta and sautéed broccoli rabe.

2 pounds beef top round steak

1 large onion, chopped

2½ cups coarsely chopped carrots

3 celery ribs, sliced

1 can (14.5 ounces) diced tomatoes

1 can (6 ounces) tomato paste

¾ cup dry red wine

1 tablespoon dried basil

2 garlic cloves, crushed through a press

Pinch of sugar (optional)

1 can (16 ounces) cannellini beans, rinsed and drained

3 to 4 tablespoons chopped fresh basil

Freshly grated Parmesan cheese

1. Trim as much fat as possible from the round steak. Cut the beef into 1- to 1½-inch cubes. Put in a 5-quart electric slow cooker.

2. Add the onion, carrots, celery, tomatoes with their juices, tomato paste, wine, dried basil, and garlic. Mix well. Cover and cook on the low heat setting for 7½ to 8 hours, until the meat is very tender.

3. Stir in the sugar, beans, and fresh basil. Cover and cook for 10 minutes longer. Pass the grated Parmesan on the side to sprinkle on top of the stew.

quick-fix pepper steak with green beans

Makes 6 to 8 servings

This is like a pepper steak stew. Serve over hot noodles, steamed rice, or mashed potatoes to soak up all the savory sauce. Accompany simply with a tossed green salad for an easy meal.

2 pounds boneless beef top round steak

1 red bell pepper, cut into strips

1 green bell pepper, cut into strips

1 yellow bell pepper, cut into strips

1 can (10 ounces) diced tomatoes and green chiles

¼ cup instant-blending flour, such as Wondra

⅓ cup dry red wine

3 cups frozen haricots verts or green beans, thawed and cut into 1-inch pieces

1½ teaspoons ground cumin

½ teaspoon smoked paprika

½ teaspoon salt

¼ teaspoon freshly ground black pepper

1. Trim as much fat as possible from the round steak. Cut the beef against the grain into thin strips. Put in a 4-quart electric slow cooker and add the bell pepper strips.

2. In a bowl, combine the tomatoes with green chiles and their juices and the flour. Stir in the wine until blended. Pour over the beef mixture and toss to mix well.

3. Cover and cook on the low heat setting for 7½ to 8 hours, until the beef is tender.

4. Stir in the haricots verts, cumin, smoked paprika, salt, and pepper. Cover and continue cooking for 30 to 60 minutes, until the beans are tender.

barbecued brisket of beef

Makes 10 to 12 servings

Here's a delicious, easy way to cook brisket. It's even better reheated the next day. Serve with mashed potatoes and buttered green beans.

1 center-cut beef brisket (4 to 5 pounds)

1 tablespoon steak seasoning, such as McCormick Montreal steak seasoning

1 tablespoon ground cumin

1 very large sweet onion, such as Vidalia, Maui, or Walla Walla, sliced

2 cups hickory barbecue sauce, or your favorite flavor

2 tablespoons yellow mustard

Cook's Note

➤ To remove even more fat, make this dish in advance. Let the whole brisket cool, then wrap and refrigerate. Transfer the sauce in the pot to a bowl, cover, and refrigerate separately. The fat will congeal in a solid layer and will be easy to skim from the top of the sauce. Slice the brisket. Before serving, reheat the meat in the sauce.

1. Trim all excess fat from the brisket. Season the meat on both sides with the steak seasoning and cumin.

2. Place half of the onion slices in a 5-quart electric slow cooker. In a bowl, whisk together the barbecue sauce and mustard. Spoon a few tablespoons over the onions in the slow cooker. Add the brisket, fat-trimmed side down. Top with the remaining onion slices and half of the remaining barbecue sauce mixture.

3. Cover and cook on the high heat setting for 2 hours. Reduce the heat setting to low and cook for 4 hours longer, or until the brisket is tender. If you prefer to just set up the brisket and walk away, you can cook the meat on the low heat setting for about 8 hours.

4. Remove the brisket to a cutting board and carve against the grain into slices. Skim as much fat as possible off the juices in the pot. Stir in the remaining barbecue sauce mixture. Serve over the sliced brisket.

If feasible, use the high heat setting for the first hour of cooking, then turn to low. However, it is safe to use the low heat setting for the entire cooking time for most dishes.

pot roast with onions, carrots, and potatoes

Makes 8 to 10 servings

Sometimes it's hard to improve on a classic. Well, the slow cooker does just that by making it easier and more convenient to make a perfect pot roast without having to pay it any attention. This recipe yields a lot of tasty sauce and contains plenty of vegetables. For extra color, you could stir in a cup of thawed frozen peas or cut-up cooked green beans shortly before serving.

4 pounds boneless beef chuck roast

2 bags (14 ounces each) small pearl onions, thawed

5 carrots, peeled and cut into 1-inch lengths

1½ pounds small white or red potatoes, scrubbed and quartered

½ cup dry red wine

⅓ cup instant-blending flour, such as Wondra

¾ teaspoon salt

½ teaspoon freshly ground black pepper

Chopped fresh parsley, for garnish

1. Trim as much excess fat from the beef as possible. Cut the meat into 3 or 4 large pieces. This allows for more even cooking.

2. In a 6-quart electric slow cooker, combine the onions, carrots, and potatoes. Toss to mix. In a small bowl, mix the wine with ½ cup of water. Whisk in the flour, salt, and pepper until smooth. Pour ¾ cup of this mixture over the vegetables in the pot. Place the cut-up roast on top of the vegetables and pour the remaining wine mixture evenly over the top of the meat.

3. Cover and cook on the high heat setting for 1 hour. Reduce the heat to low and cook for 6 to 8 hours longer, or until the meat and vegetables are very tender.

4. Remove the meat and vegetables to a platter. Garnish with chopped fresh parsley. Skim the fat off the surface of the pan juices. Season with additional salt and pepper to taste and pass this sauce on the side.

beef fajitas slow cooker style

Makes 8 to 10 servings

While the flavor of this zesty dish will remind you of beef fajitas, the texture and consistency of the meat is completely different from the grilled steak normally used in the dish. The trade-off is in the convenience of slow, hands-off cooking. Serve the meat shredded or cut in larger pieces along with the vegetables from the pot, warm flour tortillas, guacamole, sour cream, and chopped tomatoes to roll up and eat like a fajita. Alternatively, you can plate the meat and vegetables over hot cooked rice to sop up all the juices and garnish with a dollop each of sour cream, guacamole, and fresh salsa.

3½ to 4 pounds beef top round or bottom round steak
4 teaspoons fajita seasoning
2 large red bell peppers, cut into strips
2 large green bell peppers, cut into strips
2 large onions, halved and sliced
¼ cup fresh lime juice
1 teaspoon ground cumin
Salt

1. Trim all the fat from the meat. Cut the beef into 2 or 3 pieces. Pat dry with paper towels. Season with 3 teaspoons of the fajita seasoning, rubbing it into the meat.

2. In a 5- or 6-quart oval electric slow cooker, toss together the red and green bell pepper strips, onions, 1 tablespoon of the lime juice, and the remaining 1 teaspoon fajita seasoning.

3. Place the beef on top of the vegetable mixture. Sprinkle with the cumin. Drizzle the remaining 3 tablespoons lime juice into the pot.

4. Cover and cook on the low heat setting for 6 to 8 hours, until the beef is fork-tender. Season with salt to taste.

Cook's Notes

➤ Don't worry about the small amount of liquid added to the pot at the outset of cooking—you'll end up with plenty!

➤ You may wish to brighten up the dish just before serving with another 2 tablespoons lime juice and ½ teaspoon ground cumin.

ropa vieja

Makes 10 to 12 servings

This shredded meat stew is a variation on the traditional Cuban dish. Serve with rice, black beans, and fried plantains.

4 pounds beef top round roast

½ teaspoon ground ancho chile

½ teaspoon ground chipotle chile

½ teaspoon smoked paprika

2 medium onions, thinly sliced

2 medium bell peppers, preferably 1 red and 1 green, cut into thin julienne strips

1 pound russet baking potatoes, peeled and diced into small cubes

1 bottle (12 ounces) beer

3 tablespoons Dijon mustard

3 tablespoons instant tapioca

2 tablespoons sugar

½ teaspoon salt

½ teaspoon freshly ground black pepper

⅓ cup chopped fresh cilantro

1. Trim as much fat as possible from the meat. Season the roast all over with the ancho chile, chipotle chile, and smoked paprika. Cut the meat into two pieces.

2. In a 6-quart slow cooker, combine the onions, bell peppers, and potatoes. Place the seasoned meat on top. In a medium bowl, blend the beer, mustard, tapioca, sugar, salt, and black pepper. Pour a little of this mixture over the top of the roast and the rest all around the sides.

3. Cover the pot and cook on the low heat setting for 9 to 10 hours, stirring once or twice during the cooking time, if possible, until the beef is falling-apart tender. Transfer the meat to a cutting board.

4. Skim the fat off the surface of the sauce and season with additional salt and pepper to taste. Shred the beef with your fingers or two forks. Return to the sauce in the pot. Stir in the chopped cilantro just before serving.

Variation

Barbecued Beef on a Bun: After removing the meat, use a slotted spoon to lift out the vegetables. Mix ½ to ¾ of the liquid in the pot with about ¾ cup hickory-flavored barbecue sauce and toss this with the shredded beef. Spoon over split toasted hamburger buns or sourdough or French rolls. Serve the vegetables on the side.

smoky beef short ribs

Makes 8 to 10 servings

Short ribs, which require long simmering, do very well in the slow cooker. Liquid smoke provides the magic touch here. You'll find it in the spice section of your supermarket. Serve with baked or mashed potatoes and peas.

5 pounds boneless beef chuck short ribs (as lean as possible)
1 cup ketchup
¼ cup yellow mustard
2 tablespoons red wine vinegar
½ teaspoon garlic powder, or 2 garlic cloves, minced
½ teaspoon liquid smoke
1 cup warmed barbecue sauce

1. Trim off a much fat as possible from the beef ribs and put them into a 6-quart electric slow cooker. In a small bowl, mix together the ketchup, mustard, vinegar, garlic powder, and liquid smoke. Spoon this sauce over and around the ribs.

2. Cover and cook on the low heat setting for 8 to 9 hours, or until the ribs are extremely tender.

3. Transfer the ribs to a platter. Discard the sauce in the pot; it will be too fatty. Cut the meat into serving pieces and serve hot with the warmed barbecue sauce on the side.

barbecued pulled beef sandwiches

Makes 6 to 8 servings

With its slightly sweet and tangy sauce, this easy recipe is similar to a sloppy Joe. Because it employs thinly sliced rather than ground beef, it requires no browning of the meat. Everyone in the family will love it. I like to serve the sandwiches with potato salad, coleslaw, and plenty of paper napkins.

2½ to 3 pounds boneless beef top round or other lean beef,
    trimmed of all fat and cut into thin slices

1 medium onion, thinly sliced

1 cup ketchup

3 tablespoons red wine vinegar

2 tablespoons honey

1 tablespoon Worcestershire sauce

½ teaspoon smoked paprika

¼ teaspoon ground chipotle chile

6 to 8 toasted hamburger buns or kaiser rolls

1. In a 4- or 5-quart electric slow cooker, combine the beef and onion. Mix together the ketchup, vinegar, honey, Worcestershire sauce, smoked paprika, and chipotle chile until well blended. Pour over the beef and onion in the pot and stir to mix thoroughly.

2. Cover and cook on the low heat setting for 8 or 9 hours, or until the beef slices fall apart.

3. With two forks, pull the meat into shreds right in the sauce in the pot. Serve the beef with its sauce on toasted buns to make sandwiches.

easy black bean chili with beer

Makes 6 to 8 servings

There's no browning at all in this easy recipe. Instead, the meat cubes are tossed in seasoned flour and put right into the pot. A crisp, fruity wheat ale contributes deep, complex flavor. Serve with warm flour tortillas and any variety of go-withs: sour cream, picked jalapeños, shredded lettuce, chopped tomatoes, chopped scallions, sour cream, and/or shredded Cheddar cheese. And don't forget the hot sauce or spicy salsa.

2 cans (15 ounces each) black beans, rinsed and well drained

1 cup roasted red pepper strips

1 can (7 ounces) whole green chiles, rinsed, drained, and cut into ½-inch-wide strips

1 large onion, quartered and thinly sliced

1 garlic clove, crushed through a press

3 tablespoons all-purpose flour

1½ teaspoons chili powder

1½ teaspoons ground cumin

¼ teaspoon salt

1½ pounds beef top round steak or boneless pork loin, trimmed of fat and cut into 1-inch cubes or thin strips

1 cup beer or crisp fruity wheat ale, such as Samuel Adams Hefeweizen

1. In a 4-quart electric slow cooker, combine the beans, roasted peppers, green chiles, onion, and garlic. Stir gently to mix.

2. Put the flour, chili powder, cumin, and salt in a large plastic bag and mix until well blended. Add the meat cubes, seal the bag, and toss until they are evenly coated with the seasoned flour. Add to the pot along with any flour left in the bag and mix well. Stir in the beer.

3. Cover and cook on the low heat setting for 7 to 7½ hours, or until the meat is tender but holds its shape.

Cook seasonally in the slow cooker when possible. Often you can substitute fresh vegetables and fruits in season for others in recipes, providing they are similar in density.

hot dog-pineapple bean bake

Makes 6 to 8 servings

This dish is kid-friendly and proud of it. If you like, you can substitute chunks of cooked baked ham or cooked chicken or turkey sausages for the hot dogs.

1 can (28 ounces) country-style baked beans
1 can (16 ounces) pork and beans in tomato sauce
1 can (20 ounces) unsweetened pineapple chunks in juice,
   well drained
1½ tablespoons yellow mustard
1 tablespoon chipotle barbecue sauce or your favorite flavor
8 beef hot dogs (1 pound)

1. Combine the baked beans and pork and beans in a 4-quart electric slow cooker. Add the pineapple chunks, mustard, and barbecue sauce. Mix well.

2. Cut the hot dogs into pieces or leave whole. Submerge in the pineapple-bean mixture.

3. Cover and cook on the high heat setting for 1 hour. Reduce the heat to low and cook for 3½ to 4 hours longer, until hot throughout. Or cook on the low heat setting for 5½ to 6 hours. To avoid mushy hot dogs, do not overcook.

chili dogs

This easy dish can be tossed together quickly in the slow cooker, with no watching required. Chili dogs are great for a kid's party or a poker party, whenever you're looking for simple, fun food. If you're expecting a crowd, make a double batch in a 6-quart pot. Serve the hot dogs in toasted buns and top with the sauce. You'll want forks and lots of napkins. And don't forget to pass potato chips, pickles, and coleslaw on the side.

2 cans (16 ounces each) pinto beans, rinsed and drained

1 can (14.5 ounces) petite-cut diced tomatoes

1 can (6 ounces) tomato paste

1½ tablespoons chili powder

1 tablespoon ground cumin

1 medium onion, chopped

8 beef hot dogs (1 pound)

8 hot dog buns, toasted

Cook's Note

➤ To toast a large number of buns at once, use your broiler or grill.

1. In a 4-quart electric slow cooker, combine the beans, tomatoes with their juices, tomato paste, chili powder, cumin, and onion. Mix well; the sauce will be thick, but don't thin it out. Place the hot dogs on top and spoon some of the chili mixture over them.

2. Cover and cook on the high heat setting for 1 hour. Reduce the heat to low and cook for 2½ to 3 hours longer. Or cook on the low heat setting for 4½ to 5 hours.

3. Serve the hot dogs in toasted buns with a generous spoonful of chili with sauce and beans spooned on top.

apricot-mustard glazed ham

Makes 12 to 14 servings

Here's an easy way to heat up a cooked ham and free up your oven for other dishes, especially during busy holiday times. Serve with a simple sour cream and horseradish sauce.

3- to 4-pound boneless fully cooked ham
¾ cup apricot preserves
3 tablespoons Dijon mustard
Sour Cream–Horseradish Sauce (recipe follows)

1. Score the top of the ham in a diagonal crisscross pattern and place it in a 4-quart electric slow cooker.

2. In a small bowl, blend the apricot preserves with the mustard. Spoon about ⅓ cup of the mixture over the top of the ham. Spoon another ¼ cup into the bottom of slow cooker around the sides of the ham.

3. Cover and cook on the low heat setting for 5 to 6 hours, until the ham is heated through. Transfer the ham to a cutting board, spread the remaining apricot preserves and mustard over the meat and let stand for about 10 minutes. Discard any liquid in the bottom of pot; it will be too salty to eat.

4. After the ham has rested, carve into slices. Pass the Sour Cream–Horseradish Sauce on the side.

sour cream–horseradish sauce

Makes about 1 cup

1 cup sour cream

2 tablespoons Dijon mustard

1 tablespoon cream-style horseradish

In a small bowl, stir together all the ingredients. Cover and refrigerate until serving time.

alsatian pork roast with sauerkraut

Makes about 6 servings

Pork and sauerkraut team well, and both ingredients benefit from long, slow simmering. While sauerkraut is available canned, the fresher refrigerated kind is preferable, whether you buy it in bags or in a jar. Buttered rye bread makes a satisfying accompaniment to this dish.

1½ pounds golden potatoes (about 4 medium), peeled and thinly sliced into rounds

2 pounds refrigerated sauerkraut, rinsed and very well drained

1 large onion, thinly sliced

1½ tablespoons caraway seeds

1 can (14.5 ounces) diced tomatoes

1 can (6 ounces) tomato paste

¼ teaspoon freshly ground black pepper

2 pounds boneless pork sirloin tip roast or pork loin

2 tablespoons chopped fresh flat-leaf parsley

1. Arrange the potato slices on the bottom of a 5-quart electric slow cooker. Spread the sauerkraut evenly over the potatoes. Top with the onion slices. Sprinkle 1½ teaspoons of the caraway seeds evenly over the onions.

2. In a small bowl, mix together the tomatoes with their juices, tomato paste, remaining 1 tablespoon caraway seeds, and the pepper. Pour half of this mixture over the onions and place the roast in the center of the pot. Pour the remaining tomato mixture over all.

3. Cover and cook on the high heat setting for 2 hours. Reduce the heat to low and cook for 4 hours. If you'd rather the roast cook completely unattended, cook entirely on the low heat setting for 8 hours.

4. Turn off the pot and let the meat cool in the pot for 10 to 15 minutes. Transfer the roast to a cutting board and carve it into slices. Spoon the sauerkraut and potatoes onto a deep platter and arrange the pork slices on top. Garnish with the chopped parsley.

tex-mex pork and beans

Makes 5 to 6 servings

This cowboy stew is hearty and versatile. Serve topped with a little sour cream and guacamole, if you like. It also makes a good base for tostadas. Or just roll it in a large warm flour tortilla with a little shredded cheese and lettuce.

2 pounds boneless pork sirloin tip roast or boneless pork loin
1 can (28 ounces) diced tomatoes
1 can (6 ounces) tomato paste
1 large onion, chopped
1 can (4 ounces) diced green chiles
2 tablespoons ground cumin
2 tablespoons chili powder
2 garlic cloves, crushed through a press
½ teaspoon salt
½ teaspoon freshly ground black pepper
1 large can (29 ounces) pinto beans, rinsed and well drained
Sour cream, shredded Cheddar or Jack cheese, and
    avocado slices, for garnish

1. Trim any excess fat from the roast. Cut the meat into 1-inch cubes and place in a 5-quart electric slow cooker.

2. Add the tomatoes with their juices, tomato paste, onion, green chiles, cumin, chili powder, garlic, salt, and pepper. Mix well. Add the beans and stir gently to mix them in without mashing them.

3. Cover and cook on the low heat setting for 7 to 8 hours, or until the pork is tender but not falling apart. Serve garnished with sour cream, shredded cheese, and avocado slices.

instant party pork barbecue

W hether it's for a party, a family reunion, a potluck, or a post-football supper for the team, this super-easy recipe can help you out. It goes into the pot in an instant. At the end of the day, you'll have enough pork barbecue to feed a gang. Serve on rolls with baked beans and coleslaw on the side.

Makes 12 to 14 servings

2 large onions, sliced
4 pounds boneless pork sirloin tip roast (use two 2-pound roasts) or boneless pork loin, trimmed of all excess fat
2 cups hickory barbecue sauce or your favorite flavor
12 to 14 toasted hamburger buns

1. Make a bed of half the onions in a 4- or 5-quart electric slow cooker. Add the pork roast(s) and top with the remaining onions. Pour 1 cup of the barbecue sauce over the meat.

2. Cover and cook on the low heat setting for 8 hours, or until the pork is tender but not falling apart.

3. Remove the pork and onions to a serving platter. Measure out ½ cup of the cooking juices from the pot and stir into the remaining 1 cup barbecue sauce. Add more of the juices if needed. Thinly slice the pork and serve on buns, topped with the onions and sauce.

Cook's Note

➤ To toast a large number of buns at once, use your broiler or grill.

pork and hominy stew

Makes 5 to 6 servings

This recipe was given to me by a friend I met on my travels on the West Coast. Hominy is simply plumped-up corn kernels that have been specially treated to remove the outer hulls. You'll find it in supermarkets in cans, either in the bean section or with the Mexican ingredients.

1½ pounds lean boneless pork loin

1 large can (29 ounces) plus 1 smaller can (15 ounces) hominy, drained, rinsed well, and drained again

1 can (4 ounces) diced green chiles

1 can (14.5 ounces) diced tomatoes

1 cup chicken broth

1 medium onion, chopped

2 garlic cloves, crushed through a press

1 tablespoon dried oregano

½ teaspoon freshly ground black pepper

3 tablespoons yellow cornmeal

3 tablespoons chopped fresh cilantro, for garnish

Cook's Note

➤ If a thinner stew is preferred, omit the cornmeal and cook on the low heat setting for a total of 8 hours, or until the pork is very tender.

1. Trim as much fat as possible from the pork. Cut the meat into 1-inch cubes and place in a 5-quart electric slower cooker.

2. Add the hominy, green chiles, tomatoes with their juices, broth, onion, garlic, oregano, and pepper. Cover and cook on the low heat setting for about 7 hours; stir after 2 or 3 hours, if possible.

3. Stir in the cornmeal, cover, and continue cooking on low for 1 hour longer, or until the pork is very tender. Serve in bowls, topped with the chopped cilantro.

Never reheat food in the slow cooker on any setting. Refrigerated leftovers should be reheated on top of the stove, in a microwave oven, or in a conventional oven until they reach 165°F. They then can be placed in a preheated slow cooker and kept hot—at least 140°F as measured with a food thermometer—until serving.

sweet-and-sour pork with pineapple

Makes 5 to 6 servings

The majority of my recipes call for just tossing all the ingredients into the pot, but here, for best color and flavor—and to remove as much fat as possible—the onion and pork strips are browned first. Serve over hot cooked rice.

1½ to 2 pounds lean boneless pork loin

1 tablespoon vegetable oil

1 medium onion, thinly sliced

1 can (20 ounces) unsweetened pineapple chunks in juice, drained with juice reserved

¼ cup ketchup

3 tablespoons red wine vinegar

2 tablespoons brown sugar

¼ teaspoon salt

3 tablespoons cornstarch

5 medium carrots, peeled and sliced

1 large green bell pepper, cut into ¾-inch chunks or thin strips

Freshly ground black pepper

1. Trim as much fat as possible from the pork. Cut the meat into thin strips or slices. Heat the oil in a large skillet over high heat. Add the pork to the skillet, in two batches if necessary, and sauté, stirring often, until browned, 5 to 6 minutes. Transfer to a 5-quart electric slow cooker.

2. Add the onion to the same skillet and cook over medium-high heat, stirring occasionally, until browned, about 5 minutes. Add to the slow cooker.

3. In a bowl, stir together the reserved pineapple juice with 2 tablespoons of the ketchup, the vinegar, brown sugar, and salt. Stir in the cornstarch until thoroughly blended. Pour over the meat, add the carrots to the pot, and mix well.

4. Cover and cook on the low heat setting for 5 to 6 hours or on the high heat setting for 2½ to 3 hours, until the meat is cooked through and tender.

5. Stir in the remaining 2 tablespoons ketchup, the pineapple chunks, and bell pepper pieces and cook for 20 to 30 minutes longer, until hot. Season with pepper to taste.

pork carnitas style

Makes 6 servings

Traditionally, carnitas are small cubes of pork, seasoned and baked until they are both succulent and crisp, usually served with a salsa dipping sauce. Here the pork is cut into strips and stewed in salsa verde, or green chile salsa. Serve with warm tortillas and a squeeze of lime and pass bowls of chopped scallions and tomatoes and sour cream to pile on top. Paired with beans or rice, these tasty morsels also make a great filling for burritos.

2 pounds boneless pork loin chops

2 tablespoons instant-blending flour, such as Wondra

1 medium onion, thinly sliced

1 jar (12 ounces) salsa verde

¼ cup canned diced green chiles

½ teaspoon garlic powder

¼ teaspoon ground chipotle chile

1 large tomato, chopped

Kosher salt

1. Trim any fat from the chops. Cut the pork into thin strips and place in a 4-quart electric slow cooker.

2. Dust with the flour and toss until completely coated. Add the onion, salsa, green chiles, garlic powder, and chipotle chile. Stir to mix well.

3. Cover and cook on the low heat setting for 7½ to 8 hours, until the pork is very tender. Using two forks, shred the meat right in the pot. Stir in the tomato and season with salt to taste.

Variation

Beef Carnitas: Follow the recipe above, but in place of the pork, substitute 2 pounds beef top round steak, trimmed of all fat and cut into thin strips.

asian-style country ribs

Makes 6 servings

Give country ribs an Asian twist with hoisin sauce and rice wine vinegar. Add snow peas to the pot at the end of the cooking time for color. Because there's a lot of sauce, hot cooked rice sprinkled with chopped scallions is a nice accompaniment.

1 red onion, sliced

3 pounds boneless pork loin country-style ribs

$\frac{1}{3}$ cup hoisin sauce

3 tablespoons rice wine vinegar

1 tablespoon sugar

$\frac{1}{4}$ teaspoon ground ginger

2 garlic cloves, crushed through a press

$\frac{1}{2}$ pound fresh snow peas, trimmed

1. Place the red onion slices in the bottom of a 4-quart electric slow cooker. Trim as much fat from the pork as possible and arrange the ribs on top of the onions slices.

2. In a small bowl, combine the hoisin sauce, vinegar, sugar, ginger, and garlic. Mix well. Pour about ⅓ cup of this sauce over the ribs, making sure to coat them all. Refrigerate the remaining sauce.

3. Cover and cook the ribs on the low heat setting for 6½ to 7 hours, until the meat is very tender. Transfer the meat to a platter and cover with aluminum foil to keep warm.

4. Add the snow peas to the sauce remaining in the pot. Raise the heat to high, cover, and cook for 10 to 15 minutes, or until the snow peas are crisp-tender and still bright green.

5. Spoon the snow peas over and around the ribs on the platter. Moisten with some of the juices from the pot. Drizzle the remaining reserved hoisin sauce mixture over all.

Cook's Note

➤ If the reserved sauce has thickened too much in the refrigerator, heat it in a microwave oven for 20 to 30 seconds.

thai-style ribs with peanut sauce

Makes 5 to 6 servings

Peanut butter and coconut milk give these ribs their intriguing, irresistible flavor. Make this as fiery hot as you like with the crushed red pepper. Serve with steamed rice and stir-fried bok choy or steamed broccoli.

3½ pounds boneless pork loin country-style ribs

½ cup Thai peanut sauce

¼ cup crunchy peanut butter

¾ cup unsweetened canned coconut milk

¼ to ½ teaspoon crushed hot red pepper, or more to taste

Chopped scallions, for garnish

Cook's Note

➤ Thai-style peanut sauce is available in the Asian foods aisle of many supermarkets.

1. Trim as much fat as possible from the ribs. Place them in a 4-quart electric slow cooker.

2. In a bowl, combine the peanut sauce, peanut butter, and ½ cup of the coconut milk. Whisk to blend well. Add to the slow cooker and toss with the meat.

3. Cover and cook on the low heat setting for 8 to 9 hours, until the meat is very tender. Stir in the remaining ¼ cup coconut milk and the hot pepper. Serve garnished with chopped scallions.

Adapting a favorite recipe to a slow cooker can be a challenge and may take a little trial and error. Use a similar slow cooker recipe as a guide. Generally figure that you'll have to reduce the liquid by at least half or more, except in the case of soups, to compensate for the extra liquid generated by slow cooking.

sticky barbecued back ribs

This is a fabulous way to cook back ribs. First they are quickly broiled to brown them and remove excess fat; then the pot does the rest. These are literally finger-licking good. Be sure to put out plenty of napkins.

2 racks of pork loin back ribs (4 to 4½ pounds total)

1 teaspoon seasoned salt

½ teaspoon freshly ground black pepper

1¼ teaspoons smoked paprika

1 cup ketchup

3 tablespoons cider vinegar

1 tablespoon Worcestershire sauce

¼ cup packed brown sugar

⅛ teaspoon ground chipotle chile

⅛ to ¼ teaspoon crushed hot red pepper, to taste

1. Preheat the broiler. Cut the racks in half so there are 4 pieces. Place the ribs on a broiler pan, meaty side up. Dust with the seasoned salt and black pepper. Broil about 6 inches from the heat until well browned, 4 to 6 minutes. Season with 1 teaspoon of the smoked paprika, then turn over and brown the other side, 4 to 6 minutes.

2. In a bowl, combine the ketchup, vinegar, Worcestershire sauce, brown sugar, chipotle chile, crushed hot pepper, and remaining ¼ teaspoon smoked paprika. Stir to mix the sauce well.

3. Pour ¼ cup of water into the bottom of a 5- or 6- quart electric slow cooker. Add the ribs, meaty side up, smearing them with half the sauce and stacking them as necessary. Refrigerate the remaining sauce.

4. Cover and cook on the high heat setting for 1 hour. Reduce the heat to low and cook for 4 to 4½ hours longer. Or cook entirely on the low heat setting for a 6½ to 7½ hours, until the meat is very tender and almost falling off the bones. Check the ribs during cooking, especially during the last 2 hours. If there is too little liquid in the pot, pour another ¼ cup water around—not over—the ribs.

5. Transfer the ribs to a serving platter. Warm the reserved sauce and spread it over the ribs. Serve hot.

leg of lamb
braised in red wine

Makes 7 to 10 servings

Amazingly succulent and so tender you could eat it with a spoon, this savory boneless leg of lamb is braised with aromatic vegetables, fresh herbs, and an assertive red wine. A touch of honey, stirred in at the end, balances the flavors perfectly. This recipe leaves you lots of gravy, and leftovers make an incredible shepherd's pie. Serve with a roast vegetable medley or with buttered green beans and a potato gratin.

1 boned leg of lamb (4½ to 5 pounds)

1 cup finely chopped carrots

1 cup finely chopped celery

1 cup finely chopped onion

½ cup whole garlic cloves, peeled (about 2 heads)

1½ tablespoons extra virgin olive oil

2 teaspoons salt

½ teaspoon coarsely ground black pepper

¼ cup all-purpose flour

¼ cup tomato paste

3 cups full-flavored red wine, such as syrah or zinfandel

2 sprigs of fresh thyme

1 sprig of fresh rosemary

1 bay leaf

1 tablespoon honey, preferably wildflower or buckwheat

1. Trim all visible fat from the leg of lamb, removing the membrane that covers the meat where necessary. Tie the roast together with kitchen string or secure in a net bag.

2. In a 4- or 5-quart electric slow cooker, combine the carrots, celery, onion, and garlic. Toss with the olive oil, salt, and pepper. In a small bowl, make a smooth paste of the flour, tomato paste, and 1/3 cup of the wine. Mix into the vegetables. Stir in about half the remaining wine.

3. Nestle the lamb into the vegetables and pour in the rest of the wine. Add the thyme, rosemary, and bay leaf.

4. Cover and cook on the low heat setting for 7 to 8 hours; if you're around, turn the roast over after 4 or 5 hours. The dish is done when the meat is tender enough to carve with a spoon and the vegetables are soft. Remove the lamb to a carving board and cut off the strings. Carve the roast into thick slices.

5. Skim as much fat as possible off the juices in the cooker. Remove and discard the bay leaf and herbs. Stir in the honey. With a hand-held immersion blender, puree the vegetables and cooking juices to make a smooth, thick gravy. Or puree the sauce in a blender or food processor. If not serving immediately, return the meat to the sauce in the pot and leave on the warm setting for up to 2 hours.

braised lamb with moroccan flavors

Makes 6 servings

Lamb takes beautifully to braising with spices and vegetables. Serve with hot couscous and preserved lemons or lemon wedges. A carrot and radish salad would make a nice starter.

1 medium onion, chopped

2 or 3 medium zucchini, chopped

3 Roma or other large plum tomatoes, seeded and chopped

2 cans (15 ounces each) chickpeas (garbanzo beans), drained, rinsed well, and drained again

2/3 cup chicken or vegetable broth

3 tablespoons instant-blending flour, such as Wondra

2 tablespoons ground cumin

1/2 teaspoon salt

1/4 teaspoon freshly ground black pepper

Grated zest of 1 lemon

1 1/2 teaspoons ground turmeric

1 teaspoon smoked paprika

1/4 teaspoon garlic powder

1/8 teaspoon crushed hot red pepper

1/2 boneless leg of lamb (2 3/4 pounds), preferably the sirloin half, trimmed of all fat

1. In a 5-quart electric slow cooker, combine the onion, zucchini, tomatoes, and chickpeas. Whisk together the broth, flour, 1 tablespoon of the cumin, the salt, and pepper, blending until smooth. Pour over the vegetables in the slow cooker and mix well. Stir in the lemon zest.

2. In a small bowl, combine the remaining 1 tablespoon cumin, the turmeric, smoked paprika, garlic powder, and crushed hot pepper. Rub this spice mixture all over the lamb. Place the lamb on top of the vegetables in the pot.

3. Cover and cook on the low heat setting for 6 to 7 hours, until the lamb is tender. Carve the lamb into pieces and serve on top of the vegetables.

tagine of lamb with apricots and prunes

Makes 6 servings

Like *casserole*, *tagine* refers to both a cooked dish and the pot it is cooked in. A tagine is a shallow casserole with a tall conical lid. Moisture rises up from the ingredients cooking below, condenses in the lid, and falls back onto the food, ensuring delectable results. Since you get the same effect in the slow cooker, where there is no evaporation, it is ideal for preparing any meat or chicken tagine. Serve this sumptuous dish with couscous and cooked carrots.

2½ to 3 pounds boneless leg of lamb

2 tablespoons unsalted butter, melted

1 tablespoon extra virgin olive oil

2 teaspoons ground cinnamon

½ teaspoon ground ginger

½ teaspoon loosely packed saffron threads

⅛ teaspoon cayenne pepper

1 teaspoon salt

¼ teaspoon freshly ground black pepper

1 medium-large onion, thinly sliced

3 garlic cloves, finely chopped

½ pound dried apricots

½ pound prunes

1. Trim as much fat from the lamb as possible. Cut the meat into ¾- to 1-inch pieces.

2. Put the butter and oil in a 4-quart slow cooker set on the low heat setting. Add the pieces of lamb. Add the cinnamon, powdered ginger, saffron, cayenne, salt, and pepper. Toss to coat the meat with the oil and spices. Add the onion, garlic, apricots, and prunes. Pour in 1 cup of water and mix well.

3. Cover and cook on the low heat setting for 3½ to 4 hours, until the lamb is tender. If the sauce is too thick, add a little more water and adjust the seasonings.

If any finished dish turns out to have more grease on top than you might like, let it cool, then cover and refrigerate until chilled, at least 4 hours or preferably overnight. As soon as the fat solidifies, you can lift or scrape it off easily.

braised lamb with garlic and wild mushrooms

Makes 4 to 6 servings

Spoon all the aromatic pan juices from this rustic dish over hot mashed potatoes flavored with garlic or basil, over polenta, or alongside roasted potatoes. A green vegetable on the side would also be nice.

1 ounce dried mixed wild mushrooms or dried porcini or
    shiitake mushrooms
2 large onions, sliced
2½ pounds lamb sirloin steaks, cut ¾ inch thick, or
    lamb shoulder chops, trimmed of all fat
6 garlic cloves, halved
½ pound fresh cremini mushrooms, halved
¾ cup dry white wine
1 teaspoon salt
¾ teaspoon freshly ground black pepper
1 lemon
Chopped fresh flat-leaf parsley, chopped tomatoes, and
    lemon wedges, for garnish

1. Rinse the dried mushrooms briefly. Put them in a heatproof bowl, cover with hot water, and soak until softened, about 10 minutes. Drain and squeeze dry; then chop the mushrooms.

2. Cover the bottom of a 5-quart electric slow cooker with one-third of the onion slices. Add one-third of the lamb. Scatter half of the garlic cloves and another one-third of the onions over the

lamb. Add another layer of meat, using half the remaining lamb, and then add the remaining onions and garlic. Top with the rest of the lamb. Add the chopped wild mushrooms and the fresh cremini mushrooms. Season the wine with the salt and pepper and pour into the pot.

3. Cover and cook on the low heat setting for 6½ to 7 hours, until the lamb is tender. Squeeze the juice from the lemon over the lamb and season with additional salt and pepper to taste. Serve garnished with chopped parsley, tomatoes, and lemon wedges.

Variation

Braised Lamb Shanks with Garlic and Wild Mushrooms: In place of lamb steaks or chops, use 3 or 4 lamb shanks, about 3½ pounds total, trimmed of as much fat as possible. Layer half of the onions in a 5-quart electric slow cooker. Top with the garlic. Add the lamb shanks. Top with the remaining onions, the wild mushrooms, and the cremini mushrooms. As above, season the wine with the salt and pepper and pour into the pot. Cover and cook on the low heat setting for 8 to 9 hours, until the lamb shanks are very tender and the meat comes away easily from the bone. Add the lemon juice and garnish as described above.

one-pot meals

f the slow cooker is famous for anything, it's for the one-pot dish that you simply drop into the pot in the morning and return home to in the evening. Most of these recipes require anywhere from three to seven hours of cooking. Perhaps that's because some modern machines seem to cook at a higher temperature than the older ones.

If your lifestyle necessitates a morning-to-evening schedule, a few extra hours of cooking will not ruin most foods, but it won't result in maximum flavor and texture, either. So choose your priorities. Sometimes dinner right after work will trump the best taste. But here's a better solution. Try some of the recipes on weekends, or throw everything into the pot when you return home. Almost all these recipes reheat beautifully; some even improve upon standing. Reheat neatly in your microwave, in a low oven, or on a low burner, depending upon the dish.

one-pot meals

spanish rice with ground beef

A long-standing family favorite; serve with a tossed green salad and dinner is on. You can make this the night before, cool, refrigerate, and reheat just before serving, if that suits your schedule better.

Makes 6 servings

1 pound lean ground beef
1 medium onion, chopped
1½ cups converted long-grain white rice
1 green bell pepper, chopped
3 cans (14.5 ounces) diced tomatoes
1 tablespoon plus 1 teaspoon ground cumin
½ teaspoon salt
½ teaspoon freshly ground black pepper

1. In a large skillet, cook the ground beef and onion over medium-high heat, stirring occasionally to break up any large lumps of meat, until the beef is browned and crumbly, 5 to 7 minutes. Drain off any excess fat.

2. Transfer the beef and onion to a 4-quart slow cooker. Stir in the rice, bell pepper, tomatoes with their juices, cumin, salt, and pepper.

3. Cover and cook on the low heat setting for 3 to 3½ hours, or until the rice is tender. Serve hot.

stuffed bell peppers

This is an adaptation of a recipe I've been making for years. I think it tastes even better from the slow cooker than from the conventional oven. There's no need to cook the rice beforehand.

1 pound lean ground beef

½ teaspoon salt

¼ teaspoon freshly ground black pepper

⅓ cup chopped leek (white part only), rinsed well

½ cup shredded sharp Cheddar cheese

½ cup converted long-grain white rice

1 can (14.5 ounces) diced tomatoes

1 can (6 ounces) tomato paste

½ cup dry red wine

6 large green or red bell peppers

1. In a large skillet, sauté the ground beef over medium-high heat, crumbling with a fork, until well browned, 5 to 7 minutes. Drain off any excess fat. Stir in the salt, pepper, leek, cheese, and rice, mixing well.

2. In a medium bowl, combine the tomatoes with their juices, tomato paste, and wine. Stir 1 cup of the tomato mixture and 2 tablespoons of water into the beef mixture. Blend well.

3. Slice the tops off the bell peppers and carefully remove the seeds and inner ribs. Stand the peppers upright on a plate. Stuff with the beef mixture, dividing evenly and packing lightly.

4. Pour about three-quarters of the tomato-wine sauce into the bottom of a 5-quart slow cooker. Place the peppers in the slow cooker, stacking them carefully if necessary. Drizzle the remaining sauce over the tops of the peppers.

5. Cover and cook on the low heat setting for 6½ to 6¾ hours, until the rice is cooked and the peppers are tender but still hold their shape. Serve hot with the sauce from the bottom of the pot.

hamburger pie

Makes 5 to 6 servings

What could be a more comforting one-pot meal than hamburger (a.k.a. ground beef) mixed with corn, potatoes, and cheese? All you need is a green vegetable or a salad on the side.

1 pound lean ground beef

6 scallions, chopped

1 can (4 ounces) diced green chiles

Seasoned salt and freshly ground black pepper

1 large package (32 ounces) frozen hash brown shredded potatoes, thawed

1 package (16 ounces) frozen corn kernels, thawed

1 jar (16 ounces) chunky salsa

¾ cup shredded Cheddar cheese

1. In a large skillet, cook the ground beef with the scallions over medium-high heat until the meat is well browned, 5 to 7 minutes. Drain off any excess fat. Add the green chiles and season lightly with salt and pepper.

2. Place the potatoes in the bottom of a 4-quart electric slow cooker. Spread the corn evenly over the top. Thin the salsa with ½ cup of water and spoon half of it evenly over the corn. Do not stir. Cover with a layer of the ground beef mixture. Top with the remaining salsa.

3. Cover and cook on the low heat setting for 5 hours or on the high heat setting for 2½ hours, until heated through.

4. Sprinkle the cheese over the top, cover, and cook on the low heat setting for about 10 minutes, or until the cheese is melted.

beef and vegetable tamale casserole

Modern cooking makes a meal out of ingredients that have done some of the work for you. Here ready-made beef tamales are transformed into a substantial one-pot meal with some easy, savory additions. For "the works," serve topped with shredded lettuce, chopped tomatoes, sour cream, and a sprinkling of tortilla chips.

Makes 5 to 6 servings

1 large onion, chopped

2 cups chopped zucchini (about 2 medium)

1 can (15 ounces) pinto beans, rinsed and drained

1 can (6 ounces) pitted ripe olives, drained and coarsely chopped

1¼ cups red enchilada sauce

1 package (18 ounces) beef tamales

1 cup shredded Cheddar or mozzarella cheese

1. Place half of the onion in the bottom of a 4-quart electric slow cooker. Top with half of the zucchini, beans, and olives, sprinkling each on evenly. Drizzle with half the enchilada sauce.

2. Cut the tamales in half lengthwise and place them, filling side up, on top of the sauce. Add the remaining onions, zucchini, beans, and olives. Drizzle the remaining enchilada sauce over all.

3. Cover and cook on the low heat setting for 5 to 5½ hours. Sprinkle the cheese over the top, cover, and cook for 10 minutes longer, or until the cheese is melted.

beef taco salad

Makes 5 to 6 servings

Toss all of this in a pot, and the base for a salad will be ready when you are. Be sure to brown the ground beef before adding it to the pot. I always compose my taco salads with the beef on the bottom, to keep the lettuce crisp. The beef mixture reheats well in the microwave oven, so if you have any leftovers, warm them, wrap in a tortilla, and top with some lettuce, tomatoes, and cheese for another meal. Serve with tortilla chips, if you like.

1 pound lean ground beef

1 medium onion, chopped

1 can (15 ounces) red kidney beans, rinsed and drained

1 can (11 ounces) Mexicorn (corn with red and green bell peppers), drained

2 cups shredded zucchini (about 2 medium)

1 can (4 ounces) diced green chiles

1 jar (16 ounces) thick and chunky salsa, mild or hot to your taste

1 teaspoon ground cumin

3 tablespoons chopped fresh cilantro or parsley

Salt and freshly ground black pepper

Shredded Cheddar cheese, shredded iceberg lettuce, chopped tomatoes, sour cream, and corn tortilla chips

1. In a large skillet, sauté the ground beef and onion over medium-high heat, stirring often to break up any lumps of meat, until browned, 5 to 7 minutes. Drain off any excess fat.

2. Transfer to a 4-quart electric slow cooker. Mix in the beans, Mexicorn, zucchini, green chiles, salsa, and cumin. Cover and cook on the low heat setting for 4½ to 5 hours or the high heat setting for 2½ hours.

3. Stir in the cilantro and season with salt and pepper to taste. Spoon onto the center of large dinner plates and top with cheese, lettuce, tomatoes, and a dollop of sour cream. Surround the salad with tortilla chips.

tex-mex ground beef casserole

Makes 5 to 6 servings

This is a good casserole-style option when you're away for only a few hours, as it doesn't need all-day cooking.

1 pound lean ground beef

1 medium onion, chopped

1 medium zucchini, shredded (about 1½ cups)

1 can (15 ounces) black beans, rinsed and well drained

1 can (10.5 ounces) diced tomatoes with green chiles

1 can (8 ounces) tomato sauce

1 tablespoon ground cumin

6 corn tortillas (6 to 7 inches in diameter)

2 cups shredded Cheddar or Monterey Jack cheese

Chopped fresh tomatoes, avocado slices, and
    sour cream, for garnish

1. In a large skillet, cook the ground beef and onion over high heat, stirring to break up the meat into small pieces, until the beef is browned, 5 to 7 minutes. Add the zucchini, beans, tomatoes with green chiles and their juices, tomato sauce, and cumin. Mix well.

2. Cover the bottom of a 4-quart electric slow cooker with 2 tortillas, cut up as necessary to fit. Top with one-third of the beef and vegetable mixture, spreading it out evenly. Sprinkle on ¾ cup of the cheese. Add another 2 tortillas, half of the remaining beef and vegetable mixture, and another ¾ cup cheese. Top with the last 2 tortillas and the rest of the beef and vegetable mixture.

3. Cover and cook on the low heat setting for 4 to 4½ hours. Sprinkle the remaining ½ cup cheese evenly over the top; cover and cook for 10 minutes longer, until the cheese is melted. Serve hot, garnished with chopped tomatoes, avocado slices, and sour cream.

black bean and beef enchilada casserole

Makes 5 to 6 servings

Here corn tortillas are cooked right along with the beef and beans for an outstanding one-dish meal the whole family will love. Serve garnished with lots of guacamole or avocado slices, sour cream, and chopped tomatoes.

1½ pounds lean ground beef

1 large onion, chopped

1 can (15 ounces) black beans, rinsed and well drained

1 can (3.8 ounces) sliced ripe olives, well drained

½ teaspoon salt

¼ teaspoon freshly ground black pepper

1 can (14.5 ounces) diced tomatoes

1 can (10.5 ounces) diced tomatoes and green chiles

1 can (6 ounces) tomato paste

2 teaspoons ground cumin

6 corn tortillas (6 to 7 inches in diameter)

2¼ cups shredded Cheddar cheese

1. In a large skillet, sauté the beef and onion over medium-high heat, stirring often to break up the meat, until browned, 6 to 8 minutes. Drain off any excess fat. Stir in the beans, olives, salt, and pepper.

2. Meanwhile, in a medium bowl, combine the diced tomatoes with their juices, tomatoes and green chiles also with their juices, tomato paste, cumin, and ½ cup of water. Mix the tomato sauce well.

3. Oil the insert of a 4-quart oval electric slow cooker. Place 2 tortillas overlapping in the bottom. Cover evenly with one-third of the meat and bean mixture, one-third of the tomato sauce, and ¾ cup of the cheese. Layer on 2 more tortillas and half the remaining meat and bean mixture, sauce, and cheese. Top with the remaining 2 tortillas, meat, and sauce.

4. Cover and cook on the low heat setting for 6½ hours. Sprinkle the remaining ¾ cup cheese over the top of the casserole, cover the pot, and cook for 10 minutes longer, or until the cheese is melted.

sweet and tangy stuffed cabbage

Makes 4 to 6 servings

Because of the long, slow cooking, this favorite meal-in-a-dish doesn't need reheating to taste as good as it can. Serve with buttered rye or peasant bread.

1 large head of green cabbage (about 2 pounds)

1 pound lean ground beef

1 medium onion, finely chopped

2 garlic cloves, minced

1 teaspoon salt

½ teaspoon freshly ground black pepper

½ cup converted long-grain white rice

1 can (28 ounces) diced tomatoes

1 can (6 ounces) tomato paste

⅓ cup fresh lemon juice

⅓ cup golden raisins

⅓ cup packed light brown sugar

1. Rinse and core the cabbage. Remove 8 larger outer leaves from the cabbage. In a large pot of salted boiling water, cook the leaves for 4 to 6 minutes, until just limp. Remove and drain on paper towels. Chop the remaining cabbage and place in the bottom of a 6-quart electric slow cooker.

2. In a large skillet, sauté the ground beef and onion over medium-high heat, stirring to break up any lumps of meat, until the beef is browned, 5 to 7 minutes. Drain off any excess fat. Stir in the garlic, ½ teaspoon of the salt, the pepper, and the rice. Mix to blend well.

3. In another bowl, combine the tomatoes with their juices, tomato paste, and ½ cup of water. Stir to dissolve the tomato paste. Add 1 cup of this tomato sauce to the beef and rice filling and blend well.

4. Arrange the cabbage leaves on a flat surface with the stem ends facing you. Divide the filling evenly among the 8 leaves, placing it on the bottom third of each leaf near the stem end. Fold the sides of the cabbage leaves over the meat and gently roll up.

5. Place the stuffed cabbage leaves, seam sides down, on top of the chopped cabbage. Stir the lemon juice, raisins, brown sugar, and remaining ½ teaspoon salt into the remaining tomato sauce. Spoon the sauce over and around the cabbage rolls.

6. Cover and cook on the low heat setting for 6 to 6½ hours, until the cabbage and rice are tender but the rolls remain intact. Serve the stuffed cabbage with the chopped cabbage and sauce spooned on top.

ground beef and cabbage casserole

Makes 5 to 6 servings

When you're in the mood for stuffed cabbage but don't have time to fuss with all the blanching, filling, and rolling, try this easy recipe. Instead of stuffing the beef and rice inside the cabbage, the ingredients are layered , which saves a lot of time and trouble. You just turn on the slow cooker and walk away. This tastes great reheated the next day in a microwave, on top of the stove, or in the oven.

1 pound lean ground beef or ground turkey or chicken

1 medium onion, chopped

½ cup converted long-grain white rice

1 head of green cabbage (about 1½ pounds), cored and chopped

1 red bell pepper, chopped

1 can (14.5 ounces) diced tomatoes

1 can (6 ounces) tomato paste

½ cup dry red wine

1 tablespoon Worcestershire sauce

½ teaspoon garlic powder

½ teaspoon seasoned salt

¼ teaspoon freshly ground black pepper

1. In a large skillet, cook the beef and onion over medium-high heat, stirring to break up the meat, until well browned, 5 to 7 minutes. Drain off any excess fat.

2. Transfer to a 5-quart electric slow cooker. Add the rice, cabbage, and bell pepper to the beef and mix well.

3. In a bowl, combine the tomatoes with their juices, tomato paste, wine, Worcestershire sauce, garlic powder, seasoned salt, and pepper. Mix well. Stir in 1½ cups of water. Pour into the pot and stir to incorporate with the other ingredients.

4. Cover and cook on the low heat setting for 5 to 6 hours, until the rice and cabbage are tender.

beef with spinach and rice

Makes 5 to 6 servings

Usually when a recipe calls for frozen spinach, the thawed vegetable is first drained and squeezed dry. Not here. Instead, the moisture from the spinach is used as part of the liquid for the dish. To brighten the flavor, chopped fresh basil and grated Parmesan cheese are stirred in just before serving.

1 pound lean ground beef

1 package (16 ounces) frozen chopped spinach, thawed but not drained

1 can (28 ounces) crushed tomatoes with added puree and basil

6 scallions, chopped

1 garlic clove, crushed through a press

¾ cup converted long-grain white rice

½ teaspoon salt

¼ teaspoon freshly ground black pepper

¼ cup chopped fresh basil

¼ cup shredded Pecorino Romano cheese

1. In a large skillet, cook the beef over medium-high heat, stirring often to break up any lumps of meat, until crumbly and browned, 5 to 7 minutes. Drain off any excess fat.

2. Transfer to a 4-quart electric slow cooker and stir in the spinach, tomatoes, scallions, garlic, rice, salt, and pepper. Press down to create an even surface on top.

3. Cover and cook on the high heat setting for 2 hours or on the low heat setting for 4 hours, until the rice is tender. Stir in the fresh basil, sprinkle the cheese on top, and serve.

corned beef and cabbage

T o accompany the beef, pass a simple sauce made by combining plain yogurt or sour cream with Dijon mustard and creamy horseradish to taste. Serve with slices of hearty rye bread to complete the meal.

Makes 6 to 8 servings

2 pounds red potatoes, preferably organic, scrubbed and
   cut into 1-inch pieces
6 medium carrots, peeled and cut into 2-inch-long pieces
1 large onion, cut into 12 wedges
3 pounds corned beef brisket (flat cut)
3 cups beer
3 tablespoons Dijon mustard
1 head of green cabbage (about 1½ pounds), rinsed, cored,
   and cut into 10 wedges

1. Place the potatoes, carrots, and onion in a 6-quart electric slow cooker. Trim off as much fat as possible from the corned beef. Place the meat on top of the vegetables in the pot. Combine the beer and mustard, whisking until blended. Pour over the corned beef.

2. Cover and cook on the low heat setting for 7 hours. Add the cabbage to the pot and continue cooking, covered, on low heat for 2 to 3 hours longer, or until the meat and cabbage are tender.

3. Remove the corned beef to a cutting board; carve against the grain into slices. Arrange in the center of a large platter. With a slotted spoon, arrange the vegetables around the meat. Spoon some of the juices in the pot over the corned beef and vegetables. Pass some more in a sauceboat on the side.

hungarian goulash

Makes 6 servings

What could be better on a cold winter night than this fabulous stew of pork, kielbasa, and tangy sauerkraut? It is really an exceptional dish. For best results, I cook the kielbasa for a couple of minutes in a hot skillet or in the microwave to remove excess fat; then add to the pot during the last half hour or so of cooking. Serve with noodles.

1½ pounds boneless pork loin

¼ cup imported sweet Hungarian paprika

1 tablespoon all-purpose flour

¼ teaspoon salt

½ teaspoon freshly ground black pepper

3 medium red potatoes (1 to 1¼ pounds), peeled and thinly sliced

1 large onion, thinly sliced

2 bay leaves

2 pounds refrigerated sauerkraut, rinsed and well drained

½ cup chicken broth

¾ cup dry white wine

½ pound cooked Polish kielbasa, sliced

1 cup sour cream

1. Trim as much fat as you can from the pork and cut the meat into 1-inch cubes. Mix together the paprika, flour, salt, and pepper. Toss the pork cubes with the seasoned flour to coat.

2. In a 5-quart electric slow cooker, make a layer of potatoes and then onion slices. Add the pork cubes to the pot and tuck in the bay leaves. Top with the sauerkraut. Mix the broth and wine and pour over all.

3. Cover and cook on the low heat setting for 6½ to 7 hours, or until the pork and potatoes are tender but not falling apart. Remove and discard the bay leaves.

4. Tuck the kielbasa slices into the stew in the pot. Cover and cook on the high heat setting for 30 minutes longer. Stir half of the sour cream into the goulash and transfer to a serving dish. Pass the remainder at the table.

posole with pork and chicken

Makes 5 to 6 servings

This hearty dish from Jalisco, Mexico, is a cross between a soup and a stew. Traditionally served at Christmas, it is eaten as a main course. I find it soul-warming during the cold-weather months.

1 pound boneless pork loin

1 pound skinless, boneless chicken thighs

1 medium-large white onion, chopped

1 can (7 ounces) diced green chiles (or use two 4-ounce cans)

1½ teaspoons ground ancho chile

1½ teaspoons chili powder

1 teaspoon dried oregano

½ teaspoon salt

1 cup chicken broth

2 cans (15 ounces each) white hominy, rinsed and well drained

1 lime

1½ tablespoons chopped fresh cilantro

Thinly sliced scallions, shredded radishes, and lime wedges, for garnish

1. Trim as much fat as possible from the pork and chicken. Cut both meats into 1-inch cubes.

2. In a 5-quart slow cooker, combine the pork cubes, chicken cubes, onion, green chiles, ancho chile, chili powder, oregano, salt, and broth. Mix well. Stir in the hominy.

3. Cover and cook on the low heat setting for about 7 hours, until the pork and chicken are very tender but the chunks are not falling apart.

4. Just before serving, squeeze the juice from the lime into the posole and stir in the cilantro. Ladle into shallow soup plates. Pass sliced scallions, shredded radishes, and lime wedges on the side.

Why oval slow cookers? They were designed to better accommodate large roasts, hams, and whole chickens.

chicken-vegetable supper

Makes 4 servings

Here's a simple, nothing-fancy way to fix chicken quickly for a weekday dinner. Don't be tempted to add more liquid to the pot at the start of cooking; the chicken will generate plenty of juices.

2 medium zucchini, chopped

1 package (16 ounces) crinkle-cut carrot slices (coins)

1 red bell pepper, cut into julienne strips

2 medium red potatoes, peeled and diced

4 celery ribs, diagonally sliced

$\frac{1}{3}$ cup dry white wine or chicken broth

1 teaspoon dried basil

$\frac{1}{2}$ teaspoon dried thyme

$\frac{1}{2}$ teaspoon paprika

1 teaspoon salt

$\frac{1}{2}$ teaspoon seasoned pepper

1 cut-up chicken (4 to 4$\frac{1}{2}$ pounds), skin and fat removed

1 medium onion, sliced

Cook's Note

➤ You can use 6 skinless, boneless chicken breast halves instead of cut-up chicken pieces, if you prefer, though bones always add more flavor to a dish.

1. In a 6-quart electric slow cooker, combine the zucchini, carrots, bell pepper, potatoes, celery, wine, basil, thyme, $\frac{1}{4}$ teaspoon of the paprika, $\frac{1}{2}$ teaspoon of the salt, and $\frac{1}{4}$ teaspoon of the seasoned pepper. Mix well.

2. Arrange the chicken pieces on top of the vegetables. Season the chicken with the remaining $\frac{1}{4}$ teaspoon paprika, $\frac{1}{2}$ teaspoon salt, and $\frac{1}{4}$ teaspoon seasoned pepper. Scatter the onion slices on top.

3. Cover and cook on the low heat setting for 6 to 7 hours, until the chicken is cooked through and the vegetables are tender.

easy chicken and sausage jambalaya

For authentic flavor in this one-pot dish, be sure to use spicy, smoky andouille sausage. All you need to make this a complete meal is a nice tossed salad.

Makes 6 servings

1 pound cooked smoked chicken sausage with Cajun andouille seasoning, cut into ½-inch-thick slices

1 pound skinless, boneless chicken breast halves, trimmed of all fat and cut into ½- to ¾-inch pieces

1 large onion, chopped

3 celery ribs, chopped

1 teaspoon Cajun spice blend or seasoning

1 can (28 ounces) crushed tomatoes

1 can (14 ounces) reduced-sodium chicken broth

1½ cups converted long-grain white rice

1 green bell pepper, chopped

Salt

1. In a large skillet, cook the sausage over medium-high heat, stirring often, until well browned, 5 to 7 minutes.

2. In a 5-quart electric slow cooker, combine the browned sausages with the chicken, onion, celery, Cajun seasoning, crushed tomatoes, broth, rice, and bell pepper. Stir until well mixed.

3. Cover and cook on the low heat setting for 4 to 5 hours, or until the chicken is cooked through and the rice is tender but not mushy. Season with salt to taste.

chicken curry with fragrant rice

Makes 4 to 6 servings

Using a good-quality Madras curry, such as Sun brand, in place of bright yellow commercial curry powder makes all the difference in flavor. Turn supper into an Indian feast by offering assorted condiments, such as roasted peanuts, unsweetened shredded coconut, raisins, and chutney (either a bottled mango chutney or one of the recipes on pages 372 to 374).

1½ cups converted long-grain white rice

3 cups boiling water

1 tablespoon plus 1 teaspoon Madras curry powder

1 teaspoon ground cumin

¼ teaspoon ground turmeric

¼ teaspoon ground ginger

⅛ teaspoon cayenne pepper

¼ teaspoon salt

¼ teaspoon seasoned pepper

1 medium onion, chopped

4 large skinless, boneless chicken breast halves
    (about 2 pounds total)

½ cup thinly sliced red, yellow, or green bell pepper

1 cup frozen green peas or small lima beans, thawed

1. Place the rice in a 4-quart oval electric slow cooker. In a 1-quart glass measuring cup or heatproof bowl, mix together the boiling water, 1 tablespoon of the curry powder, the cumin, turmeric, ginger, cayenne, salt, and seasoned pepper. Stir into the rice along with the onion, mixing well.

2. Arrange the chicken breasts on top of the rice and sprinkle them with the remaining 1 teaspoon curry powder. Scatter the bell pepper strips over the chicken.

3. Cover and cook on the high heat setting for 2¾ to 3 hours, until the chicken is white throughout but still moist and the rice is tender but not mushy.

4. Sprinkle the peas evenly into the pot, cover, and cook for a few minutes longer to heat them. Serve immediately.

whole wheat chicken enchiladas with brown rice

Makes 6 to 8 servings

Tortillas used to mean simply flour or corn. Now there are many varieties and flavors—even low-carb—available. Whole wheat tortillas are a good nutritious option full of natural fiber, vitamins, and minerals. Make these substantial enchiladas a day ahead, if you like, and reheat them in a microwave oven. Serve with sour cream, guacamole, and a crisp salad.

2 cups cooked brown rice

2 cups diced cooked chicken breast (about ¾ pound)

1 cup cooked or canned black beans, rinsed and drained

1 can (4 ounces) diced green chiles

1¾ cups shredded sharp Cheddar cheese

1 jar (16 ounces) mild chunky salsa

Salt and freshly ground black pepper

8 whole wheat tortillas (7½ to 8 inches in diameter), warmed

1 can (14.5 ounces) diced tomatoes, drained

½ teaspoon ground ancho chile

¼ teaspoon ground chipotle chile

1. In a mixing bowl, combine the brown rice, chicken, black beans, green chiles, 1 cup of the cheese, and half of the salsa. Mix well. Season with salt and pepper to taste.

2. Place a generous ⅓ cup of the chicken and brown rice filling across the center of each tortilla. Roll up to make enchiladas.

3. Arrange a single layer of enchiladas in a 5-quart electric slow cooker. Place the second row on top at a 90-degree angle to the first. Continue stacking the enchiladas in crisscross fashion until they are all in the cooker. Combine the remaining salsa with the tomatoes, ancho chile, and chipotle chile; mix well. Pour over and around the enchiladas.

4. Cover and cook on the high heat setting for 2 to 2½ hours or on the low heat setting for 4 to 5 hours, until hot throughout. Sprinkle the remaining ¾ cup cheese on top, cover, and cook for 10 to 15 minutes longer.

Cook's Note

➤ If you're in a hurry, simply layer the tortillas and filling mixture in the pot, then top with the salsa mixture and proceed as directed in Step 4.

sweet-and-sour pineapple chicken

Makes 4 to 5 servings

Normally, you'd serve a sweet-and-sour dish over steamed rice. Well, here the rice is already included. For a change of pace, use turkey strips, available in supermarket meat sections, instead of the chicken called for here.

1 can (20 ounces) unsweetened pineapple chunks in juice

⅓ cup ketchup

¼ cup red wine vinegar

3 tablespoons brown sugar

½ teaspoon salt

¼ teaspoon freshly ground black pepper

2 large bell peppers, preferably 1 green and 1 red, cut into 1-inch cubes

1 pound chicken tenders, cut into thin strips

1 large onion, cut into thin wedges

1 cup converted long-grain white rice

1 large tomato, cut into thin wedges

1. Drain the juice from the pineapple into a bowl. Add the ketchup,
    vinegar, brown sugar, salt, pepper, and ¾ cup of water. Mix the
    sauce well.

2. In a 4- or 5-quart electric slow cooker, combine the pineapple
    chunks, bell peppers, chicken strips, onion wedges, and rice.
    Pour the sauce over all and toss well to distribute the ingredi-
    ents evenly.

3. Cover and cook on the low heat setting for 4 to 4¼ hours,
    stirring once about halfway through if possible, until the
    chicken and rice are tender. Do not overcook, or the rice will
    become too soft.

4. Just before serving, gently stir in the tomato wedges.

Refrigerate or freeze foods from the slow cooker within two hours of cooking and serving.

turkey and prosciutto rolls with basil and rice

Makes 4 servings

Packaged seasoned rice mix blended with colorful bell pepper makes the perfect base for these savory turkey rolls, stuffed with prosciutto and fresh basil. If you want to add a green vegetable to the plate, broccoli rabe or regular broccoli would be a good choice.

1 package (6 ounces) long-grain and wild rice, original recipe, with herbs and seasonings

1 bell pepper—red, yellow, or green—chopped

1 pound thinly sliced turkey breast cutlets (8 or 9)

8 or 9 large fresh basil leaves or 1½ teaspoon dried basil

4 paper-thin slices of prosciutto (.3-ounce package)

½ teaspoon smoked paprika

2 tablespoons balsamic vinegar

1½ tablespoons extra virgin olive oil

Fresh Tomato Sauce (page 108; optional)

1. In a 4-quart electric slow cooker, combine the rice with its seasoning packet, bell pepper, and 2 cups of water.

2. Lay out the turkey cutlets flat and arrange the basil leaves on top or sprinkle with the dried basil. Top with the prosciutto slices and roll up jelly-roll fashion. Place the turkey rolls, seam sides down, on top of the rice. Sprinkle the smoked paprika over the turkey.

3. Cover and cook on the low heat setting for 2¾ to 3 hours, or until the turkey is cooked through and the rice is tender but not mushy. Serve the turkey rolls over the rice. Drizzle with the balsamic vinegar and extra virgin olive oil or pass fresh tomato sauce on the side.

savory beans and greens

Not just for vegetarians, this soupy vegetable stew is so savory the entire family will love it. Ladle into bowls and serve Italian style, topped with a drizzle of extra virgin olive oil and a sprinkling of grated Parmesan cheese. If you prefer a more substantial meal, stir in a couple of cups of cooked pasta or diced cooked chicken or turkey breast just before serving.

3 cups cooked or canned Great Northern beans,
    rinsed and drained
1 medium red onion, chopped
1 cup chopped carrots
½ cup chopped fresh fennel
2 garlic cloves, crushed through a press
1½ teaspoons dried basil
Few dashes of crushed hot red pepper
½ teaspoon salt
¼ teaspoon freshly ground black pepper
1 can (14.5 ounces) diced tomatoes
1 package (9 ounces) cut-up romaine lettuce,
    preferably organic, rinsed (about 6 cups)
1 package (5 ounces) organic baby spring lettuce mix,
    rinsed (about 3 cups)
Extra virgin olive oil and freshly grated Parmesan cheese

1. In a 5-quart electric slow cooker, combine the beans, red onion, carrots, fennel, garlic, basil, crushed hot pepper, salt, black pepper, tomatoes with their juices, and romaine lettuce pieces. Mix well. Top with the baby lettuce mix but do not stir in.

2. Cover and cook on the low heat setting for 3 to 4 hours or on the high heat setting for 1½ to 2 hours, until the greens are tender, stirring once three-quarters of the way through the cooking time if possible.

3. Season with additional salt to taste. Serve in bowls, drizzled with a little extra virgin olive oil and sprinkled with grated Parmesan cheese.

asian-flavored quinoa with broccoli and chard

**Makes 4 to 6 main-dish
or 6 to 8 side-dish servings**

Quinoa is a lovely, mild nutty-flavored grain that is enhanced by toasted sesame oil. I use both the leaves and stems of the chard here. While fresh ginger is optional, it adds a very good flavor and just a touch of heat.

1 bunch (8 ounces) Swiss chard, preferably rainbow chard

8 ounces broccoli

1 medium leek (white and tender green parts)

1¾ cups chicken or vegetable broth or water

2½ tablespoons soy sauce

3 tablespoons Asian sesame oil

2 teaspoons brown sugar

⅛ teaspoon crushed hot red pepper, or more to taste

1½ teaspoons minced fresh ginger (optional)

1⅓ cups quinoa

Slow cooker wattage is indicated on the bottom of the appliance.

1. Trim the ends off the chard stems. Slice the stems very thinly; if they are thick, coarsely chop them. Cut the leaves lengthwise down the center; then cut them crosswise into thin strips. There should be about 6 cups.

2. Cut the broccoli into small pieces no larger than ½ inch. There should be 3 cups. Cut the leek lengthwise in half; then thinly slice crosswise. Swish the slices in a bowl of cold water and lift out to remove any grit.

3. In a 3½- or 4-quart electric slow cooker, combine the Swiss chard, broccoli, leek, broth, soy sauce, 2 tablespoons of the sesame oil, the brown sugar, hot pepper, and fresh ginger, if desired. Swish the quinoa around in a bowl of warm water; drain into a sieve. Repeat the rinsing and draining. Add to the pot and stir to mix.

4. Cover and cook on the high heat setting for 2 hours or on the low heat setting for 3 to 3½ hours, until the vegetables are crisp-tender and the quinoa is soft and fluffy but not mushy; when it's done the little "tails" on the grain will open out. Stir in the remaining 1 tablespoon sesame oil just before serving.

spaghetti squash marinara

Makes 4 to 5 servings

This is a terrific way to cook spaghetti squash. It holds its shape and doesn't get mushy. For dieters or people who are gluten-intolerant, this offers a fine way to enjoy your red sauce.

1 spaghetti squash (3½ pounds), outside shell rinsed and
    dried with paper towels
1 jar (26 ounces) marinara or other tomato-based pasta sauce
¼ cup dry red wine
2 tablespoons drained capers
¾ cup coarsely chopped pitted kalamata olives
Salt and freshly ground black pepper
¼ cup chopped fresh basil
2 to 3 tablespoons freshly grated Parmesan cheese or
    shaved pieces

Cook's Note

➤ Be absolutely sure to prick the spaghetti squash in several places before cooking it whole, whether in a microwave or in a regular oven. Otherwise, it may explode and make a big mess.

1. Pierce the spaghetti squash in several places with a sharp knife. Place the whole squash in a microwave oven and cook on high power for 10 minutes, or until the tough outer skin can be pierced with a large sharp knife. Split the squash lengthwise in half. Using a large tablespoon, spoon out the seeds and any stringy pieces attached to them, being careful not to remove the strands of squash.

2. Then, using a large spoon, scoop out the spaghetti squash, which will still be very firm, scraping right down to the shell. Place the squash in a 4-quart electric slow cooker. Combine the marinara sauce, wine, capers, and olives and pour over the squash, letting the sauce seep down the sides of pot.

3. Cover and cook on the low heat setting for 6 to 6½ hours, until the squash is tender but still holds its shape. Toss with the sauce in the pot. Season with salt and pepper to taste and serve hot, topped with the basil and Parmesan cheese.

vegetable-tortilla bake
with two cheeses

Makes 5 to 6 servings

Flavorful and appealing, this meatless main course is good served with sour cream, chopped tomatoes, and fresh cilantro.

1 can (27 ounces) whole tomatillos

1 cup thick and chunky salsa, mild or medium-hot to taste

1 can (15 ounces) petite-cut diced tomatoes

1 can (15.25 ounces) corn kernels, drained

1 teaspoon ground cumin

6 corn tortillas (6 to 7 inches in diameter)

1 package (6 ounces) prewashed fresh baby spinach leaves

2 cups (16 ounces) small curd cottage cheese (low fat is fine)

2 cups shredded mozzarella cheese

1. Drain the tomatillos into a colander. Rinse well under cold running water and drain again. Core and peel off the skins; coarsely chop the tomatillos.

2. In a medium bowl, combine the chopped tomatillos with the salsa, tomatoes with their juices, corn, and cumin.

3. Spread ¾ cup of the salsa mixture over the bottom of a 5-quart electric slow cooker. Top with 2 tortillas, tearing them to fit in a single layer. Layer about half of the spinach over the tortillas. Cover with half of the cottage cheese, spreading it out as evenly as possible. Add one-third of the salsa mixture (about 1⅓ cups), and finally, ¾ cup of the mozzarella cheese. Repeat with another layer of tortillas, the remaining spinach leaves and cottage cheese, half of the remaining salsa mixture, and ¾ cup of the mozzarella cheese. Top with the 2 remaining tortillas and then the remaining salsa mixture;.

4. Cover and cook on the low heat setting for 5½ to 6 hours or on the high heat setting for about 3 hours, until hot throughout.

5. Sprinkle the remaining ½ cup mozzarella cheese on top and cook, covered, for about 5 minutes, until the cheese is melted. Let the casserole stand for 10 minutes to set up before serving.

red lentil and vegetable curry

Makes 6 to 8 servings

Red lentils are clinically called "decorticated lentils," which means their outer shell has been removed. While their vibrant orange will fade when cooked, they are still attractive. Edamame, shelled fresh soybeans, are added at the end for more color and nutrition. Serve with yogurt and chutney on the side.

1 pound dried red lentils, picked over, rinsed, and well drained
1 large onion, chopped
2 cups chopped zucchini or yellow summer squash
3 celery ribs, chopped
2 cups chopped carrots
2 tablespoons Madras curry powder
1 tablespoon ground cumin
¼ teaspoon salt
½ teaspoon freshly ground black pepper
1 cup edamame (shelled fresh soybeans)

1. Put the lentils in a 4-quart electric slow cooker. Add the onion, zucchini, celery, carrots, curry powder, cumin, salt, pepper, and 3 cups of hot water. Mix well. Press down gently to submerge most of the vegetables in the water.

2. Cover and cook on the low heat setting for 6 hours, or until the lentils are tender.

3. Stir in the edamame and serve.

vegetables, grains, and side dishes

Like many people, I've cut way back on meat and often rely on vegetable-based meals. They offer great variety and colorful eye appeal. There are lots of choices; I've shared some of my favorites here. In keeping with current nutritional guidelines as well as the beautiful produce now available in supermarkets as well as specialty greengrocers and farmers' markets, I make it a point to serve my family more vegetables, beans, and whole grains.

As always, I find the electric slow cooker an enormous help, whether it's to take care of a dish while I'm out of the house; to relieve me of having yet another pot on top of the stove, especially during holiday time; or to take over so that I don't have to heat the oven.

The pot is good for many things, but none more so than beans. With dried beans, there's no soaking overnight, no parboiling. You just toss the beans into the pot with enough water and voilà: In a few hours, they are tender enough so that you can add all your seasonings and other ingredients and let them finish off at your leisure. I also include recipes for doctoring up canned beans. Everything just gets dumped into the pot, and after its long, slow simmer, no one will know they are not from scratch.

vegetables, grains, and side dishes

slow and easy beans

This is the easiest, most effortless way to cook beans—no presoaking or precooking necessary. For best results, check the label when you buy the beans to be sure they are not too old; most have a best-used-by date. Even though they're dried, a fresher crop is better. Cooking time will depend on the size of the beans, the variety, how long they've been stored, and even where they were grown. Check the beans after 3 hours to avoid overcooking.

1 package (16 ounces) dried beans—small white, Great Northern, pinto, red, black, pink, kidney, or cannellini

1. Rinse the beans and pick them over to remove any gravel or grit. Drain well. In a 4-quart electric slow cooker, combine the beans and 6 cups of water.

2. Cover and cook on the high heat setting for 3½ to 4 hours, or until the beans are tender but not falling apart. They will not absorb all the water. If you plan to use the beans in another recipe in which they will be cooked further, cook for only 3 to 3½ hours, until *al dente*, just barely tender.

3. Drain the beans into a colander and rinse with cold water. Drain well, then transfer to a covered container and refrigerate for up to 3 days.

new england baked beans with molasses and bacon

Makes 5 to 6 servings

This recipe requires two steps: first cooking the beans until they are just tender; then draining them, adding the remaining ingredients that provide all the flavor, and finishing the cooking. The results are well worth it. You can cook the beans a day or two in advance; they only improve when reheated.

1 package (16 ounces) dried pinto beans, white beans, or
   navy beans, rinsed, picked over, and well drained
3 tablespoons unsulphured molasses
2 tablespoons maple syrup
2 tablespoons brown sugar
2 tablespoons cider vinegar
1 teaspoon Dijon mustard
1 small onion, chopped
1 garlic clove, crushed through a press
½ teaspoon salt
5 slices of bacon, cooked until crisp and crumbled

1. In a 4-quart electric slow cooker, combine the beans and 6 cups of water. Cover and cook on the high heat setting for 3 to 3½ hours, until the beans are almost tender. Drain the beans into a colander and rinse quickly with cold water. Return to the cooker pot.

2. Stir in the molasses, maple syrup, brown sugar, vinegar, mustard, onion, garlic, salt, 3 strips of the crumbled bacon, and another ½ cup of water. Mix well.

3. Cover and cook on the low heat setting for 2½ to 3 hours, until the beans and sauce are hot and the beans are tender but not mushy. Stir to mix well. Sprinkle the remaining crumbled bacon over the top and serve.

If you want to substitute canned beans for dried in a recipe, figure that a pound of dried beans equals 6 to 7 cups cooked, depending on the variety. A 15-ounce can is the equivalent of about 1¾ cups drained beans. So if a recipe calls for 2 cups cooked dried beans, substitute 1 (15-ounce) can.

easiest-ever doctored-up baked beans

Makes 12 to 16 servings

Open a few cans, add a few more ingredients, throw them together, and let them steep for hours. Everyone will think you made these beans from scratch.

10 slices of bacon, cooked until crisp
1 large can (53 ounces) pork and beans in tomato sauce
1 can (28 ounces) barbecue-flavored baked beans
1 can (6 ounces) tomato paste
1 medium onion, chopped
½ cup packed brown sugar
⅓ cup unsulphured molasses
1½ teaspoons powdered mustard

1. Cut 6 of the bacon slices crosswise into 4 pieces each and use them to line the bottom of a 5-quart electric slow cooker. In a large bowl, combine the pork and beans, baked beans, tomato paste, onion, brown sugar, molasses, and powdered mustard. Mix until thoroughly blended. Carefully pour over the bacon in the pot.

2. Cover and cook on the low heat setting for 4 to 4½ hours. Remove the lid and continue cooking on low for 1 to 1½ hours longer, or until the beans have thickened slightly.

3. Crumble the remaining bacon over the top. Serve hot.

party baked beans

Makes 10 to 12 servings

Some days you just don't feel like starting from scratch. Doctoring up canned beans is a great way to go, especially with this easy recipe designed to please a crowd.

2 cans (28 ounces each) baked beans, all sauce included

1 can (29 ounces) pinto beans, rinsed and well drained

½ cup hickory-flavored barbecue sauce

1 medium onion, chopped

2 tablespoons Dijon mustard

2 tablespoons unsulphured molasses

½ cup well-drained crushed pineapple

1. In a large bowl, combine all the ingredients. Mix to blend, folding gently so as not to break the beans. Transfer to a 4-quart electric slow cooker.

2. Cover and cook on the low heat setting for 4½ to 5 hours. Remove the cover and raise the heat setting to high. Cook for 1 to 1¼ hours longer, to thicken the sauce.

lima bean succotash

Makes 10 to 12 servings

This is a choice whenever you're looking for a tasty vegetable to serve to a large group or bring to a potluck. Avoid overcooking so the beans won't lose all their green color.

2 packages (16 ounces each) frozen baby lima beans, thawed

1 package (16 ounces) frozen white or yellow corn kernels, thawed

1 medium onion, chopped

1 red bell pepper, chopped

2 celery ribs, chopped

1 to 1½ teaspoons Cajun seasoning blend, to taste

1 teaspoon smoked paprika

1 can (8 ounces) tomato sauce

Salt and freshly ground black pepper

¾ cup shredded Monterey Jack or Cheddar cheese

1. In a 5-quart electric slow cooker, combine the lima beans, corn, onion, bell pepper, celery, Cajun seasoning, smoked paprika, and tomato sauce. Mix well.

2. Cover and cook on the low heat setting for about 4 hours, until the vegetables are hot. Season with salt and pepper to taste.

3. Sprinkle the cheese over the top, cover, and cook for 5 to 10 minutes longer, until melted. Serve hot.

tangy red cabbage with apples

Makes 8 servings

This dish is reminiscent of the cabbage my German grandmother made many years ago. The pot will be stuffed with cabbage when you begin this recipe, but don't be concerned, as it cooks down considerably. The sweet-tart side dish is excellent with roast pork, turkey, or sausages. Serve hot or cold.

1 large head of red cabbage (3 pounds), chopped (about 14 cups)
2 Granny Smith apples, cored and chopped (no need to peel)
1 medium onion, chopped
¾ cup red wine vinegar
¼ cup packed brown sugar
Seasoned salt and freshly ground black pepper
Crumbled cooked bacon, for garnish

1. In a 5- or 6-quart electric slow cooker, mix together the red cabbage, apples, and onion. Stir together the vinegar and brown sugar and pour over the cabbage. Mix well.

2. Cover and cook on the low heat setting for 5½ to 6 hours, or until the cabbage is tender. Season with salt and pepper to taste. Serve topped with crisp crumbled bacon, if desired.

apricot-glazed carrots

Makes 10 to 12 servings

When you're having a party or holiday gathering, toss the carrots and flavoring ingredients into an electric pot, and you'll have a delicious vegetable to serve without any last-minute cooking.

2 bags (1½ pounds each) peeled and cut carrots
¼ cup orange juice or water
4 teaspoons grated orange zest
½ cup thick apricot preserves
Sea salt and freshly ground black pepper

1. Place the carrots in a 4-quart electric slow cooker. Pour the orange juice over the carrots and stir in 2 teaspoons of the orange zest.

2. Cover and cook on the high heat setting for 4 hours or on the low heat setting for 8 hours, until the carrots are tender but not falling apart.

3. Stir in the apricot preserves and the remaining 2 teaspoons orange zest. Season with salt and pepper to taste. Cook, uncovered, on the high heat setting for 10 minutes longer.

steamed cauliflower and leeks

This combo is good warm, drizzled with a little balsamic and salt and black pepper, or served cold in a salad with mustard vinaigrette. If you like for convenience, use packages of already cut-up and prewashed cauliflower.

Makes 6 servings

2 large leeks (white and tender green parts)
1½ pounds fresh cauliflower florets
3 tablespoons red wine vinegar
1 tablespoon extra virgin olive oil
1 teaspoon Dijon mustard
2 tablespoons balsamic vinegar
Sea salt and freshly ground black pepper

1. Trim off the roots and dark green tops of the leeks, leaving them about 5 inches in length. Cut the leeks lengthwise into thin strips. Rinse in a bowl of cold water, swishing with your hands to remove any grit. Lift out and place the leeks in a 4- or 5-quart electric slow cooker. Top with the cauliflower florets.

2. In a small bowl, whisk together the red wine vinegar, olive oil, and mustard until thoroughly blended. Pour over the leeks and cauliflower.

3. Cover and cook on the low heat setting for 3½ to 4 hours, or until tender. Drizzle the balsamic vinegar over the cooked vegetables and season with salt and pepper to taste. Serve warm or chilled.

curried cauliflower with potatoes and peas

Makes 4 to 6 servings

While this vegetable makes a wonderfully versatile side dish to serve with roast chicken, lamb, or fish, consider it as a main course for a vegetarian supper, too. Accompany with steamed basmati rice, yogurt, toasted cashews, and a chutney, such as Mango-Ginger (page 373).

1½ pounds Yukon gold potatoes, peeled and
    diced into ½-inch cubes

1 large onion, chopped

1 orange or red bell pepper, chopped

½ green bell pepper, chopped

2 Roma or large plum tomatoes, chopped

1 can (6 ounces) tomato paste

2 tablespoons curry powder

1½ teaspoons ground cumin

1 garlic clove, crushed through a press

½ teaspoon salt

1 large head of cauliflower, cut into 1-inch florets

1 cup frozen peas, thawed

1. In a 4-quart electric slow cooker, toss together the potatoes, onion, orange and green bell peppers, and tomatoes. Stir in the tomato paste, curry powder, cumin, garlic, salt, and ½ cup of water. Mix well. Place the cauliflower florets on top.

2. Cover and cook on the low heat setting for 7 to 8 hours, or until the pieces of potato are tender but still hold their shape.

3. Stir in the peas, increase the heat to the high setting, and cook, covered, for 10 to 15 minutes longer.

Add thawed frozen vegetables like peas to a dish during the last 30 minutes or so of cooking time for bright color and crisp-tender texture.

corn on the cob

Makes 8 servings

Everyone loves corn on the cob, but when you're serving a lot of it, that big pot on the stove can get in the way of other food preparation. Here's the easy way: Husk the corn and remove the silk; then simply pop all the ears into your slow cooker a couple of hours before you plan to serve dinner. This is also a good way to prep the corn if you'd like to cook it ahead and finish it off on the grill.

8 ears corn on the cob, husked
1 cup boiling water
Butter, for serving

1. Place the corn in a 5- or 6-quart quart electric slow cooker. Pour the boiling water over the corn.

2. Cover and cook on the high heat setting for 2 to 2½ hours, or until the corn is just tender. Do not overcook.

3. Serve hot, with butter on the side.

Cook's Note

➤ For a spicy flavored butter for corn, mix 1 stick (4 ounces) softened butter with ½ teaspoon ground cumin and ⅛ teaspoon ground chipotle chile, or more to taste, until well blended. Form into a log and refrigerate or freeze until needed.

creamed corn with jalapeño peppers

An upscale steak house chain zips up their popular creamed corn with jalapeño, an idea I incorporated here with delicious results. Make it hot, hotter, or hottest to suit your own taste.

Makes 6 to 8 servings

2 cups half-and-half

3 tablespoons all-purpose flour

3 packages (16 ounces each) frozen white corn,
    thawed and drained

1 medium onion, chopped

2 to 3 teaspoons chopped fresh jalapeño peppers or
    1 can (4 ounces) mild diced green chiles

1 cup shredded Gruyère or Cheddar cheese

Sea salt and freshly ground black pepper

1. In a bowl, whisk together ½ cup of the half-and-half and the flour until smooth. Whisk in the remaining 1½ cups half-and-half.

2. In a 4-quart electric slow cooker, mix together the corn, onion, and jalapeños. Stir in the half-and-half mixture. Cover and cook on the high heat setting for 3 hours, stirring twice during the cooking time.

3. Stir in ½ cup of the cheese and season with salt and pepper to taste. Top with the remaining ½ cup cheese. Cover and cook for 10 to 15 minutes longer, until the cheese is melted.

corn pudding with bacon

Makes 6 to 8 servings

This old-fashioned recipe is a great dish to tote to a potluck. Depending upon your taste, use plain or vegetable-flavored cracker crumbs. Do not add any extra salt before cooking, because the crumbs tend to be quite salty.

2 packages (16 ounces each) frozen corn kernels,
 thawed and drained
1 medium red onion, chopped
4 slices of bacon, cooked until crisp and crumbled
2 teaspoons sugar
1 cup heavy cream
1 cup half-and-half
3 large eggs
¼ teaspoon freshly ground black pepper
Pinch of cayenne pepper
1½ cups crushed buttery crackers, such as Ritz

1. In a 4-quart electric slow cooker, combine the corn, red onion, crumbled bacon, and sugar. Mix well.

2. In a bowl, whisk together the cream, half-and-half, and eggs until thoroughly blended. Season with the black pepper and cayenne. Pour over the corn and stir to blend. Last, mix in 1¼ cups of the crushed crackers.

3. Cover and cook on the high heat setting for 2½ to 3 hours, or until the pudding is set. Uncover and sprinkle the remaining ¼ cup crushed crackers over the top. Serve hot.

fennel, potatoes, onions, and peppers

S erve hot as a side dish with meats, fish, or poultry. Or top with crumbled cheese for a vegetarian entree.

Makes 5 to 6 servings

1 large fennel bulb

1 pound baby Dutch yellow potatoes, scrubbed and thinly sliced

1 red bell pepper, chopped

1 package (14 to 16 ounces) frozen petite whole onions,
    thawed and drained

3 tablespoons balsamic vinegar

2 tablespoons extra virgin olive oil

½ teaspoon salt

¼ teaspoon freshly ground black pepper

Crumbled feta or goat cheese, for garnish

1. Trim the top stalk and very bottom from the fennel bulb. Cut the bulb lengthwise into 6 pieces. Then cut the wedges crosswise into slices.

2. In a 4-quart electric slow cooker, combine the fennel, potatoes, bell pepper, onions, 2 tablespoons of the vinegar, 1 tablespoon of the olive oil, the salt, black pepper, and ⅓ cup of water. Toss well.

3. Cover and cook on the high heat setting for about 4½ hours, or until the potatoes and vegetables are tender.

4. Stir in the remaining 1 tablespoon each vinegar and olive oil. Season with additional salt and pepper to taste. Serve hot, topped with crumbled feta cheese, if desired.

balsamic-glazed onions

Makes about 6 cups

Slow is the easy way to make savory sweet-tart onions. These are a marvelous addition to burgers, sandwiches, salads, and pizza. They are the perfect accompaniment to grilled steak, salmon, or calf's liver. You also can chop them up to make an instant relish and spoon them over hot dogs.

3 pounds red or yellow onions (or some of each), cut into
  ¼- to ⅜-inch-thick slices
4 tablespoons balsamic vinegar
3 tablespoons packed brown sugar
½ teaspoon salt
¼ teaspoon freshly ground black pepper

1. Place the onions in a 4- or 5-quart electric slow cooker. Mix together 3 tablespoons of the vinegar with the brown sugar, salt, and pepper.

2. Cover and cook on the high heat setting for 3¼ to 3½ hours, or until the onions are tender. If you are around, stir the mixture once after about 2 hours.

3. Stir in the remaining 1 tablespoon vinegar and season with additional salt and pepper to taste. Remove the onions with a slotted spoon, but reserve some of the liquid from the bottom of the pot to moisten them.

herb-roasted potatoes with onions

Makes 6 to 8 servings

These savory potatoes are wonderfully simple. They go beautifully with roast chicken, beef, pork, or lamb.

3 pounds small new potatoes, preferably organic,
    scrubbed and quartered
1 package (14 to 16 ounces) frozen petite whole onions,
    thawed and drained
2 tablespoons extra virgin olive oil
1½ teaspoons fresh thyme leaves or 1 teaspoon dried
Sea salt and freshly ground black pepper

1. In a 4-quart electric slow cooker, toss together the potatoes, onions, and olive oil.

2. Cover and cook on the low heat setting for 6 to 7 hours, or until the potatoes are tender but not falling apart.

3. Gently stir in the thyme. Season with salt and pepper to taste. Serve hot or at room temperature.

slow scalloped potatoes

Makes 6 to 8 servings

Everyone loves creamy, cheesy scalloped potatoes. They are so simple yet so good, comfort food at its best. Use mild or sharp Cheddar cheese, depending upon your family's preference.

2½ pounds baking potatoes, peeled and thinly sliced

1 medium onion, halved and thinly sliced

5½ tablespoons butter

⅓ cup all-purpose flour

2 cups half-and-half

Sea salt and freshly ground black pepper

⅔ cup shredded Cheddar cheese

Vegetables like carrots and potatoes take longer to cook, so cut them into smaller pieces and place in the bottom and around the sides of the slow cooker. Place meats and poultry on top because they tend to cook faster.

1. In a 4-quart electric slow cooker, toss together the potato and onion slices.

2. In a 1½-quart saucepan, melt the butter over medium heat on top of the stove until bubbly. Whisk in the flour until thoroughly blended, then cook, whisking often, for 1 to 2 minutes to make a roux. Gradually whisk in the half-and-half. Bring to a boil, whisking until the sauce is smooth and thick. Reduce the heat and simmer, stirring, for 1 to 2 minutes longer. Season the cream sauce with salt and pepper to taste.

3. Pour the cream sauce over the potatoes and onions. Gently mix with a wooden spoon to coat all the potato slices with sauce. Press down on the potato mixture with the back of the spoon or with a wide spatula so the slices lie flat on top.

4. Cover and cook on the high heat setting for 3½ to 3¾ hours, or until the potatoes are fork-tender. Sprinkle the cheese over the potatoes, cover, and cook for 5 minutes longer, or until the cheese melts.

mediterranean
warm potato salad

Makes 6 to 8 servings

love the Mediterranean-inspired flavorings here: peppers, capers, and fresh basil. For a variation, stir in ½ cup chopped kalamata olives after cooking and instead of the bacon, sprinkle ¼ cup crumbled feta cheese on top along with the chopped tomatoes and basil.

3 pounds Yukon gold potatoes, peeled and cut into
   ½- to ¾-inch pieces
1 red bell pepper, chopped
½ green bell pepper, chopped
1 medium onion, chopped
3 tablespoons drained capers
½ cup red wine vinegar
3 tablespoons extra virgin olive oil
¼ cup plus 3 tablespoons chopped fresh basil
½ teaspoon salt
¼ teaspoon seasoned pepper
Crisply, cooked crumbled bacon, chopped tomatoes, and
   fresh basil leaves, for garnish

1. In a 4-quart electric slow cooker, combine the potatoes, red and green bell peppers, onion, and capers. In a glass measuring cup, mix together the vinegar, olive oil, ¼ cup of the chopped basil, the salt, seasoned pepper, and ¼ cup of water. Pour over the potato mixture and toss until mixed.

2. Cover and cook on the high heat setting for 3 to 3½ hours or on the low heat setting for 6 to 7 hours, until the potatoes are tender but not falling apart.

3. Stir in the remaining 3 tablespoons chopped basil and more salt and pepper to taste. Serve warm or cold, garnished with crumbled bacon, chopped tomatoes, and basil leaves.

set it and forget it baked potatoes

Makes 8 servings

Serve these easy potatoes piping hot, split, and filled with butter, sour cream, crumbled cooked bacon, and chopped scallions or chives. Or add your favorite cheese. These fully cooked potatoes can also be used to make potato salad, potato cakes or croquettes, or mashed potatoes.

8 medium russet or Idaho baking potatoes, scrubbed and dried well

1. Prick the potatoes in several places with a fork or the tip of a sharp knife. Stack the potatoes in a 3½- or 4-quart electric slow cooker. Do not add any water.

2. Cover and cook on the high heat setting for 3 to 4 hours or on the low heat setting for 6 to 8 hours, until fork-tender.

Cook's Note

➤ Sweet potatoes can also be cooked this same way.

spiced sweet potato sticks

S piked with chili powder and cumin, all these sweet and zesty potato sticks lack is the frying. In fact, steaming seals in both their flavor and nutritional value. Serve with all kinds of grilled meats or poultry. For convenience and to save time, buy the sweet potatoes already peeled, cut up, and washed in bags in market produce sections.

Makes 4 to 6 servings

2¼ pounds sweet potatoes, peeled and cut into
    1½- to 2-inch sticks about ½ inch thick, or 2 pounds
    packaged cut-up raw sweet potato fries
2 tablespoons extra virgin olive oil
1 teaspoon chili powder
½ teaspoon ground cumin
1 tablespoon fresh lime juice

1. Place the sweet potatoes in a 4-quart oval electric slow cooker. Add the olive oil, chili powder, cumin, and lime juice. Toss gently to coat evenly.

2. Cover and cook on the low heat setting for about 3 hours, until the sweet potatoes are tender but still hold their shape.

candied sweet potatoes with pecans

Makes 10 to 12 servings

This is the simplest way ever to make sweet potatoes for the holiday table or any time you roast a turkey. For best results, use dark-skinned sweet potatoes, usually labeled as yams; they have a brighter orange color and sweeter flavor.

4 pounds sweet potatoes or yams, peeled
1 stick (4 ounces) butter
1½ cups packed brown sugar
2 tablespoons grated orange zest
⅓ cup fresh orange juice
2½ teaspoons ground cinnamon
1 cup coarsely chopped pecans, toasted

Cook's Notes

➤ When grating orange or lemon zest, keep in mind you only want the colored outer part of the peel, with none of the bitter white pith inside.

➤ If marshmallows are a must with your sweet potatoes, after cooking, sprinkle ¾ to 1 cup miniature marshmallows around the edge of the pot. Cover and let melt for a minute or two.

1. If the potatoes are large, cut them lengthwise in half. Slice them ⅜ inch thick. Place the sweet potato slices in a 5-quart electric slow cooker.

2. In a glass bowl or large glass measuring cup, melt the butter in a microwave oven on high power for 30 to 60 seconds. Or melt in a small saucepan over low heat. Stir in the brown sugar, orange zest, orange juice, cinnamon, and ¾ cup of the toasted pecans. Mix well.

3. Pour the orange-pecan butter over the sweet potatoes and toss gently but thoroughly to coat the slices.

4. Cover and cook on the low heat setting for 7 to 7½ hours or on the high heat setting for 3½ to 3¾ hours, until the sweet potatoes are fork-tender. Serve with the remaining ¼ cup pecans sprinkled on top.

ratatouille

With its slow, even heat, the electric pot does a great job of maintaining the integrity of the vegetables that go into this tantalizing mélange. Of course it's a dish best made in season, when eggplant, peppers, zucchini, and tomatoes are garden fresh. Serve warm or at room temperature, alongside grilled fish, poultry, eggs, or sausage. For another variation, try crumbling feta or fresh white goat cheese on top of the warm ratatouille. It also makes a good bruschetta topping over toasted rustic bread slices.

1 eggplant (1¼ pounds), peeled and sliced

Salt

2 medium onions, chopped

2 large red bell peppers, cut into ½-inch pieces

5 large plum tomatoes, preferably Roma, seeded and
   coarsely chopped

3 medium zucchini, cut into ½-inch cubes

2 garlic cloves, crushed through a press

1 tablespoon extra virgin olive oil

½ teaspoon freshly ground black pepper

4 teaspoons dried basil

½ teaspoon dried oregano

¼ teaspoon dried thyme leaves

3 tablespoons chopped fresh basil or parsley,
   for garnish

1. Sprinkle the eggplant slices on both sides with salt. Spread out on several thicknesses of paper towels (or in a colander) and let stand for 30 to 60 minutes to drain. Press out excess moisture with additional paper towels. Rinse the eggplant thoroughly to remove the salt and pat dry with paper towels. Cut the eggplant slices into ½-inch cubes.

2. In a 5-quart electric slow cooker, combine the eggplant with the onions, bell peppers, tomatoes, zucchini, garlic, olive oil, black pepper, basil, oregano, and thyme. Mix well. (Do not add any liquid, as the vegetables exude plenty during cooking).

3. Cover and cook on the high heat setting for about 3 hours or on the low heat setting for 5½ to 6 hours, until the vegetables are tender but still hold their shape.

4. Add salt and pepper to taste, if needed. Sprinkle the top with fresh basil before serving hot, at room temperature, or chilled, discarding any excess liquid in the pot.

At high altitudes—above 3,500 feet—it may be necessary to increase cooking times in recipes.

spanish pistou

Makes 4 to 6 servings

This tangy zucchini salad makes an excellent accompaniment to all kinds of grilled foods or roast chicken. Sprinkled with crumbled feta or ricotta salata cheese, it can be enjoyed as a vegetarian main course. Note: This dish is best served at room temperature.

1½ pounds zucchini (3 medium-large), cut into ⅜-inch dice
1 large green bell pepper, cut into ⅜-inch dice
1 large onion, chopped
3 garlic cloves, finely chopped
1 teaspoon salt
½ teaspoon freshly ground black pepper
¼ teaspoon crushed hot red pepper
¼ cup extra virgin olive oil
1 can (14.5 ounces) diced tomatoes, drained
1½ tablespoons fresh lemon juice

1. In a 4-quart electric slow cooker, combine the zucchini, bell pepper, onion, garlic, salt, black pepper, hot pepper, olive oil, tomatoes, and lemon juice.

2. Cover and cook on the low heat setting for 5 hours, stirring two or three times if possible, until the onion is softened and the zucchini is tender but still has some resistance.

3. Transfer to a bowl and stir in the lemon juice. Season with additional salt to taste. While the dish can be eaten warm, it is traditional to serve it slightly chilled or at room temperature.

vegetable medley

Makes 6 to 8 servings

You could think of this easy dish as a contemporary version of succotash: beans, corn, and tomatoes. Here popular edamame, or shelled soybeans, are used, along with frozen corn and fresh tomatoes. No need to peel and seed. Zucchini adds its mellowing influence as well. Serve with chopped fresh basil or parsley sprinkled on top and add a drizzle of extra virgin olive oil, if you like.

1 package (16 ounces) frozen shelled edamame (soybeans), thawed

1 package (16 ounces) frozen white corn, thawed

1 medium onion, chopped

1 medium-large zucchini, cut into ⅜-inch dice

4 Roma or other large plum tomatoes, chopped

½ teaspoon salt

½ teaspoon freshly ground black pepper

2 tablespoons extra virgin olive oil

3 tablespoons chopped fresh basil or parsley

1. In a 4- or 5-quart electric slow cooker, combine the edamame, corn, onion, zucchini, tomatoes, salt, pepper, and olive oil. Mix well.

2. Cover and cook on the low heat setting for 4 to 4½ hours or on the high heat setting for 2 to 2½ hours, until the onion is softened and the zucchini is tender.

3. Add the basil. Season with additional salt and pepper to taste.

slow-roast fall vegetables

Makes 8 to 10 servings

A lovely mix of late-summer and early-fall vegetables are steam-baked in the pot, moistened only with a douse of good olive oil until they are soft and creamy but still hold their shape. Serve with roast chicken, beef, lamb, or pork.

2 pounds baby red new potatoes, preferably organic,
    no more than 1½ inches in diameter, scrubbed

1½ pounds parsnips, peeled and cut on the diagonal into
    1½-inch pieces

1 pound large carrots, peeled and cut on the diagonal into
    1½-inch pieces

1 large fennel bulb (¾ to 1 pound), trimmed and cut
    lengthwise into 10 or 12 wedges

6 to 8 whole garlic cloves, peeled

3 sprigs of fresh thyme, preferably lemon thyme, or
    ½ teaspoon dried thyme leaves

¼ cup extra virgin olive oil

2 teaspoons coarse salt

½ teaspoon coarsely cracked black pepper

1. Put all the ingredients into a 5- or 6-quart electric slow cooker. Toss gently to mix and coat the vegetables lightly with the oil.

2. Cover and cook on the high heat setting for 3 hours, or until the vegetables are tender but not mushy when pierced with the tip of a knife. If you are around, stir them once or twice while they are cooking, moving the bottom pieces up to the top and vice versa.

3. Serve hot, with the juices on the bottom of the pot sprinkled over the vegetables. If you make this dish in advance and want to reheat it, let the vegetables return to room temperature. Spread them out on a baking sheet and drizzle the juices over them. Broil about 4 inches from the heat, stirring once, until they are hot, about 5 minutes. The touch of caramelization will add extra flavor.

barley casserole with artichokes and tomatoes

Makes 8 to 10 servings

This is a terrific accompaniment to broiled or grilled meats, fish, or chicken. You can easily turn it into a one-pot meal by adding some cut-up pieces of rotisserie chicken from the market.

1½ cups pearl barley

1 can (13.75 ounces) artichoke hearts

1 medium onion, chopped

3½ cups chicken broth

3 tablespoons dry sherry

1½ teaspoons dried basil

½ teaspoon seasoned salt

¼ teaspoon freshly ground black pepper

2 medium tomatoes, halved, seeded, and chopped

3 tablespoons chopped fresh basil

⅓ cup crumbled feta cheese

1. Rinse the barley in several changes of cold water; drain well. Drain the artichokes, rinse them well to remove all their brine, and drain again. Quarter the artichoke hearts.

2. In a 4-quart electric slow cooker, combine the barley, quartered artichoke hearts, onion, broth, sherry, dried basil, seasoned salt, and pepper. Mix well.

3. Cover and cook on the low heat setting for 4½ to 5 hours, or until the barley is tender but not mushy and all the liquid is absorbed.

4. Stir in the chopped tomatoes and fresh basil. Serve with the feta cheese sprinkled over the top.

polenta slow cooker style

Makes 6 to 8 servings

Best results are achieved when cooking polenta on the high-heat setting, which allows the starch in the grain to expand and cook properly. Unlike polenta cooked on top of the stove, no stirring is required. This makes a great foil for sausages and peppers, marinara sauce, or sautéed mushrooms.

1½ cups fine polenta or yellow cornmeal, preferably stone-ground
3 tablespoons freshly grated Parmesan cheese
2 tablespoons butter
Sea salt

1. Pour 4½ cups of water into a 3-quart electric slow cooker. Gradually whisk in the polenta until it is well blended and there are no lumps.

2. Cover and cook on the high heat setting for 2¾ to 3 hours, until the polenta is thickened and the grains are tender.

3. Add the Parmesan cheese and butter. Stir until melted and smooth. Season with salt to taste. Serve at once.

Cook's Note

➤ Polenta can be made in advance, but it will thicken and set, which allows it to be reheated with even more flavor: Spread out the soft polenta in a baking dish and let cool completely. Wrapped well, the polenta can be refrigerated overnight. Shortly before cooking, cut the polenta into squares, diamonds, or triangles. Fry in olive oil or butter until crisp and golden brown; or dot with a little more cheese and butter and broil until hot and browned on top.

creamy polenta with fontina cheese

It's almost magical how the slow cooker produces perfect, smooth polenta with almost no stirring.

2 cups fine polenta or yellow cornmeal, preferably stone-ground
1 tablespoon extra virgin olive oil
1½ teaspoons salt
Dash of cayenne pepper
2 tablespoons heavy cream (optional)
1½ to 2 cups shredded Italian fontina cheese

1. Put the cornmeal in a 3½- or 4-quart electric slow cooker. Gradually stir in 5 cups of cold water until very well blended. Stir in the olive oil, salt, and cayenne.

2. Cover and cook on the high heat setting for 2½ to 3 hours, until the polenta is soft and thickened and has lost any trace of a pasty taste. If you're around, give the mixture a quick stir every half hour or so.

3. Stir in the cream, if desired, and the cheese and cook for 30 minutes longer. If you're not ready to serve, paint the top with a little more oil to prevent a skin from forming and leave on the warm setting.

slow cooker quinoa

Makes 8 to 12 servings

A staple grain of the ancient Incas that is very high in protein, quinoa has a delicate nutty flavor and cooks to a light fluffy texture. The only key to cooking quinoa is to rinse it first to remove an outer coating that can be slightly bitter. Serve quinoa as a side dish the same way you would rice or another grain. Leftovers can be added to salads, soups, and cooked vegetables.

2 cups quinoa, preferably organic
4 cups chicken broth or water
Salt and freshly ground black pepper
Butter or Asian sesame oil (optional)

1. Rinse the quinoa in several changes of warm water. Drain into a sieve.

2. In a 4-quart electric slow cooker, combine the quinoa and broth. Cover and cook on the low heat setting for 2½ to 3 hours, until all the broth is absorbed and the quinoa is soft but not mushy and the little white rings, or halos, become visible around the outside edges of the grain.

3. Season with salt and pepper to taste. Toss the hot quinoa with a little butter or sesame oil, if desired.

slow cooker rice

T he slow cooker does an amazing job of cooking rice. Although it takes longer to cook, there's no problem with sticking or boiling over. And for a party, the machine allows you to free up another burner. For the best, most consistent results, be sure to use converted rice. I often stir in a tablespoon or two of butter before serving.

Makes 8 servings

2 cups converted long-grain white rice, such as Uncle Ben's
4 cups boiling water
½ teaspoon salt

1. Place the rice in a 4-quart slow cooker. Stir in the boiling water and salt

2. Cover and cook on the high heat setting for 1¼ to 1½ hours or on the low heat setting for 2 to 2¼ hours, until all the water is absorbed and the rice is tender but not mushy.

3. Transfer the rice to a serving dish and fluff with a fork.

Cook's Note

➤ If you don't want to fuss with boiling water, follow the recipe above using water from the tap, but cook on the high heat setting for 1¾ to 2 hours or on the low heat setting for 2½ to 3 hours.

warm rice salad

Rice salad makes a pleasant alternative to potato or pasta salad, and this one is so good warm, you'll want to serve it with everything: chicken, pork, turkey, even beef. While it's excellent as soon as it comes out of the pot, the salad is equally good at room temperature or even slightly chilled. To transform from a side dish to the main event, simply toss in about 2 cups diced cooked chicken, turkey, or shrimp.

1½ cups converted long-grain white rice

5 tablespoons red or white wine vinegar

½ cup chopped dried apricots

⅓ cup raisins

2 bell peppers, preferably 1 red and 1 yellow, chopped

1 tablespoon Dijon mustard

¼ teaspoon salt

¼ teaspoon freshly ground black pepper

¼ cup extra virgin olive oil

2 scallions, thinly sliced

¼ cup chopped toasted almonds

1. Put the rice into a 4-quart electric slow cooker. Add 2 table-spoons of the vinegar, the dried apricots, raisins, bell peppers, and 3 cups of water. Mix well.

2. Cover and cook on the low heat setting for 2½ to 3 hours, or until the rice is tender and the liquid is absorbed. Do not over-cook the rice. Remove the stoneware insert from the pot and fluff the rice with a fork.

3. In a glass measuring cup or small bowl, whisk together the remaining 3 tablespoons vinegar with the mustard, salt, and pepper. Gradually whisk in the olive oil until the dressing is well blended.

4. Pour the vinaigrette over the rice. Add the scallions and toss to mix well. Sprinkle the almonds on top.

Follow regular food-safety precautions when preparing foods for the slow cooker. Wash hands and surfaces often. Keep raw meats and poultry separate from cooked foods—and never put them on the same cutting board unless it has been thoroughly washed, cleaned, and disinfected in between.

tex-mex rice and corn casserole

Makes 10 to 12 servings

Give rice south-of-the-border flair in this simple creation. Serve alongside other fiesta-style fare—or with almost any grilled meats.

1 jar (16 ounces) thick and chunky salsa, mild or
   medium-hot to taste
2 cups corn kernels (about 16 ounces)
2 cups converted long-grain white rice
1 small onion, chopped
½ teaspoon salt
¼ teaspoon freshly ground black pepper
⅓ cup canned diced green chiles
1 cup shredded Cheddar cheese
¼ cup chopped fresh cilantro, for garnish

1. In a 4-quart electric slow cooker, mix together the salsa, corn, rice, onion, salt, pepper, and 2 cups of water.

2. Cover and cook on the low heat setting for 2½ to 3 hours, or until the rice is tender but not mushy. Stir in the chiles and cheese. Garnish with a sprinkling of cilantro.

black beans and rice

Makes 6 to 8 servings

Orange juice, lime juice, and grated orange peel give this dish good flavor. Serve with grilled meats, fish, or poultry. Salsa makes a nice condiment to accompany the dish. Reheat any leftovers in the microwave oven.

2 cans (15 ounces each) black beans, rinsed and drained

1 cup converted long-grain white rice

1 small onion, chopped

½ cup thawed frozen orange juice concentrate

1 can (4 ounces) diced green chiles

3 tablespoons fresh lime juice

1½ teaspoons ground cumin

½ teaspoon salt

¼ teaspoon freshly ground black pepper

1 teaspoon grated orange zest

1. In a 4-quart electric slow cooker, combine the beans, rice, onion, orange juice concentrate, chiles, 2 tablespoons of the lime juice, the cumin, salt, pepper, and 1½ cups of water. Mix well.

2. Cover and cook on the low heat setting for 2¾ to 3 hours, until the rice is tender but not mushy. Stir in the remaining 1 tablespoon lime juice and the orange zest and serve.

curried rice pilaf

Makes 8 to 10 servings

This fabulous rice is a family holiday tradition in my home whenever ham is served. It's also good with shrimp, grilled fish, and chicken or with roasted or grilled vegetables. If you need to feed a few more, stir in 1 pound of thawed frozen baby peas at the end of the cooking time, cover, and cook for a few minutes longer to heat through. Making this in a slow cooker streamlines the conventional technique and avoids the need to cook the rice and onions in butter before adding the liquid and spices. This recipe is not forgiving, so watch and cook until the rice is just tender and the grains separate.

2 cups converted long-grain white rice
1 large onion, quartered and thinly sliced
4 tablespoons butter, melted
1½ tablespoons Madras curry powder
1¼ teaspoons ground cumin
½ teaspoon ground turmeric
¼ teaspoon ground ginger
⅛ teaspoon ground chipotle chile
¼ teaspoon freshly ground black pepper
¼ teaspoon seasoned salt
⅓ cup chopped fresh parsley

1. In a 4-quart electric slow cooker, combine the rice, onion, melted butter, curry powder, cumin, turmeric, ginger, chipotle chile, and pepper. Stir in 4 cups of water.

2. Cover and cook on the low heat setting for 2¾ to 3 hours or on the high heat setting for 2 to 2¼ hours, until the liquid is absorbed and the rice is tender and cooked through but not mushy.

3. Stir in the seasoned salt and parsley. Serve immediately.

smoky red beans and rice

Makes 8 servings

Spanish smoked paprika is readily available at supermarkets now; several of the major spice companies include it in their line. I love the way the smoky flavor livens up this dish.

1 cup converted long-grain white rice, such as Uncle Ben's
2 cans (15 ounces each) red kidney beans, rinsed and drained well
1 can (10 ounces) diced tomatoes and green chiles
1 medium onion, chopped
1 red bell pepper, chopped
1 tablespoon ground cumin
1 tablespoon smoked paprika
Sea salt and freshly ground black pepper

1. In a 4-quart electric slow cooker, combine the rice, beans, tomatoes and chiles, onion, bell pepper, cumin, smoked paprika, and 2½ cups of water. Stir well.

2. Cover and cook on the low heat setting for 3¼ to 3½ hours, or until the liquid is absorbed and the rice is tender but still retains it shape.

3. Season with salt and pepper to taste. Serve immediately.

artichoke-parmesan risotto

Makes 5 to 6 servings

Risotto in a slow cooker? You bet! It's a great way to make real Italian risotto effortlessly. There's no stirring in the pot and no guesswork. But you must be home to take this out of the cooker as soon as it is done.

2 tablespoons extra virgin olive oil

1 small onion, chopped

1½ cups Arborio rice

¾ cup dry white wine

3½ cups chicken broth

1 cup chopped thawed frozen artichoke hearts, well drained

½ cup freshly grated Parmesan-Romano cheese blend

Sea salt and freshly ground black pepper

1. In a large skillet, heat the olive oil. Add the onion and cook over medium heat, stirring occasionally, until soft, 3 to 4 minutes. Stir in the rice and cook, stirring often, for 3 to 4 minutes, until the grains turn opaque. Stir in the wine and heat to boiling.

2. Turn the hot rice mixture into a 4-quart electric slow cooker. Stir in the broth and artichoke hearts.

3. Cover and cook on the high heat setting for 2¼ to 2½ hours, until all the liquid is absorbed but the rice is still moist. Stir in the cheese and season with salt and pepper to taste. Serve immediately.

slow cooker brown rice

Makes about 6 cups cooked rice; 8 servings

Be sure to start with boiling water here to jump-start the cooking. Otherwise you'll end up with an undesirable result—very mushy rice. Note: Do not add butter to the cooked rice if you plan to use leftovers in salads, soups, or other dishes.

1½ cups long-grain brown rice
3 cups boiling water
¼ teaspoon salt
2 tablespoons butter

1. Place the brown rice in a 3-quart electric slow cooker. Stir in the boiling water.

2. Cover and cook on the high heat setting for about 1½ hours or on the low heat setting for 2¼ to 2½ hours, until all the water is absorbed and the rice is tender with the grains separate, but not mushy.

3. Season with the salt and stir in the butter until melted. Serve immediately.

Variation

Mexican Fiesta Brown Rice: Instead of stirring in the salt and butter after the rice has finished cooking, stir in ¾ cup sour cream, ¾ cup chunky prepared salsa, and 1 cup shredded Cheddar or Jack cheese. Cover and cook on the low heat setting for 10 to 20 minutes, stirring once, until the cheese is melted.

wild rice with apricots and almonds

Makes 4 to 6 servings

Wild rice takes a long time to cook on top of the stove, and it needs monitoring to make sure the liquid doesn't evaporate. Cooking it slowly in the pot makes a lot more sense. Just put it in and walk away. This recipe dresses up the wild rice with crunchy almonds and tangy dried fruit. It's a nice dish to serve with turkey or pork.

1 cup wild rice, rinsed well and drained
2¼ cups hot water
1 medium onion, finely chopped
1 cup chopped celery
¼ cup sliced almonds
¼ cup chopped dried apricots or dried cherries
Kosher salt and freshly ground black pepper

1. In a 3- or 3½-quart electric slow cooker, combine the wild rice, hot water, onion, and celery. Stir to mix.

2. Cover and cook on the low heat setting for about 3 hours, or until the water is absorbed and the wild rice is cooked through and tender; the dark grains will start to split and show their white interiors.

3. Fluff with a fork. Stir in the almonds and apricots and season with salt and pepper to taste.

almost-instant mixed vegetables and rice

Makes 6 servings

Here's a quickie for when you need to throw dinner together in a flash. Toss a couple of packages in the pot, and you've got your starch and vegetables. It saves prep time and is a good way to make a side dish for holidays or other times when you don't have room on top of the stove or you don't want to heat up the kitchen.

1 package (6 ounces) long-grain and wild rice mix
    (Uncle Ben's original recipe with herbs and seasonings)
2 cups boiling water
1 bag (16 ounces) frozen vegetable blend (preferably a
    mix of julienne carrots, cut baby corn, water chestnuts,
    broccoli florets, mushrooms, sugar snap peas, red peppers,
    and onions), thawed and drained
1 tablespoon butter
Lemon pepper

1. In a 3-quart electric slow cooker, combine the rice and contents of the seasoning packet from the rice box, the boiling water, and the thawed and drained vegetables.

2. Cover and cook on the low heat setting for 2¾ to 3 hours, or until all the water is absorbed and the rice is tender.

3. Add the butter and toss until melted. Season with lemon pepper to taste.

When seasoning mixes included in packaged foods are called for, no additional salt is listed in the recipe, since there is usually a generous amount included. Of course, you can always season with salt and pepper to taste before serving.

slow-cooked buttermilk cornbread

Makes 10 to 12 servings

No one will guess this didn't come out of an oven. It's a moist and flavorful cornbread with a lovely golden brown crust. Serve warm, with plenty of butter.

6 tablespoons butter, cut into pieces

1½ cups buttermilk

2 large eggs

½ cup sugar

2 cups yellow cornmeal

1 cup all-purpose flour

2 teaspoons baking powder

½ teaspoon salt

The crockery inserts in most pots are microwave-, oven-, and dishwasher-safe (up to around 400°F or so, depending on the manufacturer—check your manual), but should not be used on top of the stove unless specifically designed to do so, in which case it will be indicated in the manufacturer's instruction book.

1. Line a buttered 4-quart electric slow cooker with a piece of non-stick aluminum foil, cut to fit the bottom.

2. In a large glass bowl, melt the butter in a microwave oven on high power for 20 to 30 seconds. Or melt in a small saucepan on top of the stove over low heat and pour into a large bowl.

3. Whisk in the buttermilk, eggs, and sugar until well blended. Then whisk in the cornmeal, flour, baking powder, and salt quickly until just well blended. Transfer the batter to the cooker, spreading it out evenly.

4. Cover and cook on the high heat setting for 1½ to 1¾ hours, or until a cake tester or pick inserted in the center comes out clean. Watch carefully to avoid overcooking. Remove the insert and run a knife around the edges to loosen the bread. Let cool slightly, then cut into slices or wedges.

savory sausage stuffing

Makes 8 to 10 servings

Don't wait for the holidays to enjoy a tasty bread stuffing. This fabulous recipe is versatile and flexible. If you like a hint of sweetness in your dressing, include ½ cup dried cherries or diced dried apricots. If you like nuts, you can also add a generous ¾ cup toasted pecans.

12 to 14 ounces fully cooked sun-dried tomato sausages, Polish kielbasa, or spicy Southwestern-style sausages
1 medium onion, chopped
2 cups chopped celery
¾ cup chicken broth
1 box (12 ounces) seasoned dressing or stuffing mix
1 stick (4 ounces) unsalted butter, melted
¼ cup plus 1 tablespoon chopped fresh parsley
½ teaspoon freshly ground black pepper

Cook's Notes

➤ If your box of stuffing has two packages inside, use them both. You need to include the full contents of the 12-ounce box.

➤ Do not season the stuffing with salt; seasoned packaged dressings contain plenty.

➤ If you're not using homemade chicken broth, try to buy broth that is 99 percent fat free and reduced sodium.

1. Peel off the sausage casings. Chop the sausages. Add to a large skillet along with the onion and celery. Cook over medium-high heat, stirring often, until the sausages are browned and the onion is softened, 7 to 8 minutes. Drain off all but about 1 tablespoon of the fat.

2. Transfer the sausage mixture to a large bowl. Pour the broth into the skillet and bring to a boil, using a wooden spoon or spatula to scrape up all the browned bits from the bottom of the pan. Pour the broth over the sausage.

3. Add the dressing or stuffing mix, melted butter, ¼ cup of the chopped parsley, and the pepper to the bowl. Mix well. Transfer to a 4-quart electric slow cooker.

4. Cover and cook on the low heat setting for about 4 hours. Serve with the remaining 1 tablespoon chopped parsley sprinkled on top.

breakfast and brunch

Mornings are a great time to take advantage of your slow cooker. You can put up your flavored oatmeal the night before, or pop a colorful egg strata, French Toast Bake, Chunky Chicken Hash, or even Blueberry Coffee Cake into the pot first thing in the morning and greet your guests a few hours later with a hot brunch in a cool kitchen. The reason you cannot leave some of these dishes overnight in the pot is that eggs cook best on the high heat setting.

breakfast and brunch

slow-cooked steel-cut oats

Makes 3 to 4 servings

Cooking oatmeal overnight opens up a whole new world of breakfast when you want it— and cuts down on prep time when you're in a hurry in the morning. I like it best sprinkled with chopped nuts, drizzled with maple syrup, or sprinkled with brown sugar and doused with milk or cream, if I'm splurging. Refrigerate any leftovers in a covered container; reheat in a microwave oven before serving.

1 cup steel-cut oats or Irish oatmeal
1 teaspoon ground cinnamon
¼ to ½ teaspoon grated nutmeg

1. In a 3- or 4-quart electric slow cooker, combine the oats, cinnamon, nutmeg, and 4 cups of water. Whisk together until thoroughly combined.

2. Cover and cook on the low heat setting for 8 hours, or until the oats are tender. Stir well and serve.

Variation

Stir ⅓ cup dried fruit, such as raisins, chopped apricots, cherries, or cranberries, into the pot at the outset of cooking.

overnight oatmeal with cinnamon and bananas

Makes 4 servings

Start this just before you go to bed at night—and you'll wake up to a pot of oatmeal, ready to embellish and eat in the morning. This yields a medium-thick porridge. If you like your oatmeal thinner, add an additional ½ to ¾ cup water at the outset of cooking.

2 cups old-fashioned 100 percent whole-grain rolled oats (*not* quick-cooking oats)
1 teaspoon ground cinnamon
¼ teaspoon ground nutmeg
2 bananas, peeled and sliced
Brown sugar and milk or cream, as accompaniments

1. In a 4-quart electric slow cooker, combine the oats, cinnamon, nutmeg, and 4 cups of water, whisking well to thoroughly combine.

2. Cover and cook on the low heat setting for 7½ to 8 hours, or until the oats are tender and the porridge is a medium-thick consistency. Stir well.

3. Spoon the oatmeal into bowls and top with banana slices and a sprinkling of brown sugar. Pass a pitcher of milk on the side.

Variation

The oatmeal can also be cooked without the cinnamon and nutmeg and served plain with the milk—and no fruit, if desired.

french toast bake

Makes 6 servings

Serve this easily assembled French toast casserole for breakfast or brunch. Pass additional maple syrup or a fruit syrup on the side, or top with a sprinkling of powdered sugar and accompany with fresh seasonal fruits.

12 slices of raisin bread
6 tablespoons butter, melted
2 teaspoons ground cinnamon
⅓ cup packed brown sugar
4 large eggs
2 cups milk
2 tablespoons maple syrup
1 teaspoon vanilla extract

1. Cover the bottom of a 4-quart electric slow cooker with 3 slices of bread, cutting them to fit as necessary. Combine the melted butter, cinnamon, and brown sugar; mix well. Dab about 2 tablespoons over the bread in the slow cooker, spreading to cover. Add another 3 bread slices and drizzle with more of the butter. Add 3 more bread slices and another drizzle of butter mixture. Top with the 3 remaining bread slices and the remaining butter.

2. In a medium bowl, whisk the eggs until well blended. Whisk in the milk, maple syrup, and vanilla. Pour over the bread in the slow cooker and press the bread down into the egg mixture.

3. Cover and cook on the high heat setting for 2½ to 3 hours, or until puffed and set. Remove the lid and let stand for 5 minutes before serving.

chunky chicken hash

Rely on convenient frozen hash browns to streamline preparations for this meal-in-a-pot. For color, garnish with chopped fresh tomatoes and parsley. Serve with fruit salad for brunch or with a spinach salad or steamed broccoli for a light supper.

1 pound skinless, boneless chicken thighs

1 large package (32 ounces) frozen hash-brown potatoes, thawed

1 can (14.5 ounces) petite-cut diced tomatoes with sweet onions and roasted garlic

1 can (4 ounces) mushroom stems and pieces, drained

1 can (4 ounces) diced green chiles

1 can (3.8 ounces) sliced ripe olives, well drained

2 teaspoons Cajun seasoning mix or 1 teaspoon each ground cumin and chili powder

Salt and freshly ground black pepper

To avoid burning your fingers, use pot holders or mitts to remove the stoneware insert when cooking is complete.

1. Pat the chicken thighs dry with paper towels. Trim off as much fat as possible. Cut the meat into ¾-inch pieces.

2. In a 4-quart electric slow cooker, combine the chicken chunks with the potatoes, tomatoes with their juices, mushrooms, chiles, olives, and Cajun seasoning until blended.

3. Cover and cook on the low heat setting for 4½ to 5 hours, or until the chicken is cooked through and the potatoes are tender. Season with salt and pepper to taste.

Variation

Sprinkle ¾ cup shredded Cheddar cheese over the top for the last 10 minutes of cooking time.

chicken enchilada casserole

Mexican food makes wonderful brunch food. This dish has all the exciting flavor of Mexican enchiladas layered in a casserole. If there are any leftovers, they reheat well in a microwave oven. Be sure to garnish with some bright bits, such as red bell pepper, black olives, or green cilantro, for an attractive presentation.

2 cups canned green enchilada sauce

6 corn tortillas (6 to 7 inches in diameter)

1 pound diced cooked skinless, boneless chicken breast
   (about 3½ cups)

2 cups shredded mozzarella or Monterey Jack cheese

¾ cup thick and chunky salsa

Sour cream, guacamole, and chopped tomatoes, for topping

1. In a 3- to 4-quart electric slow cooker, spread ½ cup of the green enchilada sauce evenly over the bottom of the pot. Add 2 tortillas, tearing as necessary to fit in a single layer. Spread ¾ cup of the enchilada sauce evenly over the tortillas. Scatter half the chicken over the sauce and 1 cup of the cheese over the chicken. Top with 2 more tortillas, again tearing to fit. Repeat with another layer of the remaining enchilada sauce, chicken, and cheese. Top with the last 2 tortillas and drizzle the salsa over all, spreading to cover.

2. Cover and cook on the low heat setting for 4 to 5 hours or on the high heat setting for 2 to 2½ hours, until very hot and bubbly. Serve hot, topped with sour cream, guacamole, and tomatoes.

chicken-tortilla casserole

Makes 6 servings

Everyone loves an easy one-pot dish, especially when it's topped with sour cream, chopped tomatoes, and avocado slices. Be sure to serve the casserole like a lasagna, cutting down into the dish so everyone gets some of each layer.

3¾ cups (about two 16-ounce jars) chunky tomato salsa, mild or medium

5 or 6 whole wheat, regular flour, or corn tortillas (7 to 8 inches in diameter)

1 bag (16 ounces) frozen white corn kernels, thawed and well drained

3 cups diced cooked skinless, boneless chicken breast (about 1 pound)

3½ cups shredded Mexican cheese blend or a combination of half Cheddar and half Monterey Jack

Sour cream, chopped tomatoes and avocado slices, for garnish

1. Spoon 2 tablespoons of the salsa evenly over the bottom of a 4-quart oval electric slow cooker. Add a layer of 1½ to 2 tortillas, tearing if necessary to fit into the cooker insert.

2. Stir together 3 cups of the salsa with the corn and spoon one-third of the mixture over the tortillas in the pot. Sprinkle 1 cup of the chicken and then 1 cup of the cheese over the corn mixture. Repeat these layers two more times. Top with the remaining salsa, spreading it evenly.

3. Cover and cook on the low heat setting for 4 to 4½ hours. Sprinkle the remaining ½ cup cheese over the top. Cover and cook for 5 to 15 minutes longer, until the cheese is melted. Serve topped with sour cream, chopped tomatoes, and sliced avocado.

cheddar strata with artichokes and green chiles

Makes 6 to 8 servings

Serve this delicious brunch or supper dish with assorted fresh fruits or a tossed salad.

1 tablespoon butter, softened

8 large slices of Italian or sourdough bread, cut into 1-inch cubes

3 cups shredded sharp Cheddar cheese

1 can (4 ounces) diced green chiles

1 can (13.75 ounces) artichoke hearts, rinsed, well drained, and quartered

4 large eggs

2½ cups milk

1 tablespoon Dijon mustard

½ teaspoon seasoned salt

¼ teaspoon seasoned pepper

Tomato salsa, for garnish

1. Grease a 4-quart electric slow cooker with the softened butter. Place half of the bread cubes in the bottom of the pot. Sprinkle 1½ cups of the cheese evenly over the bread. Top with half of the green chiles and half of the quartered artichoke hearts. Add another layer of the remaining bread cubes and then the remaining artichoke hearts and chiles. Sprinkle the remaining cheese on top.

2. In a medium bowl, beat the eggs lightly. Whisk in the milk, mustard, seasoned salt, and seasoned pepper. Beat until well blended. Pour the eggs over the cheese and bread mixture in the slow cooker.

3. Cover and cook on the high heat setting for 2½ to 2¾ hours, or until the strata is cooked through, set, and puffed. Let stand for 5 minutes before serving. Top with a dollop of salsa.

ham and cheese brunch strata

Makes 8 to 10 servings

Finding a good egg bread, such as brioche or challah, will make all the difference in flavor here. Since the strata cooks for such a long time, you needn't worry whether the bread is stale or not. Any leftover strata can be stored in the refrigerator and reheated in a microwave oven in a very short time.

1 loaf (16 ounces) egg bread, such as brioche or challah, cut into
 ¾-inch cubes

1½ cups shredded mozzarella, Monterey Jack, or Manchego cheese

1½ cups shredded Cheddar cheese

1 can (4 ounces) diced green chiles

⅔ cup chopped roasted red peppers

¾ cup pimiento-stuffed olives, coarsely chopped

2 cups diced flavorful cooked ham, such as Black Forest

6 large eggs

3 cups milk

1 teaspoon smoked paprika

½ teaspoon seasoned pepper

1. Scatter one-third of the bread cubes evenly over the bottom of a 5-quart electric slow cooker. Mix together both cheeses. Sprinkle 1½ cups of the cheese and half each of the green chiles, roasted peppers, olives, and ham over the bread in the cooker. Add half the remaining bread cubes, sprinkling them evenly with the remaining cheese, green chiles, red peppers, olives, and ham. Top evenly with the remaining bread cubes.

2. In a medium bowl, beat the eggs lightly. Then whisk in the milk, ½ teaspoon of the smoked paprika, and the seasoned pepper until well blended. Pour over the bread mixture in the slow cooker, pressing the cubes down lightly to submerge them in the custard. Sprinkle the remaining ½ teaspoon smoked paprika over the top.

3. Cover and cook on the high heat setting for 2¾ to 3 hours, or until the strata is puffed and cooked through. Remove the cover and cook for 10 minutes longer. Let stand for 5 to 10 minutes to cool and set up before serving.

two-cheese strata with prosciutto, red peppers, and basil

Makes 6 to 8 servings

Perfect for brunch or even a weekend lunch, this savory bread pudding needs only a green salad and maybe a mimosa beforehand. It's a sophisticated dish that would be perfect for company.

1 tablespoon butter, softened

6 to 8 slices of Italian bread

¼ pound very thinly sliced prosciutto

1 jar (12 ounces) roasted red peppers, rinsed, well drained, and cut into large pieces

4 ounces fresh white goat cheese, crumbled

2¾ cups shredded Gruyère or sharp Cheddar cheese

¼ cup chopped scallions

14 large fresh basil leaves

4 large eggs

1½ tablespoons Dijon mustard

2 cups half-and-half

½ teaspoon salt

¼ teaspoon freshly ground black pepper

1. Grease a 4-quart oval electric slow cooker with the softened butter. Line the bottom with 2 bread slices, cutting the pieces to fit. Arrange one-third of the prosciutto slices over the bread. Top with half of the roasted red pepper pieces. Sprinkle half of the goat cheese and then 1 cup of the Gruyère over the peppers. Add half of the scallions and half of the basil leaves, distributing them evenly. Cover with a second layer of bread slices. Then layer on the remaining red peppers, half of the remaining prosciutto, another 1 cup Gruyère, the remaining scallions, and the rest of the basil leaves. Finally, top with the remaining bread slices and then the remaining prosciutto slices

2. In a medium bowl, beat the eggs to break them up, then whisk in the mustard until blended. Gradually whisk in the half-and-half, salt, and pepper, beating until well blended. Pour evenly over the top, then press down on the bread with a wide flat spatula to submerge them in the custard.

3. Cover and cook on the high heat setting for 2½ to 2¾ hours, or until the strata is puffed and almost set. Sprinkle the remaining ¾ cup Gruyère cheese over the top and cook on high, covered, for 15 minutes longer. Uncover and let stand for at least 10 and up to 30 minutes to firm up before serving. Serve the strata hot, warm, or at room temperature.

pastrami and rye reuben casserole

Makes 6 to 8 servings

f you love deli, you'll really enjoy this casserole, which incorporates all the flavors of a Reuben sandwich in a strata. It's great for supper or for a substantial brunch dish, especially if it's Super Bowl Sunday. Serve with a tomato salad.

8 slices of rye bread

6 tablespoons Thousand Island dressing (use your favorite brand)

½ pound thinly sliced lean pastrami, regular or hickory-smoked turkey pastrami, or corned beef

2 pounds jarred crispy sauerkraut, rinsed and well drained

1 teaspoon caraway seeds

3 dill pickles, thinly sliced lengthwise

2¾ cups shredded Swiss cheese (10 to 12 ounces)

4 large eggs

1¾ cups milk

2 tablespoons prepared yellow mustard

1. Cover the bottom of a 5-quart electric slow cooker with 3 slices of the bread, tearing or cutting as necessary to fit in a single layer. Dollop 2½ tablespoons Thousand Island dressing over the bread and spread evenly. Cover with half of the pastrami slices. Top the meat with half of the sauerkraut, ½ teaspoon caraway seeds, and half of the pickles. Sprinkle with 1 cup of the cheese. Cover with 3 more bread slices, another 2½ tablespoons dressing, and the remaining pastrami, sauerkraut, caraway seeds, and pickles. Sprinkle with another 1 cup of the cheese. Spread the remaining 1 tablespoon dressing over the last 2 bread slices and cut into 1-inch cubes. Scatter them evenly over the top of the casserole.

2. In a medium bowl, whisk together the eggs, milk, and mustard until well mixed. Pour into the pot. Press the bread cubes down gently to submerge them in the egg mixture.

3. Cover and cook on the high heat setting for 2½ to 2¾ hours, or until the eggs are cooked through and set. Sprinkle the remaining ¾ cup cheese on top and continue cooking, uncovered, for 10 to 15 minutes longer, until the cheese is melted.

4. Let the strata cool and set for 10 minutes before serving.

spinach-cheese torte

Serve this as an entree for brunch, lunch, or dinner. Accompany with warm Canadian bacon slices and fresh fruit, skewered attractively or cut up to make a salad.

5 large eggs

1 container (16 ounces) cottage cheese

2 tablespoons all-purpose flour

1 package (9 ounces) prewashed fresh spinach, finely chopped

4 scallions, chopped

¾ cup freshly grated Parmesan and Pecorino Romano cheese blend

½ teaspoon seasoned salt

½ teaspoon freshly ground black pepper

Cook's Note

➤ Although 9 ounces of spinach doesn't sound like much, it measures about 9 cups. To make chopping easy, pulse in your food processor, in two batches if necessary. You should end up with 4 cups of chopped spinach.

1. Line an 8-inch springform pan with aluminum foil.

2. In a medium bowl, whisk together the eggs until well beaten. Blend in the cottage cheese and flour. Stir in the spinach, scallions, cheese, seasoned salt, and pepper. Pour the mixture into the lined pan.

3. Place the pan on a rack in the bottom of a 5-quart electric slow cooker. Do not add any water to the pot.

4. Cover and cook on the high heat setting for 3½ to 4 hours, or until set in the center; do not use low heat for this recipe. Let the torte stand for 10 to 15 minutes before serving.

Remember to unplug the slow cooker when cooking is complete.

raspberries and cream brunch strata

Makes 5 to 6 servings

For those who would rather eat coffee cake than bread and cheese, this is yummy and on the sweet side, which makes it perfect for a special, late, and leisurely weekend breakfast. Serve with fresh fruit salad and big mugs of freshly brewed coffee or hot chocolate.

1 tablespoon butter, softened

8 large slices of shepherd's bread or egg bread, cut into 1-inch cubes (about 8 cups)

1 package (8 ounces) cream cheese, cut into ¾-inch cubes

⅓ cup raspberry jam

1 small container (6 ounces) fresh raspberries, rinsed and dried

6 large eggs

1 teaspoon vanilla extract

3 tablespoons granulated sugar

1½ cups milk

Confectioners' sugar, for topping

1. Grease a 4-quart oval electric slow cooker with the softened butter. Arrange half of the bread cubes over the bottom of the pot. Scatter the cream cheese cubes evenly over the bread. Dot with the jam, spreading it out as much as possible. Sprinkle half of the raspberries over the jam and top with the remaining bread cubes and raspberries.

2. Beat together the eggs, vanilla, and granulated sugar until well blended. Beat in the milk until thoroughly combined. Pour over the bread in the slow cooker.

3. Cover and cook on the high heat setting for 2¼ to 2½ hours, or until set. Remove the cover and let the strata stand for 5 minutes to set up. Then dust confectioners' sugar liberally over the top and serve.

applesauce cake with raisins and walnuts

Makes 8 to 10 servings

B e sure to use the high heat setting and to check the cake as it nears the end of the cooking time to avoid overbaking. Serve this homey, old-fashioned dessert with whipped cream or a scoop of your favorite ice cream.

1 stick (4 ounces) butter, melted

1 cup granulated sugar

2 large eggs

1½ cups unsweetened applesauce

2 teaspoons ground cinnamon

½ teaspoon ground nutmeg

2 teaspoons vanilla extract

2 cups all-purpose flour

1½ teaspoons baking soda

¼ teaspoon baking powder

½ cup raisins, dried cranberries, or dried cherries

¾ cup chopped walnuts

Confectioners' sugar

1. Line a 4-quart electric slow cooker with nonstick aluminum foil, covering the bottom and about three-quarters of the way up the sides. Smooth out the foil as much as possible.

2. In a large glass bowl or 2-quart microwave-safe glass measuring cup, melt the butter in a microwave oven on high power for 50 to 60 seconds. Whisk in the granulated sugar and eggs until smooth. Beat in the applesauce, cinnamon, nutmeg, and vanilla. Then whisk in the flour, baking soda, and baking powder until blended. Stir in the raisins and walnuts.

3. Turn the batter into the foil-lined pot and smooth the top evenly. Cover and cook on the high heat setting for 2¼ to 2½ hours, or until a cake tester inserted in the center comes out clean. (Do not attempt this recipe on the low heat setting.) Remove the lid and let the cake stand in the slow cooker for a few minutes to set.

4. Using the foil to assist, carefully lift the cake out of the pot in one piece and transfer to a plate. Let cool for 10 to 15 minutes. Dust the top with confectioners' sugar. Serve warm or at room temperature, cut into slices.

blueberry coffee cake

**Makes 1 coffee cake;
6 to 8 servings**

With a taste reminiscent of blueberry muffins, this tender cake is a breeze to bake in the slow cooker pot. Note, though, that the batter will not rise as high as a conventional quick bread. Serve cut into wedges either warm or at room temperature.

1 stick (4 ounces) plus 3 tablespoons butter, softened

½ cup granulated sugar

2 large eggs

1 teaspoon vanilla extract

½ teaspoon grated nutmeg

1½ teaspoons ground cinnamon

1¼ cups plus 1½ tablespoons all-purpose flour

1 teaspoon baking powder

¼ teaspoon baking soda

Few dashes of salt

½ cup nonfat plain yogurt

1 cup fresh or partially thawed frozen blueberries

¾ cup chopped walnuts

¼ cup packed light brown sugar

1. Use 1 tablespoon of the butter to grease a 4-quart round electric slow cooker.

2. In a large bowl with an electric mixer, beat together 1 stick of the butter and the granulated sugar until light and fluffy. Beat in the eggs, vanilla, nutmeg, and 1 teaspoon of the cinnamon until thoroughly blended. On low speed, beat in 1¼ cups of the flour, the baking powder, baking soda, and salt. Add the yogurt and beat just until blended.

3. Toss the blueberries with the remaining 1½ tablespoons flour to coat them lightly. Add to the batter along with ½ cup of the walnuts, folding them in by hand. Turn into the buttered pot.

4. Melt the remaining 2 tablespoons butter and mix with the brown sugar and the remaining ½ teaspoon cinnamon and ¼ cup walnuts. Sprinkle evenly over the top of the cake batter.

5. Cover and cook on the high heat setting for about 2 hours, or until a cake tester or pick inserted in the center comes out clean. Do not overcook. Carefully run a knife around the sides of the pot to loosen the cake. Let the cake cool in the pot for 15 minutes. Then with a big spatula, gently ease the cake out of the pot in one piece and transfer to a serving plate. Let cool completely before cutting into wedges.

cream cheese-pecan pound cake

Makes 1 cake; 10 servings

You'll be surprised how well pound cake turns out in a slow cooker. The crust is thicker than conventionally baked, but the flavor is excellent. I love this cake by itself, toasted with butter and jam, or sliced and topped with fresh berries and a spoonful of whipped cream.

2 sticks (8 ounces) unsalted butter, softened

1 package (8 ounces) cream cheese, softened

1½ cups granulated sugar

2 teaspoons vanilla extract

4 large eggs

2 cups all-purpose flour

2 teaspoons baking powder

Dash of salt

1 cup chopped pecans

Confectioners' sugar

1. Butter the bottom of a 4-quart electric slow cooker. Line the bottom and about three-quarters of the way up the sides with a piece of nonstick aluminum foil. Smooth out the foil as much as possible.

2. In a large bowl with an electric mixer, beat together the butter and cream cheese until soft and creamy. Beat in the granulated sugar and vanilla until light and fluffy. Beat in the eggs, one at a time; don't worry if the batter looks curdled at this point. Beat in the flour, baking powder, and salt until blended. By hand, stir in the nuts. Turn the batter into the cooker, spreading it evenly.

3. Cover and cook on the low heat setting for 3½ to 3¾ hours, or until a cake tester inserted in the center comes out clean. If the slow cooker has a hot spot, pick up the stoneware insert using potholders and turn it around in the base about halfway through the cooking to avoid overbrowning the crust.

4. When the cake is done, turn off the cooker, remove the insert, and let stand for 10 to 15 minutes. Then carefully lift out the cake, using the foil to assist, and place on a serving plate to cool. Peel off the foil and dust the top of the cake with confectioners' sugar. Cut into wedges and serve.

hot orange-sauced fruit

Makes 8 to 10 servings

Here's an unusual fruit cocktail to serve at breakfast or brunch. Mixed canned fruit in a marvelous orange sauce also makes a delicious accompaniment to brunch dishes like waffles or pancakes, ham, or turkey, especially during cold weather or winter months. Serve as a side dish on a brunch or lunch buffet, or offer as a dessert topping for ice cream, pound cake, or angel food cake.

2 large cans (29 ounces each) yellow cling peach slices,
   well drained
1 large can (20 ounces) pineapple chunks, well drained
1 large can (29 ounces) Bartlett pear halves, well drained
   and cut into chunks
¾ cup frozen orange juice concentrate, thawed
2 tablespoons cornstarch
⅔ cup packed brown sugar
2 tablespoons Grand Marnier or other orange-flavored liqueur

1. Put the drained fruits into a 4-quart electric slow cooker.

2. In a small microwave-safe bowl or 4-cup glass measuring cup, whisk together the orange juice concentrate, cornstarch, and ¼ cup of cold water until well blended. Microwave on high power for 1 minute. Whisk until blended. Continue to microwave for 30 to 60 seconds longer, until the sauce is smooth and thickened when whisked. Whisk in the brown sugar until well blended. Add the orange sauce to the fruits in the slow cooker and toss gently.

3. Cover and cook on the high heat setting for about 2½ hours, until the sauce is thickened and bubbly around the edges.

4. Remove the cover and cook for 15 to 20 minutes longer, to thicken slightly. Stir in the orange liqueur. Let cool for at least 10 minutes before serving hot, warm, at room temperature, or even chilled.

To avoid breaking or cracking the stoneware insert, cool completely before cleaning. Do not put a hot ceramic pot in cold water. Never immerse the metal housing in water.

preserves, chutneys, and salsas

One of the best ways to dress up the simplest cooking—a grilled chicken breast, steak, chop, fish fillet, or even burger—is with a drizzle or dollop of a homemade condiment. All of these jams, jellies, chutneys, and salsas are small-batch preserves, resulting in 2 to 3 pints (that's 4 to 6 cups). Recipes like Corn and Black Bean Salsa and Roasted Red Pepper and Onion Relish are meant to be enjoyed fresh. Others, like Apricot-Pineapple Jam, Cherry-Apple Chutney, and Tangy Peach Salsa, can be used fresh or refrigerated or frozen for longer storage. No water-canning processing is necessary.

Many of these condiments are colorful. Besides using them to dress up your own table, they make wonderful house gifts or additions to Christmas baskets of homemade treats. Wrap a decorative square of cloth around the top of the jar, secure it with a ribbon, and attach a small greeting card, which indicates whether the preserve needs refrigeration.

preserves, chutneys, and salsas

apricot-pineapple jam

This jam is particularly good on toasted brioche, whole-grain bread, or a croissant. Since it's made with dried apricots, you can enjoy it year-round.

Makes about 5½ cups

1 pound dried apricots
1 can (20 ounces) unsweetened pineapple chunks in juice
1½ cups orange juice
1 cup sugar

1. Put the apricots into a food processor and pulse to chop into small pieces. Transfer to a 3- or 4-quart electric slow cooker.

2. Drain the pineapple juice from the can into the slow cooker. Cut the pineapple chunks into roughly ¼-inch pieces. Add to the cooker along with the orange juice and sugar.

3. Cover and cook on the low heat setting for 4 hours. Uncover and cook on the high heat setting for 1 to 1¼ hours longer, or until thickened.

4. Let the jam cool, then transfer to jars, cover with lids, and refrigerate for up to 6 weeks or freeze for up to 3 months.

fiery green pepper jelly

Makes about 5 cups

This bright green jelly made the rounds years ago, but recently, fans have started serving it again. You can adjust the heat by how much fresh jalapeño you add. It's a great hors d'oeuvre, most popular spooned atop softened cream cheese or whipped cream cheese on crackers or over a Cheddar cheese spread.

1 medium green bell pepper, seeded and chopped
1 can (4 ounces) mild whole green chiles, rinsed and seeded
1 to 2 tablespoons canned jalapeño peppers, rinsed and seeded
1¼ cups cider vinegar
5 cups sugar
5 drops of green food coloring
1 pouch (3 ounces) liquid fruit pectin, such as Certo

1. In a food processor or blender, combine the bell pepper, green chiles, and jalapeños. Puree until as smooth as possible. Add the vinegar and blend again until even smoother. Transfer to a 4-quart electric slow cooker. Stir in the sugar.

2. Cover and cook on the high heat setting for 2½ hours, stirring twice, until bubbling around the edges. Do not overcook, or the jelly will taste burnt. Remove the stoneware insert. Stir in the food coloring and mix well; the dull color will brighten. Then add the pectin and stir until completely dissolved.

3. Carefully ladle the jelly into clean hot glass jars or plastic containers. Let cool to room temperature. Then cover with lids and refrigerate for up to 1 month; do not freeze.

maple-pumpkin butter

This autumnal spread is nice to have tucked away for holiday company. I like it with cream cheese on crackers. You can also serve it on toast or English muffins or with biscuits. Be sure to use canned pumpkin; fresh contains too much moisture.

Makes about 5½ cups

1 can (29 ounces) plus 1 can (15 ounces) pure pumpkin puree
2 cups packed brown sugar
¼ cup maple syrup
1 tablespoon fresh lemon juice
1½ teaspoons pumpkin pie spice
¼ teaspoon ground nutmeg

1. Combine all the ingredients in a 4-quart electric slow cooker. Mix well. Smooth the top of the mixture.

2. Cover and cook on the high heat setting for 2½ hours. Remove the cover and cook for 30 minutes longer, or until the butter is thickened slightly.

3. Let the pumpkin butter cool in the pot. Transfer to plastic containers, cover with lids, and refrigerate for up to 3 weeks or freeze for up to 3 months.

Cook's Note

➤ For more texture, stir in ½ cup finely chopped pecans or walnuts after cooling.

roasted red pepper and onion relish

Makes about 6 cups

Use this deliciously sweet and tangy condiment to accompany grilled meats or poultry, or serve it as a dip with crackers or even as a topping for bruschetta. The relish is also good mixed with cream cheese for a spread or spooned over a block of cream cheese for a simple appetizer.

3 cans (14.5 ounces each) diced tomatoes, well drained

1 jar (12 ounces) roasted red peppers, rinsed, well drained, and chopped

1 can (4 ounces) mild diced green chiles

2 medium-large onions, chopped (about 3 cups)

½ cup finely chopped celery

⅓ cup finely chopped green bell pepper

1 to 2 teaspoons finely chopped jalapeño pepper, or to taste

¼ cup cider vinegar

⅔ cup sugar

3 tablespoons instant tapioca

¼ teaspoon salt

¼ teaspoon freshly ground black pepper

Cook's Note

➤ This is a fresh relish and is not meant to be stored for a long time, even in the refrigerator. You can serve it as soon as it is cooled.

1. Combine all the ingredients in a 4-quart electric slow cooker. Stir to blend well. With the back of a spoon, smooth the top of the mixture.

2. Cover and cook on the low heat setting for 6 to 7 hours, or until the relish is thickened. Ladle into hot jars. Let cool, then cover with lids and refrigerate for up to 2 weeks.

cranberry-raspberry relish

This beautiful tart relish, which thickens as it cools, is great with holiday meals, as a spread on sandwiches, or alongside turkey, chicken, or pork. Make it weeks in advance and keep it stashed in the freezer. If you want to embellish the relish even further, stir in some chopped dried apricots and walnuts or pecans after cooking.

Makes about 3 cups

1 bag (12 ounces) fresh cranberries, rinsed and picked over
1 bag (12 ounces) frozen unsweetened raspberries, thawed
1 cup packed brown sugar
Grated zest of 1 orange

1. In a 3- or 4-quart electric slow cooker, mix together the cranberries, raspberries with their juices, brown sugar, and orange zest.

2. Cover and cook on the low heat setting for 3½ to 4 hours, or until the cranberry skins pop. Let cool, then transfer to a container, cover, and refrigerate for up to 1 week or freeze for up to 2 months.

cherry-apple chutney

Makes about 6 cups

Tangy and sweet, this makes an excellent condiment to serve with grilled chicken, turkey, lamb, or pork, or with Indian curries. It's a fine choice to pack up and give as a house gift. Don't be put off by the tapioca. It leaves the chutney with an especially shiny, nicely thickened consistency.

1 pound dried tart (Montmorency) cherries
2 Granny Smith apples, peeled, cored, and chopped
1 cup raisins
1 medium onion, chopped
½ cup apple cider vinegar
1 cup packed brown sugar
2 tablespoons instant tapioca
Dash of cayenne pepper, or more to taste

1. In a 4-quart electric slow cooker, combine the dried cherries, apples, raisins, onion, vinegar, brown sugar, tapioca, cayenne, and 1 cup of water. Mix well.

2. Cover and cook on the low heat setting for about 4 hours, or until the chutney is glossy and thickened. Let cool. Ladle into freezer jars or plastic containers. Cover with lids and refrigerate the chutney for up to 1 month or freeze for up to 3 months.

mango-ginger chutney

C hutneys are very easy to make in the slow cooker and more economical than store bought. Of all the chutneys, mango is probably the most popular. Serve with roast chicken, pork, lamb, or almost any curry.

Makes about 4 cups

2 large ripe mangoes, peeled, pitted, and cut into ¾-inch cubes
   (about 3½ cups)
1 medium onion, chopped
1 red bell pepper, chopped
¾ cup golden raisins
1¼ cups packed brown sugar
½ cup red wine vinegar
1 garlic clove, crushed through a press
1 teaspoon finely grated fresh ginger
3 tablespoons instant tapioca
Few dashes of cayenne pepper, or to taste
3 tablespoons fresh lime juice

1. In a 4-quart electric slow cooker, combine the mangoes, onion, bell pepper, raisins, brown sugar, vinegar, garlic, ginger, tapioca, cayenne, and 2 tablespoons of the lime juice. Mix well.

2. Cover and cook on the low heat setting for 4 hours, or until the chutney is glossy and slightly thickened. Remove the stoneware insert. Stir in the remaining 1 tablespoon lime juice and let cool to room temperature. Transfer to jars, cover with lids, and refrigerate the chutney for up to 1 month.

Cook's Note

➤ The chutney may seem a little thin while it's still hot. It will set up and thicken when chilled.

easy apricot chutney

Makes about 5 cups

Serve this lovely chutney as an accompaniment to a curry or as a spread on crackers or sandwiches. It makes an excellent appetizer spooned over a round of Brie cheese and heated in the oven until the cheese is warm, soft, and slightly runny.

2 cups chopped fresh pitted apricots (about 8)
2 cups chopped dried apricots (1 pound)
1 cup chopped onion
3 to 4 tablespoons diced mild green chiles
2 teaspoons minced fresh ginger
1 garlic clove, minced
½ cup golden raisins
¾ cup packed brown sugar
1 cup cider vinegar
½ teaspoon powdered mustard
½ teaspoon salt
¼ teaspoon freshly ground black pepper

Cook's Note

➤ To chop the dried apricots easily, pulse them in a food processor.

1. In a 3½- or 4-quart electric slow cooker, combine the fresh and dried apricots, onion, chiles, ginger, garlic, golden raisins, brown sugar, vinegar, powdered mustard, and salt. Mix well.

2. Cover and cook on the high heat setting for 2¾ to 3 hours or on the low-heat setting for 5½ to 6 hours, until the fruits and onion are tender but still retain some shape. Stir in the pepper. Season with additional salt to taste.

3. Let cool to room temperature. Transfer to jars, cover with lids, and refrigerate for up to 1 month.

corn and black bean salsa

Makes about 6 cups

Serve this as a salsa with tortilla chips for dipping or as a relish alongside grilled steak, chicken, or shrimp. Or use as a base for a tostada-style salad, piled high atop a crisp corn tortilla with chopped lettuce, tomatoes, avocados, and shredded cheese.

2 cans (15 ounces each) black or pinto beans, rinsed
   and drained
1 package (16 ounces) frozen corn kernels, thawed
1 can (10 ounces) diced tomatoes and green chiles
1 can (8 ounces) tomato sauce
1 medium onion, chopped
1½ teaspoons ground cumin
½ teaspoon chili powder
½ cup shredded pepper Jack or Cheddar cheese
Thinly sliced scallions and coarsely chopped ripe olives,
   for garnish

1. In a 4-quart electric slow cooker, combine the beans, corn, tomatoes with chiles and their juices, tomato sauce, onion, cumin, and chili powder.

2. Cover and cook on the low heat setting for 5½ to 6 hours, until hot.

3. Sprinkle the cheese over the top; it will melt quickly. Serve warm, with sliced scallions and chopped olives sprinkled on top. Refrigerate any leftovers.

tangy peach salsa

Makes about 5¾ cups

like to spoon this mildly sweet salsa over chicken before roasting or over shrimp or ribs after grilling. It's also fine as a dip with corn tortilla chips or as a condiment to dress up simple grilled chicken, fish, or pork.

2 cans (14.5 ounces each) diced tomatoes

4 fresh peaches, peeled and coarsely chopped

1 small onion, finely chopped

1 medium green bell pepper, finely chopped

1 can (4 ounces) diced green chiles

⅓ cup tomato paste

¼ cup red wine vinegar

6 tablespoons brown sugar

½ teaspoon ground cumin

¼ teaspoon salt

Dash of crushed hot red pepper, or more to taste

1. Drain 1 can of the tomatoes well. Include all the juices from the second can. Combine them both in a 4-quart electric slow cooker. Add the peaches, onion, bell pepper, chiles, tomato paste, vinegar, brown sugar, cumin, salt, and hot pepper.

2. Cover and cook on the high heat setting for 3 hours or on the low heat setting for 6 hours, until hot and saucy. Let cool. Transfer to jars, cover with lids, and refrigerate for up to 2 weeks.

tomatillo salsa

Makes about 3¾ cups

Also known as *salsa verde,* this tart relish is based on tomatillos, sometimes called "Mexican green tomatoes," rather than on ripe red tomatoes. While like tomatoes, tomatillos are technically a fruit; they are close relatives of the gooseberry and not a tomato at all. Serve this salsa as a dip with tortilla chips, or use it to top salads, enchiladas, or tacos. As a condiment, it goes especially well with chicken and fish.

1½ pounds fresh tomatillos
1 can (4 ounces) mild diced green chiles
1 to 2 tablespoons diced fresh or canned jalapeño peppers, to taste
1 medium onion, chopped
½ teaspoon salt

1. Peel off the papery husks from the tomatillos; rinse well. Cut out the cores and chop the tomatillos; there will be about 4½ cups.

2. Place the chopped tomatillos in a 4-quart electric slow cooker. Add the green chiles, jalapeños, onion, salt, and ⅓ cup of water. Mix well.

3. Cover and cook on the high heat setting, stirring once or twice, for about 2½ hours, until the tomatillos are softened. Let them cool slightly.

4. In batches, transfer the tomatillo mixture with its liquid to a food processor or blender and pulse to produce a coarse puree. Season with additional salt to taste. Transfer to a container, let cool, cover with a lid, and refrigerate for up to 1 week or freeze for up to 3 months.

Cook's Note

➤ When purchasing fresh tomatillos, look for firm fruit that is green with dry husks. Unlike red tomatoes, tomatillos should be refrigerated as soon as you bring them home from the market.

great slow cooker desserts

Have a sweet tooth? I do, for sure, which is why it was a delight to create these easy-to-prepare sweets for the electric slow cooker. They are so good that your guests will have a hard time believing these were fast-fix recipes. And you'll be amazed at the variety of desserts you can whip up without turning on the oven. Fruit desserts range from poached fruit and fruit sauces to fruit slumps, fruit crumbles, and fruit cobblers. There is rice pudding, bread pudding, and a choice of crème brûlées.

But of all the desserts developed for this book, I am particularly fond of the cakes.

These range from scratch recipes like Pineapple-Carrot Cake, Coconut-Zucchini Cake, and Chocolate-Raspberry Pudding Cake to doctored-up mixes that result in Moist Lemon Cake, Golden Apricot Nectar Cake, and Chocolate-Orange Cake. Speaking of chocolate, how about trying Chocolate Chip Cheesecake in a chocolate cookie crust, Bittersweet Fudge Brownies, Flourless Chocolate Torte, or Chocolate-Pecan Bread Pudding? There's even a Warm Chocolate Lava Cake, just like they serve in restaurants.

Most cakes require lining the stoneware insert so that you can remove the dessert in one piece. Here's a great trick I leaned from my mother, which can be used for any kind of baking or cake pan: Turn the stoneware insert upside down on the countertop and mold a piece of nonstick aluminum foil large enough to reach about three-quarters of the way up the sides over the *outside* of the pot, pressing and smoothing the foil against the walls. Gently lift off this foil mold. Turn the insert right side up and carefully tuck the foil into the pot, pressing firmly against the bottom and sides.

great slow cooker desserts

golden apricot nectar cake

Makes 12 to 14 servings

Turning cake baking into an instant art by doctoring up mixes has become extremely popular. On top of never guessing this luscious cake was made from a mix, no one will believe it was "baked" in a slow cooker. If desired, glaze the top with some apricot jam, heated to liquid consistency in a microwave oven for 30 to 60 seconds, or sprinkle with confectioners' sugar.

1 package (18.25 ounces) butter recipe yellow cake mix

1 stick (4 ounces) butter, melted and cooled slightly

1¼ cups apricot nectar

4 large eggs

2 tablespoons grated orange zest

1 package (8 ounces) cream cheese, softened

⅓ cup sugar

1 teaspoon vanilla extract

½ cup sweetened shredded coconut

1. Butter a 4-quart round electric slow cooker. Line the bottom and about three-quarters of the way up the sides with nonstick aluminum foil. Smooth out the foil as much as possible.

2. In a large mixing bowl, combine the cake mix, butter, apricot nectar, and 3 of the eggs. With an electric mixer, beat on low speed until evenly blended, about 30 seconds. Increase the speed to medium and continue beating for 2 minutes, scraping down the bowl once or twice. Stir in 1 tablespoon of the orange zest.

3. In a medium bowl, combine the cream cheese, sugar, vanilla, and remaining 1 egg and 1 tablespoon orange zest. Beat until smooth. Stir in the coconut.

4. Transfer half of the cake batter to the lined pot, spreading it out evenly. Gently spoon all of the cream cheese mixture all over the batter. Top with the remaining cake batter.

5. Cover and cook on the high heat setting for about 2½ hours, or until the cake is set and a cake tester inserted near the center comes out clean. (Do not attempt this recipe on the low heat setting.)

6. Let the cake cool and set in the pot for 5 to 10 minutes. Then, using the edges of the foil to assist, carefully remove the cake on the foil to a serving plate. Let cool before slicing. Refrigerate any leftover cake.

chocolate-orange cake

Makes 10 to 12 servings

Here's a doctored-up mix recipe that will leave them guessing. Rich and fudgy, studded with chocolate chips, the dessert boasts an orange accent both in the cake and glaze. It's a fabulous choice for a casual gathering.

1 package (18.25 ounces) chocolate fudge cake mix
1 package (3.9 ounces) instant chocolate fudge pudding
    and pie filling mix
1 cup sour cream
4 large eggs
½ cup vegetable oil
1½ tablespoons grated orange zest
1 cup semisweet chocolate chips
Chocolate-Orange Glaze (recipe follows)

1. Butter the stoneware insert of a 4-quart round electric slow cooker. Line the bottom only with a round of nonstick aluminum foil cut to fit the bottom.

2. In a large bowl with an electric mixer, beat together the cake mix, pudding and pie mix, sour cream, eggs, oil, and ½ cup of water on low speed until well mixed. Beat on medium speed for 2 minutes. By hand, stir in the orange zest and chocolate chips. Turn the batter into the prepared pot, spreading the top evenly.

3. Cover and cook on the high heat setting for about 2½ hours, or until a cake tester inserted in the center comes out clean. (Do not attempt this recipe on the low heat setting.) Watch

carefully to avoid overcooking and too much browning around the edges.

4. Remove the cover and the stoneware insert. Carefully run a knife all around the edges to loosen the cake. Let cool in the pot for 15 to 20 minutes. Then run the knife around the edge of the cake again and invert onto a serving plate. Do this carefully to remove the cake in one piece, using a wide spatula to help pry out the cake from the bottom, if necessary. Peel off the foil and carefully turn the cake right side up. Let cool completely.

5. To frost, spread the Chocolate-Orange Glaze over the top of the cake and let it drip down the sides like icicles. Refrigerate until set before slicing.

chocolate-orange glaze

Heat ½ cup heavy cream in a glass bowl or measuring cup in a microwave oven on high power for 1 minute, or until very hot. Or heat in a small saucepan on top of the stove. Add 1 cup semisweet chocolate chips and whisk until smooth and well blended. Stir in 2 teaspoons grated orange zest. **Makes 1 cup.**

chocolate fudge cake with peanut butter ganache

Makes 10 to 12 servings

For easy removal of this cake, be sure to butter the slow cooker pot and then line the bottom with a round of nonstick aluminum foil cut to fit. It's not a mistake that you see no eggs in the ingredient list. There are no eggs in this cake, but it's so rich and moist no one will ever guess. The acid in the vinegar helps cut the gluten in the flour, which makes the crumb exceptionally tender.

2¼ cups all-purpose flour
1½ cups sugar
⅓ cup unsweetened cocoa powder
1½ teaspoons baking soda
Dash of salt
1 stick (4 ounces) butter, melted
1 tablespoon cider vinegar
1 tablespoon vanilla extract
⅓ cup semisweet chocolate chips
Peanut Butter Ganache (recipe follows)

1. Butter the bottom and sides of a 4-quart round electric slow cooker. Line the bottom with a round of nonstick aluminum foil cut to fit the bottom of the pot.

2. In a large bowl, combine the flour, sugar, cocoa powder, baking soda, and salt. Whisk gently to blend the dry ingredients. Add the melted butter, vinegar, vanilla, and 1½ cups of cold water.

Whisk vigorously until the batter is well blended and smooth. Stir in the chocolate chips.

3. Turn the batter into the lined pot, spreading it out evenly. Cover and cook on the low heat setting for 4½ to 5 hours, or until a cake tester inserted in the center comes out clean. (Do not cook on the high heat setting, or the cake will burn around the sides.)

4. Uncover and remove the insert from the cooker. Carefully run a knife all around the edges to loosen the cake. Let cool in the pot for 15 to 20 minutes. Then run the knife around the sides again before gently turning the cake out of the pot. You may have to coax it a bit with a spatula. Peel off the foil and carefully turn the cake right side up on a serving plate. Let cool completely.

5. Spread the warm Peanut Butter Ganache over the top and sides of the cake. Use a small offset spatula or a dinner knife to draw swirls or a patterned design on top of the cake. Let cool until set. Refrigerate until serving time.

peanut butter ganache

In a glass bowl or a 2-cup glass measuring cup, combine 1 cup semisweet chocolate chips, ⅓ cup chunky peanut butter, and ¼ cup heavy cream. Heat in a microwave oven on high power for about 1½ minutes, or until the chocolate is melted when stirred. Mix until the ganache is smooth and well blended. Let stand or refrigerate briefly until the frosting is of spreading consistency. **Makes about 1 cup.**

warm chocolate lava cake

Makes 8 servings

Top this decadent creation with scoops of coffee or mocha chip ice cream or with sweetened whipped cream. Refrigerate any leftovers and reheat for 20 to 30 seconds in a microwave oven.

2 cups semisweet chocolate chips

1½ sticks (6 ounces) butter, cut up

⅔ cup sugar

6 large eggs

2 teaspoons vanilla extract

2 tablespoons all-purpose flour

1. Butter the bottom and sides of a 4-quart round electric slow cooker. In a large glass bowl or 2-quart microwave-safe glass measuring cup, combine the chocolate and butter. Heat in a microwave oven on high power for 1½ to 2½ minutes, or until melted and smooth when stirred.

2. Whisk in the sugar, eggs, and vanilla until smooth. Whisk in the flour until smooth and well mixed. Turn the chocolate batter into the cooker, spreading evenly.

3. Cover and cook on the high heat setting for 2 to 2¼ hours. (Do not attempt this recipe on the low heat setting.) When done, the edges will be set but the center still slightly runny. Immediately scoop the "cake" into bowls or dessert dishes. Serve immediately.

flourless chocolate torte

**Makes one 8-inch cake;
10 to 12 servings**

As elegant as any cake that ever came out of an oven, this intense dessert, deep and rich, will be the star of any dinner party or dessert table. To ensure the best texture, make sure that the dessert is served at warm room temperature, not cold.

2 cups semisweet chocolate chips
2 ounces unsweetened chocolate, coarsely chopped
2 sticks (8 ounces) unsalted butter
6 large eggs
1½ tablespoons sugar
Raspberry Sauce (recipe follows)
Fresh raspberries and whipped cream, as accompaniments

1. In a large glass bowl, combine the chocolate chips, unsweet-ened chocolate, and butter. Heat in a microwave oven on high power for 1½ to 2 minutes, or until melted and smooth when stirred. Or melt in a double boiler over hot water. Whisk in the eggs and sugar.

2. Wrap the outside of an 8-inch springform pan with aluminum foil to prevent any leakage. Turn the chocolate mixture into the pan and spread it out evenly. Cover the top of the springform with foil. Place the pan on a vegetable steamer or other low rack set in the bottom of a 5-quart round electric slower cooker. Do not add any water to the cooker.

3. Cover and cook on the high heat setting for 2¾ to 3 hours. (Do not attempt this recipe on the low heat setting.) The edges should be softly firm, but the center of the cake should still be

soft and moist; it will set up when chilled. Turn the cooker off and remove the cover. Let the springform pan stand in the cooker until it is cool enough to handle.

4. Remove the springform pan from the pot and remove the foil. Let the torte cool for 1 hour. Then cover again and refrigerate until chilled and set, at least 3 hours or overnight. Bring to room temperature before serving. Serve sliced, with a drizzle of Raspberry Sauce. Garnish with a few fresh raspberries, if you have them, and whipped cream.

raspberry sauce

In a food processor or blender, combine 2 packages (12 ounces each) individually frozen unsweetened raspberries, partially thawed, and 1/3 cup confectioners' sugar. Puree as smooth as possible. Taste and add a little more sugar if you think the sauce needs it. If you want to remove the seeds, press the sauce through a sieve. Refrigerate until serving time. **Makes about 2 cups.**

chocolate-raspberry pudding cake

Makes 6 to 8 servings

Chocolate pudding with a hint of raspberry ends up underneath a layer of chocolate cake in this comforting, old-fashioned dessert that bakes up so well in a slow cooker. A dollop of whipped cream offers just the right soft foil to the intense flavor of the cake.

1 cup all-purpose flour

¾ cup granulated sugar

½ cup unsweetened cocoa powder

2 teaspoons baking powder

½ teaspoon salt

½ cup half-and-half

3 tablespoons butter, melted

½ cup semisweet chocolate chips

¾ cup packed brown sugar

1¾ cups boiling water

2 tablespoons seedless raspberry jam

Whipped cream

1. In a mixing bowl, combine the flour, granulated sugar, ¼ cup of the cocoa powder, the baking powder, and salt. Whisk gently until well blended. Add the half-and-half and melted butter and stir until smooth. Fold in the chocolate chips. Turn the batter into a 3- or 3½-quart electric slow cooker, spreading it out evenly.

2. In another bowl, stir together the brown sugar and remaining ¼ cup cocoa powder until well blended. Sprinkle this mixture evenly over the top of the batter.

3. In a medium bowl, pour the boiling water over the jam and whisk until it is completely dissolved. Gently pour evenly all over the top of the batter in the pot. Do not stir.

4. Cover and cook on the high heat setting for 2 to 2¼ hours, or until a cake tester inserted in the cake portion on top of the dessert comes out clean. (Do not attempt this recipe on the low heat setting.) Let the cake stand for 10 to 15 minutes before serving it warm, topped with whipped cream.

Variation

Chocolate Peanut Pudding Cake: Follow the recipe directions above but add ¾ cup unsalted or reduced-salt peanuts to the batter along with the chocolate chips. Spread evenly in a 3- or 3½-quart electric slow cooker. Sprinkle with the brown sugar–cocoa mixture as directed above. In place of the raspberry jam, mix the 1¾ cups boiling water with 2 tablespoons chunky peanut butter. Gently pour evenly all over the top. Do not stir. Cover and cook as directed above.

chocolate-zucchini cake

Makes 12 servings

Everyone knows zucchini makes a great moist quick bread. So why not try a cake, and make it even better by adding chocolate? This is a good way to use up some of that extra zucchini from the garden.

1 stick (4 ounces) butter

1¾ cups granulated sugar

3 large eggs

2 teaspoons vanilla extract

2 cups all-purpose flour

¾ cup unsweetened cocoa powder

1 teaspoon baking soda

½ teaspoon baking powder

¼ teaspoon salt

2 cups shredded zucchini (3 small or 2 medium)

¾ cup semisweet chocolate chips

Sifted confectioners' sugar

1. Butter the bottom of a 4-quart electric slow cooker. Line the bottom and about three-quarters of the way up the sides with nonstick aluminum foil. Press the foil to smooth out as much as possible.

2. In a large glass bowl or 2-quart microwave-safe glass measuring cup, heat the butter in a microwave oven on high power for about 1 minute, until melted. Whisk in the granulated sugar, eggs, and vanilla until well blended. Whisk in the flour, cocoa powder, baking soda, baking powder, and salt until thoroughly blended. Stir in the zucchini until well blended. Stir in the chocolate chips.

3. Turn the batter into the lined pot, spreading it evenly. Cover and cook on the high heat setting for 2¼ to 2½ hours, until a cake tester inserted in the center comes out clean. (Do not attempt this recipe on the low heat setting.)

4. Let the cake cool and set in the pot for 10 minutes. Then using the edges of the foil to assist, remove the cake to a platter and let cool completely. Before slicing, dust the top with confectioners' sugar.

bittersweet
fudge brownies

Makes 12 to 16 servings

Dark, decadent, and rich, these are for those who like their brownies fudgy and ultra-chocolaty. For deepest flavor, use bittersweet rather than semisweet chips, now readily available in markets.

²/₃ cup plus ½ cup bittersweet or semisweet chocolate chips

1 stick (4 ounces) butter

1 cup sugar

1 teaspoon vanilla extract

2 large eggs

½ cup all-purpose flour

¼ cup unsweetened cocoa powder

Pinch of salt

½ cup chopped walnuts

Some desserts are steamed, and for best results, a vegetable steamer or other low rack placed in the slow cooker is a must. Check that the pan and rack fit into the insert prior to cooking.

1. Butter an 8-inch springform pan. In a 2-quart microwave-safe glass bowl, combine ⅔ cup of the chocolate chips and the butter. Heat in a microwave oven on high power for 1½ to 2 minutes, until just melted and smooth when stirred.

2. Add the sugar, vanilla, and eggs and whisk until well blended. Whisk in the flour, cocoa powder, and salt until well mixed. Stir in the nuts and remaining ½ cup chocolate chips. Turn into the springform pan, spreading the top evenly. Place on a vegetable steamer or other low rack in the bottom of a 5-quart round electric slow cooker. Do not add any water.

3. Cover and cook on the high heat setting for 3½ to 3¾ hours, or until almost set; the outside edges should be set, the center still moist and sticky. (Do not attempt this recipe on the low heat setting.) Turn the cooker off and remove the cover. Let the springform pan remain in the cooker until it is cool enough to handle. Remove the pan and let the brownies cool in the pan.

4. To serve, run a knife around the edges of the springform to loosen the brownies before removing the sides. Cut into wedges.

Cook's Note

➤ This is a one-bowl recipe that takes advantage of the microwave to melt the chocolate. If you prefer, you can use a double boiler over hot water.

moist lemon cake

Makes 10 to 12 servings

Designed for lemon lovers, this desert is fabulous and moist. A simple glaze is poured over the cake while it's still warm. No other frosting is needed.

1 package (18.25 ounces) lemon cake mix (pudding included)

1 package (3 ounces) lemon-flavored gelatin

3 large eggs

½ cup vegetable oil

1 tablespoon butter, melted

¾ cup sifted confectioners' sugar, plus more for dusting

2 tablespoons fresh lemon juice

If you opt for making cakes in the slow cooker, watch and check carefully. Be around near the end of the cooking time or you risk over-cooking. You don't want to return late only to find a burned cake, which may have cooked only an hour longer than called for.

1. Butter the insert of a 4-quart round electric slow cooker. Line the bottom and about three-quarters of the way up the sides with nonstick aluminum foil. Smooth out the foil as much as possible.

2. In a large bowl with an electric mixer, beat together the cake mix, gelatin powder, eggs, oil, and 1 cup of water on low speed until well mixed. Raise the speed to medium and beat for 2 to 3 minutes. Turn the batter into the pot. Smooth out evenly.

3. Cover and cook on the high heat setting for about 2 hours, until a cake tester inserted in the center comes out clean. Watch carefully to avoid overcooking. (Do not attempt this recipe on the low heat setting.)

4. After baking, uncover and remove the stoneware insert. While the cake is still very warm, use a thin skewer to poke deep holes all over the cake.

5. In a small glass or ceramic bowl, blend the melted butter with the confectioners' sugar and lemon juice. Heat in a microwave oven on high power for 30 to 40 seconds, until very hot. Stir the glaze and pour all over the top of the hot cake, which will absorb it. Let cool. Then remove the cake from the insert by using the foil to assist. Peel off the foil and place the cake, glazed side up, on a serving plate. Dust a little additional confectioner's sugar over the top.

orange-pumpkin cake

Makes 10 to 12 servings

This is an especially nice dessert to whip up during the fall season or over the winter holidays. I like to keep one of these cakes handy in the freezer for when friends drop by unexpectedly.

1 package (18.25 ounces) yellow cake mix

3 large eggs

1 can (15 ounces) pure pumpkin puree

2 teaspoons ground cinnamon

½ teaspoon ground nutmeg

½ cup plus 1 tablespoon orange juice

4 tablespoons butter, softened

1 cup confectioners' sugar

Once cooked and cooled, some slow cooker cakes can be split in half horizontally and filled and frosted. No one will guess they were "baked" in an electric pot.

1. Butter a 4-quart oval electric slow cooker. Line the bottom and about three-quarters of the way up the sides with nonstick aluminum foil. Smooth out the foil as much as possible.

2. In a large bowl with an electric mixer, beat together the cake mix, eggs, pumpkin, cinnamon, nutmeg, and ½ cup of the orange juice on low speed until well mixed. Increase the speed to medium and continue to beat for 2 to 3 minutes. Turn the batter into the lined pot, spreading the top evenly.

3. Cover and cook on the high heat setting for about 2½ hours, until a cake tester inserted in center comes out clean. Watch carefully to avoid overcooking. (Do not attempt this recipe on the low heat setting.)

4. Remove the stoneware insert with the cake. Let cool. Then remove the cake, using the foil to assist. Carefully peel off the foil and place the cake on a serving plate. Make a frosting by blending the softened butter with the confectioners' sugar and remaining 1 tablespoon orange juice until smooth and well blended. Spread the frosting evenly over the top of the cake. Let stand until set. To serve, cut into wedges or slices. Refrigerate any leftovers.

pineapple-carrot cake

Makes 12 servings

mpossible to guess this awesome carrot cake was baked in a slow cooker. It looks great and even boasts the traditional cream cheese frosting.

2 cups sugar

3 large eggs

1 cup buttermilk

1 stick (4 ounces) unsalted butter, melted

2 teaspoons vanilla extract

2 cups all-purpose flour

1 tablespoon ground cinnamon

2 teaspoons baking soda

¼ teaspoon salt

¾ cup drained unsweetened crushed canned pineapple

2 cups shredded carrots

2⅓ cups sweetened shredded coconut

1 cup chopped walnuts

Cream Cheese Frosting (recipe follows)

1. Butter the bottom of a 4-quart round electric slow cooker. Line the pot as follows: Tear off two 12-inch-long sheets from an 18-inch-wide roll of nonstick heavy-duty aluminum foil. Fold each foil strip into thirds, nonstick side out, so you end up with strips 4 inches wide and 18 inches long. Center one foil strip in the bottom of the pot and up the sides, with an equal amount of foil overhang at the top of both sides. Center the second foil strip at a right angle to the first in the same fashion so that you end up with crisscrossed foil strips. Smooth them to make sure the strips are flat in the pot.

Cook's Note

➤ Since baking soda goes into action as soon as it is combined with a liquid, be sure to line the pot before mixing up the batter.

2. In a large bowl, whisk together the sugar, eggs, buttermilk, melted butter, and vanilla until thoroughly mixed. Whisk in the flour, cinnamon, baking soda, and salt until well blended. Stir in the pineapple, carrots, 2 cups of the coconut, and the nuts. Turn the batter into the prepared pot, spreading it out evenly. Fold back the ends of the foil strips so they are below the cover.

3. Cover and cook on the high heat setting for 3 to 3¼ hours, or until a cake tester inserted in the center comes out clean. (Do not attempt this recipe on the low heat setting.) Uncover and remove the stoneware insert. Let the cake cool completely in the pot.

4. Run a knife around the rim of the cake to loosen it. Carefully ease the cake out of the pot with the help of the foil. Peel off the foil and place the cake, right side up, on a serving plate.

5. With a sharp knife, split the cooled cake in half horizontally. Frost the bottom layer with about one-third of the Cream Cheese Frosting. Top with the other cake layer and cover the top and sides with the remaining frosting. Sprinkle the remaining ⅓ cup coconut over the top of the cake. Refrigerate until set. Cut into slices to serve. Refrigerate any leftovers.

cream cheese frosting

In a medium bowl, combine 1 package (8 ounces) cream cheese, softened, with 4 tablespoons softened butter, 1 package (16 ounces) confectioners' sugar, 2 teaspoons vanilla extract, and 2 teaspoons grated orange zest. Beat until smooth. **Makes 2⅔ cups.**

raspberry pudding cake

Makes 6 to 8 servings

Here's another flavor rendition of the ever-popular pudding-cake theme. The cake and raspberry mixtures swap places during cooking, and the raspberries end up underneath the cake.

1 cup all-purpose flour

1¾ teaspoons baking powder

Dash of salt

1 cup granulated sugar

½ cup half-and-half or light cream

1 large egg

1 stick (4 ounces) butter, melted

1 teaspoon vanilla extract

1 package (12 ounces) frozen unsweetened raspberries, only partially thawed; do not drain

2 tablespoons cornstarch

Sifted confectioners' sugar, for garnish

Whipped cream, as accompaniment

1. In a medium bowl, whisk together the flour, baking powder, salt, and ½ cup of the granulated sugar until blended. Whisk in the half-and-half, egg, melted butter, and vanilla until mixed.

2. Turn the batter into a 3- or 3½-quart electric slow cooker, spreading it out evenly. Mix together the raspberries with their juices, the remaining ½ cup granulated sugar, and the cornstarch until well blended. Pour evenly over the batter in the pot.

3. Cover and cook on the high heat setting for 2¼ to 2½ hours, or until a cake tester inserted in the cake portion of the dessert on top comes out clean. (Do not attempt this recipe on the low heat setting.) Dust the top with confectioners' sugar. Serve warm, topped with whipped cream, if desired. Refrigerate any leftovers.

When cooking many cakes in the slow cooker, butter and then line the stoneware insert or part of it with nonstick aluminum foil, such as the product made by Reynolds, to help ease the cooked cake out in one piece. You can line the bottom of the insert with a piece cut to fit, line the pot with a sheet of foil, or fold the foil into strips.

coconut-zucchini cake

Makes 12 servings

Have a garden? Don't know what to do with all that zucchini? Here's a terrific idea; the cake freezes well, too. This is a favorite dessert, converted to the slow cooker—and it's just as delicious! Use nonstick aluminum foil strips to get the cake out of the pot in one piece.

1 package (8 ounces) cream cheese, softened

2 cups sugar

3 large eggs

1½ sticks (6 ounces) butter, melted

Grated zest of 1 large orange

1½ tablespoons ground cinnamon

2 teaspoons vanilla extract

3 cups all-purpose flour

1 teaspoon baking soda

¼ teaspoon baking powder

¼ teaspoon salt

¾ cup packed sweetened shredded coconut

½ cup golden raisins

2 cups packed shredded zucchini (2 medium)

1 cup chopped walnuts

Cream Cheese Icing (recipe follows)

1. Line a 4-quart round electric slow cooker as follows: Butter the bottom of the slow cooker insert. Tear off two 12-inch-long sheets from an 18-inch-wide roll of nonstick aluminum foil. Fold each foil strip into thirds, nonstick side out, so you end up with strips 4 inches wide and 18 inches long. Center one foil

strip in the bottom of the pot and up the sides, with an equal amount of foil overhang at the top on each side. Center the second foil strip at a right angle to the first in the same fashion so that you end up with crisscrossed foil strips. Smooth them to make sure the strips are flat in the pot.

2. In a large mixing bowl with an electric mixer, beat together the cream cheese, sugar, eggs, butter, orange zest, cinnamon, and vanilla until thoroughly blended. Add the flour, baking soda, baking powder, and salt. Beat for 2 to 3 minutes. By hand, stir in the coconut, raisins, zucchini, and walnuts until well mixed. Turn the cake batter into the pot, spreading it out evenly. Fold down the ends of the foil strips so they are below the pot cover.

3. Cover and cook on the high heat setting for 3¼ to 3½ hours, or until a cake tester inserted in the center comes out clean. (Do not attempt this recipe on the low heat setting.) Uncover, remove the stoneware insert, and let the cake cool completely in the pot.

4. Run a knife around the edges of the cake to loosen it. Carefully ease the cake out of the pot with the help of the foil. Peel off the foil and place the cake, right side up, on a serving plate. Frost the top and sides of the cake with the Cream Cheese Icing. Let stand until set. To serve, cut into wedges. Refrigerate any leftovers.

cream cheese icing

Mix 4 ounces cream cheese (half of an 8-ounce package) softened with 1 tablespoon heavy cream, 2 teaspoons grated orange zest, and ⅓ to ½ cup confectioners' sugar until smooth. **Makes about ¾ cup.**

chocolate chip cheesecake

Makes one 8-inch cheesecake; 8 to 10 servings

Chocolate chips and cheesecake: What's not to like? A rich chocolate cream glazes the top, adding a wonderful hit of dark chocolate as well as a very attractive covering.

1 cup chocolate cookie crumbs
3 tablespoons butter, melted
3 packages (8 ounces each) cream cheese, softened
¾ cup sugar
2 large eggs
2 teaspoons vanilla extract
¾ cup semisweet chocolate chips
Chocolate Cream (recipe follows)

1. In a small bowl, combine the cookie crumbs and melted butter; mix well. Press into the bottom and ½ inch up the sides of an 8-inch springform pan. In a large bowl with an electric mixer, beat together the cream cheese, sugar, eggs, and vanilla until well blended and smooth. Stir in the chocolate chips. Turn the cheese mixture into the crust in the pan.

2. Place the cheesecake on a vegetable steamer or other low rack set in the bottom of a 5-quart round electric slow cooker. Do not add any water to the cooker.

3. Cover and cook on the high heat setting for 3 to 3¼ hours, or until the cake is set in the center. (Do not attempt this recipe on the low heat setting.) Remove the cover and turn the slow cooker off. Let the cheesecake stand in the cooker until cool enough to handle.

4. Remove the springform pan from the insert and let the cheese-cake cool to room temperature. Then spread the Chocolate Cream evenly over the top. Refrigerate until chilled and fully set, several hours or overnight.

5. To serve, run a knife around the edge of the cheesecake to loosen it. Remove the side of the springform pan. Cut the cheesecake into slices. Refrigerate any leftovers.

chocolate cream

In a glass bowl or cup, heat ½ cup whipping cream in a microwave oven on high power 45 to 60 seconds or longer, until very hot. Stir in 1 cup semisweet chocolate chips until melted and smooth. Cool until slightly thickened. **Makes about 1 cup.**

pineapple–coconut–macadamia cheesecake

Makes one 8-inch cheesecake; 10 to 12 servings

No one will guess this fabulous dessert came from a slow cooker. It's absolutely delicious and simple to cook in a springform pan placed on a vegetable steamer or other low rack in a slow cooker.

2 cups sweetened flaked or shredded coconut

3 packages (8 ounces each) cream cheese, softened

¾ cup sugar

3 large eggs

⅓ cup heavy cream

1 teaspoon vanilla extract

¾ cup well-drained coarsely chopped canned pineapple chunks (½-inch pieces)

¾ cup coarsely chopped dry-roasted unsalted macadamia nuts

Whipped cream, toasted coconut, and macadamia nuts, for garnish

1. Line the bottom of an 8-inch springform pan with 1 cup of the coconut, pressing it down firmly. In a large bowl with an electric mixer, beat together the cream cheese and sugar until light and fluffy. Beat in the eggs, cream, and vanilla and continue beating until the batter is smooth and fluffy, about 5 minutes. By hand, stir in the remaining 1 cup coconut and the pineapple and macadamia nuts. Spoon evenly over the coconut crust.

2. Place the cheesecake on a vegetable steamer or other low rack set in the bottom of a 5- or 6-quart round or oval electric slow cooker. Do not add any water to the pot. Cover and cook on the high heat setting for 3½ to 4 hours, or until the cheesecake is set in the center. (Do not attempt this recipe on the low heat setting.)

3. Remove the cover and turn the cooker off. Let the cheesecake stand in the cooker until the springform is cool enough to handle. Then remove the cake pan and let cool to room temperature. Cover and refrigerate until chilled and set, at least 4 hours or overnight

4. To serve, remove the side of the springform pan. Garnish the cheesecake with whipped cream, toasted coconut, and macadamia nuts. Refrigerate any leftovers.

slow "baked" apples

Makes 4 servings

f you're a fan of baked apples, here's an effortless way to cook them. Timing will vary depending on the variety of apple, size, and texture. Serve hot, warm, or chilled, with a splash of crème fraîche or heavy cream, if you like.

4 tart-sweet baking apples
2 tablespoons brown sugar
4 teaspoons dark raisins or dried tart cherries
1 cup natural raspberry soda or unsweetened apple juice

1. Core each apple, starting at the top but leaving the bottom of the apple intact. Remove the seeds, but do not cut all the way through.

2. Stand the apples upright in a 4-quart electric slow cooker. Spoon 1½ teaspoons brown sugar and then 1 teaspoon raisins into the center of each apple. Pour the soda over and around the apples.

3. Cover and cook on the low heat setting for 4 to 5 hours, until the apples are soft but still hold their shape. Serve warm, at room temperature, or chilled, with some of the cooking liquid spooned over the fruit.

apple-pecan crunch

Warm and fragrant, this easy dessert is bound to please apple fans. It tastes like apple pie, but there's no crust to fuss with. Serve with vanilla ice cream or whipped cream.

6 Granny Smith apples, peeled, cored, and sliced
1½ tablespoons fresh lemon juice
1½ teaspoons ground cinnamon
3 tablespoons brown sugar
Pecan-Streusel Topping (recipe follows)

1. In a 4-quart oval electric slow cooker, toss together the apple slices, lemon juice, cinnamon, and brown sugar until well mixed. Sprinkle the Pecan-Streusel Topping over the apples.

2. Cover and cook on the low heat setting for 3½ to 4 hours, until the apples are tender but still hold their shape. Serve hot or warm.

pecan-streusel topping

In a food processor, mix together ½ cup rolled oats, ¼ cup all-purpose flour, and ⅓ cup packed brown sugar. Add 6 tablespoons butter, cut into pieces, and pulse just until the pieces are the size of peas and the mixture is crumbly. Transfer to a bowl and stir in ¾ cup coarsely chopped pecans by hand. **Makes about 1½ cups.**

fresh apricot-coconut crumble

Makes 8 servings

When fresh apricots are in season, this is a wonderful way to use them. It's not necessary to peel the apricots, so the dessert is really simple to prepare. Sprinkle additional toasted coconut over the top before serving. I like to top this with a scoop of coconut or butter pecan ice cream.

2½ pounds fresh apricots (about 15), pitted and sliced

½ cup granulated sugar

1 tablespoon cornstarch

1 tablespoon fresh lemon juice

⅓ cup packed brown sugar

⅓ cup quick-cooking rolled oats

⅓ cup sweetened flaked or shredded coconut

2 tablespoons all-purpose flour

3 tablespoons butter, melted

1. Put the apricot slices in a 3- or 3½-quart electric slow cooker. Sprinkle the granulated sugar and cornstarch over the fruit and toss to mix well. Stir in the lemon juice.

2. To make the coconut crumble topping, stir together the brown sugar, oats, coconut, and flour with a fork until well blended. Drizzle on the melted butter, stirring until the topping is moistened and crumbly. Sprinkle the topping evenly over the apricots in the pot.

3. Cover and cook on the high heat setting for about 2¼ hours, until the dessert is slightly thickened and the apricot mixture is bubbly around the edges. (Do not attempt this recipe on the low heat setting.) Serve the crumble warm, at room temperature, or chilled.

Once food is cooked, it should be held hot, at or above 140°F in the slow cooker. Holding food hot for extended periods may reduce the quality.

berry berry cobbler

made this cobbler with frozen berries on purpose, so it could be enjoyed all year round. Accompany with whipped cream, crème fraîche, or vanilla ice cream. Note: If you prepare the recipe only through Step 2, you will end up with an excellent berry sauce, which can be spooned as a topping over ice cream, angel food or pound cake, or cheesecake.

2 bags (16 ounces each) frozen unsweetened berry medley (a combination of blueberries, raspberries and blackberries), thawed but not drained

½ cup plus 2 teaspoons granulated sugar

2 tablespoons cornstarch

1¼ cups all-purpose flour

3 tablespoons brown sugar

1 teaspoon baking powder

¼ teaspoon ground nutmeg

5 tablespoons cold unsalted butter, cut up

4 to 5 tablespoons heavy cream

1. Put the thawed berries with their juices into a 3- to 4-quart electric slow cooker. Mix together ½ cup of the granulated sugar and the cornstarch. Gently stir into the berries until thoroughly blended.

2. Cover and cook on the high heat setting for 2¼ hours, or until slightly thickened, stirring once if possible. (Do not attempt this recipe on the low heat setting.)

3. In a food processor, combine the flour, brown sugar, baking powder, and nutmeg. Pulse to mix. Add the butter and pulse until the dough looks like coarse meal. Add ¼ cup of the cream and pulse 6 times. If the dough does not come together, add the remaining 1 tablespoon cream and process until the dough just forms a ball.

4. Remove the dough from the machine and divide it into 10 equal balls. With the palm of your hand, quickly flatten to ½-inch disks and arrange evenly on top of the hot berry mixture in the slow cooker. Sprinkle the remaining 2 teaspoons granulated sugar over the dough.

5. Cover and cook on the high heat setting for 1 to 1¼ hours, until the biscuit topping is cooked through. Serve warm, making sure everyone gets some of the berry mixture and some cobbler topping.

peach-apricot crumble

Makes 8 to 10 servings

Because it's so hard to find stone fruits at the peak of ripeness and flavor, this recipe uses a mix of fresh and frozen. To peel the peaches, dip them in a pot of boiling water for 30 to 60 seconds, depending upon ripeness; the skins will slip right off. Serve with whipped cream or vanilla ice cream.

5 medium peaches, peeled and sliced (about 3 cups)

1 package (1 pound) frozen unsweetened sliced peaches, thawed with juices reserved

6 fresh apricots, pitted and sliced (about 2 cups)

1 tablespoon fresh lemon juice

3 tablespoons instant tapioca

½ cup packed light brown sugar

Oatmeal Crumble (recipe follows)

1. In a 4-quart electric slow cooker, combine the fresh and frozen peaches with their juices, the apricots, lemon juice, tapioca, and brown sugar. Mix well.

2. Cover and cook on the high heat setting for 1½ to 2 hours, until bubbly. Remove the cover and stir.

3. Sprinkle the Oatmeal Crumble evenly over the top. Cover again and cook on the high heat setting for 1 hour longer. Serve warm or at room temperature.

oatmeal crumble

In a food processor, combine ½ cup all-purpose flour and ½ cup packed light brown sugar. Add 4 tablespoons butter, cut into 8 pieces, and process until crumbly. Add ½ cup quick-cooking rolled oats, ½ teaspoon ground cinnamon, and ¼ teaspoon ground nutmeg. Process until mixed and crumbly. **Makes about 1 cup.**

peach slump

Whatever you call this—a slump or grunt—it's an irresistible dumpling-topped fruit dessert. Dollops of rich batter are added to the partially cooked fruit in the slow cooker to steam in the sweet juices. Serve warm with a splash of cream or whipped cream.

2½ to 3 pounds fresh peaches, peeled and sliced (about 4 cups)

½ cup plus 3 tablespoons sugar

2 tablespoons cornstarch

¾ cup all-purpose flour

1 teaspoon grated orange zest (optional)

¾ teaspoon baking powder

½ cup heavy cream

2 tablespoons butter, melted and slightly cooled

⅛ teaspoon ground cinnamon

1. In a 4-quart electric slow cooker, combine the peaches, ½ cup sugar, and the cornstarch. Toss gently to mix well.

2. Cover and cook on the high heat setting for 2 hours. (Do not attempt this recipe on the low heat setting.) Stir; the mixture should be thickened.

3. For the topping, combine the flour, orange zest, 2 tablespoons of the remaining sugar, and the baking powder; mix well. Stir together the cream and melted butter. Pour into the flour mixture and stir until blended.

4. Drop the dough in 8 large dollops on top of the peaches, spacing the dumplings evenly. Mix together the remaining 1 tablespoon sugar and the cinnamon. Sprinkle the cinnamon sugar over the top of the dumplings.

5. Cover and continue cooking on the high heat setting for about 1 hour, or until the dumplings are cooked through. Serve warm.

poached pears with dried cherries and gorgonzola

Makes 4 to 6 servings

After a big meal, especially one that is on the sophisticated side, many people like to serve fruit and cheese in place of a heavy, sweet dessert. This slow cooker special combines both: fragrant fresh pears poached in red wine along with dried cherries and Gorgonzola. Feel free to substitute Roquefort, or one of our excellent American blues, such as Maytag or Point Reyes.

4 to 6 firm, ripe pears, preferably Bartlett

¾ cup cabernet sauvignon or other dry red wine

¼ cup sugar

¼ cup dried cherries

½ to ¾ cup crumbled Gorgonzola cheese

1. Peel the pears. Core them from the bottom, leaving the tops intact with their stems attached. In a bowl, combine the wine and sugar, stirring to dissolve the sugar. Stand the pears up in a 4-quart electric slow cooker. Pour the wine mixture over the pears.

2. Cover and cook on the high heat setting for 1 hour. Reduce the heat setting to low and continue to cook for 1 to 2 hours longer, until the pears are tender but still hold their shape well.

3. Transfer the pears to individual dessert dishes or bowls. Add the dried cherries to the hot wine and then spoon some over each pear. Sprinkle 2 tablespoons crumbled Gorgonzola cheese on top of each.

Variation

Poached Pears with Raspberry Fudge Sauce: Prepare the recipe as directed above, but omit the cheese. Instead, after spooning the wine and cherries over the pears, drizzle 2 tablespoons warmed Raspberry Fudge Sauce (page 441) over each.

wiki wiki pineapple dessert

Makes 10 to 12 servings

Wiki wiki means "quick, quick" in Hawaiian. This old standby is probably one of the fastest desserts you can put together in the slow cooker. It tastes like a cobbler, but it's made with a box of cake mix and a can of crushed pineapple.

1 can (20 ounces) crushed pineapple packed in juice
1 package (18.25 ounces) yellow cake mix
1 stick (4 ounces) butter, melted
½ cup sliced almonds
Whipped cream or ice cream, for serving

Cleaning a slow cooker insert is easy, especially if you soak it for a while and use warm soapy water and a soft sponge. Or you can wash it in the dishwasher. While disposable slow cooker plastic liners are sold in supermarkets, they can be a nuisance.

1. Spread the pineapple with all its juices over the bottom of a 4-quart oval electric slow cooker. Sprinkle the dry cake mix evenly over the pineapple. Drizzle on the melted butter. Sprinkle the almonds evenly on top.

2. Cover and cook on the high heat setting for 2 to 2½ hours, or until the cake is cooked through. Serve hot or cold, with whipped cream.

Cook's Note

➤ Because this dessert is made with pineapple packed in juice, the cake will be a little tart. If you prefer things very sweet, use crushed pineapple in syrup instead.

raspberry-blackberry cobbler

Makes 8 to 10 servings

Because this recipe uses frozen berries, you can enjoy the dessert all year round. Serve with whipped cream, crème fraîche, or ice cream.

2 bags (16 ounces each) frozen unsweetened raspberries, thawed but not drained

2 bags (16 ounces each) frozen unsweetened blackberries, thawed but not drained

¾ cup granulated sugar

¼ cup instant tapioca

1 cup all-purpose flour

4 tablespoons brown sugar

1¼ teaspoons baking powder

4 tablespoons butter, cut into 6 pieces

½ cup heavy cream

1 tablespoon grated orange zest

¼ cup plus 2 tablespoons finely chopped pecans

1. In a 4-quart electric slow cooker, combine the berries with their juices, granulated sugar, and tapioca; mix thoroughly. Cover and cook on the high heat setting for 1½ hours.

2. Meanwhile, in a food processor, combine the flour, 3 tablespoons of the brown sugar, the baking powder, and the butter. Pulse until the mixture looks crumbly. Add the cream, orange zest, and ¼ cup chopped pecans. Pulse until the dough forms a ball.

3. Stir the fruit in the pot. Divide the dough into walnut-size pieces, roll each into a ball, and flatten with your fingers into 2-inch rounds. Place the pieces of dough on top of the fruit. Sprinkle the remaining 1 tablespoon brown sugar and 2 tablespoons chopped pecans on top.

4. Cover and cook on the high heat setting for 1 to 1¼ hours longer, until the dough is cooked through. Turn off the cooker, remove the cover, and let the dessert cool in the pot for at least 10 minutes. Spoon into bowls and serve hot, at room temperature, or cold.

chocolate-pecan bread pudding

Makes 8 to 10 servings

Yes, this is as good as it sounds—yummy, irresistible comfort food that is perfectly sweet. Serve with whipped cream or a drizzle of caramel sauce and a sprinkle of salt, if you happen to be so inclined.

1 loaf of firm-textured white bread (1 pound)

3 cups milk

6 ounces unsweetened chocolate

3 large eggs

1¼ cups sugar

2 teaspoons vanilla extract

1 cup chopped pecans

¾ cup semisweet chocolate chips

1. Butter the bottom and sides of a 5-quart electric slow cooker. Cut the bread into ¾- to 1-inch cubes; no need to remove the crust.

2. In a 2-quart glass bowl, combine the milk and unsweetened chocolate. Heat in a microwave oven on high power for 6 to 8 minutes, stirring every 2 minutes, until the chocolate is melted and the mixture is smooth. Whisk in the eggs, sugar, and vanilla until smooth. Add the bread cubes and pecans and stir until well mixed.

3. Transfer the bread mixture to the slow cooker. Sprinkle the chocolate chips over the top, pressing them in lightly.

4. Cover and cook on the high heat setting for about 2½ hours, or until set in the center. (Do not attempt this recipe on the low heat setting.) Uncover and let stand for about 10 minutes. To serve, scoop out with a large spoon. Refrigerate any leftovers.

Variations

➤ Stir 2 to 3 tablespoons bourbon or Grand Marnier into the milk mixture along with the eggs.

➤ Instead of pecans, use ¾ cup pitted dried tart cherries and 1½ tablespoons grated orange zest.

coconut bread pudding
with dried apricots

Makes 6 to 8 servings

Bread pudding is a crowd-pleaser to begin with. Adding coconut and dried apricots just makes it even better. Bread pudding, however, is not the most beautiful dessert in the world, so be sure to dress it up when you dish it out. In addition to the accompaniments suggested below, you could also top the pudding with some whole dried or glacéed apricots or a drizzle of caramel sauce.

1 loaf of firm-textured white bread (1 pound), crust removed,
    cut into 1-inch cubes
1 cup sweetened shredded coconut
½ cup chopped dried apricots
5 large eggs
½ cup granulated sugar
3 cups half-and-half or light cream
1 tablespoon vanilla extract
Confectioners' sugar and whipped cream or
    vanilla ice cream, for serving

1. Butter the bottom and sides of a 5-quart electric slow cooker. Spread half of the bread cubes over the bottom. Sprinkle on half of the coconut and all of the dried apricots. Cover with the remaining bread cubes and then the remaining coconut.

2. In a medium bowl, whisk the eggs until well blended. Beat in the sugar, half-and-half, and vanilla. Pour the custard evenly over the bread.

3. Cover and cook on the low heat setting for 3½ to 4½ hours, or until the pudding is set. Remove the cover and let cool slightly. Sprinkle with confectioners' sugar just before serving. Top each portion with a dollop of whipped cream or a scoop of vanilla ice cream. Refrigerate any leftovers.

gingerbread

Makes 10 servings

This is an old-fashioned comfort cake at its best—moist and full of flavor. Serve warm, topped with whipped cream or vanilla bean or coffee ice cream, if you like.

1½ sticks (6 ounces) butter, at room temperature

1 cup packed dark brown sugar

1 large egg

¾ cup unsulphured molasses

2¼ cups all-purpose flour

1½ teaspoons baking soda

2 teaspoons ground ginger

1 teaspoon ground cinnamon

¼ teaspoon ground cloves

¼ teaspoon salt

¾ cup hot brewed coffee or boiling water

Cook's Note

➤ Baking soda rather than baking powder is essential here because of the acidity of the molasses.

1. Butter the bottom and sides of a 4-quart electric slow cooker. Line the bottom and about three-quarters of the way up the sides of the pot with nonstick aluminum foil. Smooth out the foil as much as possible.

2. In a large bowl, cream together the butter and brown sugar. Beat in the egg and molasses. In another bowl, mix together the flour, baking soda, ginger, cinnamon, cloves, and salt. Add to the creamed mixture alternately with the coffee, beating well after each addition.

3. Turn the batter to the foil-lined pot, spreading it evenly. Cover and cook on the high heat setting for 2¾ to 3 hours, or until a cake tester inserted near the center comes out clean. (Do not attempt this recipe on the low heat setting.) Let stand until cool in the pot before removing.

cinnamon-raisin
rice pudding

Make 8 to 10 servings

This is delicious, traditional comfort food. Be sure to stir once or twice during the cooking time for best results. Serve in bowls, topped with a drizzle of heavy cream.

2 cups converted long-grain white rice

¾ cup sugar

½ to ¾ cup dark or golden raisins

5¼ cups whole milk

2 teaspoons ground cinnamon

¾ teaspoon grated nutmeg

2 teaspoons vanilla extract

If you're in the market to buy a slow cooker, research the features desired and buy the one that suits your needs. The 4-quart pot is probably the most all-purpose.

1. Place the rice in a 4-quart electric slow cooker. Mix in the sugar and raisins. In a small saucepan on top of the stove, heat 4½ cups milk until just boiling. Whisk in the cinnamon and nutmeg. Pour over the rice in the slow cooker and mix well.

2. Cover and cook on the low heat setting, stirring once or twice, for 2½ to 3 hours, or on the high heat setting for about 1½ hours, until the liquid is absorbed and the rice is tender but not mushy.

3. Stir in the vanilla and remaining ¾ cup milk. Serve warm or chilled. Refrigerate any leftovers.

Variation

Dried Cherry and Orange Rice Pudding: Prepare the recipe as directed above, but in place of the cinnamon and nutmeg, use the grated zest of 1 large orange and substitute ⅓ cup pitted dried tart cherries for the raisins.

crème brûlée

Makes 4 servings

This recipe comes from Amy Golino, culinary analyst at Rival, the company that invented the electric slow cooker and trade-marked it the Crock-Pot®. It's one of her favorite things to make in a slow cooker.

    2 cups heavy cream

    1 vanilla bean, split lengthwise in half

    ½ cup granulated sugar

    5 large egg yolks

    3 to 4 tablespoons brown sugar

Cook's Note

➤ Vanilla beans are very expensive these days. If you prefer, you can substitute 2 teaspoons vanilla extract by heating just the cream and sugar in Step 2 until the sugar dissolves and whisking in the vanilla in Step 4 along with the egg yolks.

1. Arrange 4 individual 6-ounce soufflé dishes or ramekins (3½ inches in diameter and 1¾ to 2 inches high) on the bottom of a 6- or 7-quart electric slow cooker.

2. Combine the cream, vanilla bean, and granulated sugar in a medium saucepan on top of the stove. Bring to a boil over medium heat, stirring to dissolve the sugar; immediately remove from the heat. Let cool to room temperature, allowing the vanilla bean to steep in the cream. When cool, pick out the vanilla bean and, with the tip of a small knife, scrape the tiny seeds into the cream; discard the pod.

3. Whisk the egg yolks together until well blended. Whisk the yolks into the vanilla cream. Strain the custard through a fine sieve. Ladle the custard into the ramekins in the slow cooker.

4. Carefully pour hot water around the ramekins to reach halfway up the sides of the dishes. Cover and cook on the high heat setting for 2 to 2¼ hours, or until the custard is set but the centers are still soft and a bit jiggly. Turn off the pot and remove the cover. Remove the dishes from the stoneware insert as soon as they are cool enough to handle. Let cool, then cover and refrigerate until chilled, at least 3 hours or up to a day in advance.

5. Just before serving, preheat the broiler. Generously cover the tops of the custards with an even layer of brown sugar. Broil the custards 3 inches from the heat for 2 to 3 minutes, or until the brown sugar is melted. Watch carefully to avoid burning. Or use a kitchen blowtorch to melt the sugar; it will harden as it cools. Serve immediately.

chocolate crème brûlée

Makes 4 servings

For those who cannot get enough crème brûlée and for those who are always looking for another way to enjoy chocolate, here is a recipe that unites the two. Use your best bittersweet chocolate, preferably 65 to 70 percent cacao. It has just the right balance of chocolate and sugar to make this a stupendous dessert.

4 ounces bittersweet chocolate, broken up or
    coarsely chopped
½ cup granulated sugar
1¾ cups heavy cream
1 teaspoon vanilla extract
5 large egg yolks
3 to 4 tablespoons brown sugar

1. Arrange 4 individual 6-ounce soufflé dishes or ramekins (3½ inches in diameter and 1¾ to 2 inches high) on the bottom of a 6- or 7-quart electric slow cooker.

2. In a 4-cup glass measuring cup or bowl, combine the chocolate, granulated sugar, and ¾ cup of the cream. Heat in a microwave oven on high power for 45 to 60 seconds, whisking until the chocolate is melted and smooth.

3. Whisk in the remaining 1 cup cream and the vanilla. Beat the egg yolks until well blended. Gradually whisk them into the chocolate cream until thoroughly blended. Strain the chocolate cream through a mesh sieve. Ladle into the soufflé dishes or ramekins in the cooker. Carefully pour in enough hot water to reach about halfway up the sides of the dishes.

4. Cover and cook on the high heat setting for about 2 hours, or until most of the custard is set but the centers are still soft and a bit jiggly. Turn off the pot and remove the cover. Remove the dishes from stoneware insert as soon as they are cool enough to handle. Let cool, then cover and refrigerate until chilled, at least 3 hours or up to a day in advance.

5. Just before serving, preheat the broiler. Generously cover the tops of the custards with an even layer of brown sugar. Broil the custards about 3 inches from the heat for 2 to 3 minutes, or until the brown sugar is melted. Watch carefully to avoid burning. Or use a kitchen blowtorch to melt the sugar; it will harden as it cools.

hot caramel sauce

Makes about 1²/₃ cups

No worry about standing and stirring or scorching with this easy homemade sauce. Serve over fresh fruits, ice cream, or bread pudding. Or use as a dessert fondue dip.

1½ cups packed brown sugar
1¼ cups heavy cream
2 teaspoons butter
1 teaspoon vanilla extract

1. In a 1½-quart electric slow cooker, mix together the brown sugar and cream. Cover and cook on the low heat setting for 2½ hours, stirring once or twice.

2. Uncover and cook for 30 to 60 minutes longer, until thickened slightly. Stir in the butter and vanilla. Refrigerate any leftovers.

raspberry fudge sauce

This versatile chocolate sauce, with its subtle raspberry undertone, can be used like a fondue for dipping fruits, marshmallows, cake cubes, and the like or for topping ice cream, cakes, and fresh fruit. Keep a batch handy in the fridge to reheat in a microwave oven on a moment's notice for ice cream sundaes.

Makes about 3 cups

18 ounces bittersweet chocolate, cut up or broken into pieces
1 cup heavy cream
⅓ cup seedless raspberry jam
1 teaspoon vanilla extract

1. In a 1½-quart electric slow cooker, combine the chocolate, cream, and jam. Cover and cook on the low heat setting for 1½ to 2 hours, stirring 2 or 3 times, until the chocolate is melted and the sauce is smooth and hot.

2. Whisk in the vanilla. Refrigerate any leftover sauce in a covered container for up to 2 weeks. Reheat in a microwave oven or on top of the stove over very low heat.

Cook's Note

➤ The flavor of this sauce can be varied by using apricot preserves or orange marmalade in place of the raspberry jam.